教科書ガイド

三省堂 版

クラウン English Communication Ⅱ

TEXT BOOK GUIDE

文研出版

はじめに

本書は、三省堂発行の高等学校の教科書『CROWN English Communication Ⅱ』で英語を学習するみなさんの予習と演習のために書かれました。

教科書の学習は、教室でみなさんに直接英語を教えられる先生方のご指導によらなくてはなりませんが、英語の勉強は事前に自ら調べたり、また、授業のあとで復習し演習することで、学習した内容を確かなものにすることができます。本書はこうした予習・演習をより効果的に進めることを目的に作られた案内書であり、問題の解答をそのまま与えるものではありません。

本書では、教科書の内容を正しく理解するだけでなく、教科書で扱われる表現を文法の体系からわかりやすく解説し、さらに多くの例題を解くことにより応用力をつけることを目指しました。本書を教科書学習の理解に役立たせるばかりでなく、積極的に英語でコミュニケーションをはかる手がかりとして利用していただければ幸いです。

2023年2月

編集部

本書の構成と学習の進め方

本書では、教科書本文の１セクションを１つの単位として取り上げ、重要項目ごとに解説をつけました。

次のような流れで学習できるように、構成されています。

■教科書本文

教科書本文の１セクションを１単位として転載しています。

セクション分けされていない課は、便宜的にいくつかのまとまりに区切り、それぞれを１単位として転載しています。

■このセクションの内容

そのセクションの概要がつかめているか、空所補充問題で確認できるようになっています。

解答は、次ページのいちばん下に掲載されています。

■解説

教科書本文を理解する上で重要な箇所を取り上げ、文型、文法、および語句や表現の観点からわかりやすく解説しています。

解説が理解できたかどうかをチェックするために、解説のあとに、適宜基本的な演習問題を入れています。解説が理解できているかを確認しましょう。

■Grammar for Communication

各課で新たに学習する文法事項を詳しく解説しています。

文法の決まりや文構造をより深く理解し、定着を図るために、基本的な例文を多く示しています。

■確認問題

次のような項目ごとに、段階を踏んで英語の理解を総合的に確認しましょう。

語彙・表現

教科書で学んだ語彙・発音・表現などについて、さまざまな形式の問題を解くことで確認します。

文のパターン・文法

教科書本文で学んだ文法・語法・表現を演習します。

総合

教科書本文を掲載し、英文和訳・和文英訳・整序問題など、さまざまな形式の問題を付しました。文法や内容の理解を総合的に確認します。

CONTENTS

Lesson 1 Lost in Translation

教科書p.8　Section 1

- □ translation [trænsléɪʃən]
- □ tempt [témpt]
- □ be tempted to ～
- □ translate ～ into ...
- □ professor [prəfésər]
- □ warning [wɔ́:rnɪŋ]
- □ ～ come into *one's* mind
- □ completely [kəmplí:tli]
- □ bilingual [baɪlíŋgwəl]
- □ expression [ɪkspréʃən]
- □ every time ～
- □ loss [lɔ́:s]
- □ be at a loss for words
- □ assumption [əsʌ́mpʃən]
- □ corresponding [kɔ̀:rəspándɪŋ]
- □ be true for ～

①When you study English, you may be tempted to translate English into Japanese. A professor of translation studies from Canada gives a warning.

1

②You find yourself wanting to say something in English. ③However, the words just don't come into your mind. ④You want to say "*Mata ashita*" in English, but you don't know how. ⑤You want to be understood completely. What do you do? Well, you may simply ask your bilingual friend, "⑥How do you say '*Mata ashita*' in English?" She will answer, "See you tomorrow." The problem is solved.

⑦The expression "How do you say ... in English?" is so useful that you may want to use it every time you are at a loss for words. ⑧There's nothing wrong with that, but the assumption behind this question could be wrong. ⑨Japanese expressions may not always have exactly corresponding expressions in English. ⑩And the same is true for English. English expressions may not have exactly corresponding expressions in Japanese. ⑪As you will see, translation sometimes fails.

このセクションの内容

言いたいことを英語でどう言えばよいかわからないときは、2か国語を話す友人にHow do you say ～ in English?とたずねればよい。この表現は（A.　　　　　）ので、困ったときはいつでも使いたくなるだろうが、たとえ翻訳しても、日本語の表現と英語の表現が常に正確に（B.　　　　　）するとは限らない。つまり、翻訳が（C.　　　　　）することもあるのだ。

① When you study English, you may be tempted to translate English into Japanese.

▶ be temptedはtempt「(人)を誘惑する」の受け身。be tempted to *do*で「～したくなる」の意味を表す(≒ feel like V-ing「～したい気がする」)。

▶ translate ～ into ... は「～を…に翻訳する」。

② You find yourself wanting to say something in English.

▶〈find *oneself* V-ing〉は「～している…自身を発見する」→「～している自分に気づく」。

③ However, the words just don't come into your mind.

▶ the words「その言葉」とは②の文のsomethingを表す言葉、つまり「言いたいことを表現する英語」のこと。

▶ justは、否定語の前で「まったく(～しない)」。

▶～come into *one's* mindは「～が(人の)心に浮かぶ」(≒ think of ～「～を思いつく」)。

④ You want to say "*Mata ashita*" in English, but you don't know how.

▶ howはhow you should say "*Mata ashita*" in English「『また明日』を英語でどう言うべきか」を１語で表したもの。

⑤ You want to be understood completely.

▶ to be understoodは、名詞的用法の不定詞to understandの受け身で、「理解されること」の意味を表す。 ⇒p.19 G-❷

例 This bike needs *to be repaired.* (≒ This bike needs repairing.)
「この自転車は修理される[修理する]必要がある」

✍ 次の英文を日本語に直しなさい。

I was happy to be invited to her birthday party.
私は彼女の誕生日パーティーに ________________________ 。

⑥ How do you say '*Mata ashita*' in English?

▶ How do you say ～ in English? は、「あなたは～を英語でどのように言いますか」と、表現方法をたずねる言い方。

✍ 英文を完成させなさい。

「ありがとう」を韓国語で何と言いますか。
(　　　) do you (　　　) "*Arigato*" in Korean?

▶〈物の名称〉をたずねるときは、What do you call ～? を使う。

例 *What* do you *call* this fish in English?
「この魚を英語で何と言いますか[呼びますか]」

このセクションの内容 の答え→ A. とても役に立つ B. 対応 C. 失敗

⑦ The expression "How do you say ... in English?" is so useful that you may want to use it every time you are at a loss for words.

▶ so ～ that ...「とても～なので…」の構文。

▶ may want to use it「それを使いたくなるかもしれない」のitは、The expression "How do you say ... in English?"を指す。

▶ every time (that) ～は「～するときはいつも[必ず]」という意味で、接続詞と似た働きをする。似た表現のeach time (that) ～は、「～するたびに」と1回ごとの行動を強調して使う。

例 *Every time* she goes out, she takes this bag with her.
「外出するときはいつも、彼女はこのバッグを持って行く」

▶ at a lossは「困って、途方に暮れて」。be at a loss for wordsで「言葉に困っている」→「何と言っていいかわからない」の意味を表す(≒ do not know what to say)。

⑧ There's nothing wrong with that, but the assumption behind this question could be wrong.

▶ There's nothing wrong with ～. は「～には何の問題もない」の意味。問題があることを伝える場合は、There's something wrong with ～.「～はどこか調子[具合]が悪い、～には問題がある」と言う。

▶ thatは「"How do you say ... in English?"という表現を使うこと」を指す。

▶ the assumption behind this question「この質問の背後にある想定」とは、「いつもこの質問を使えば完全に翻訳できるという思い込み」のこと。

▶ couldは、現在または未来に対する〈可能性・推量〉を表し、could be wrongで「間違っている可能性がある」という意味になる。

⑨ Japanese expressions may not always have exactly corresponding expressions in English.

▶ not always ～は部分否定で、「常に～とは限らない」。

▶ exactly corresponding expressionsは「正確に対応する表現」。語句のニュアンスの違い、文化的な背景の違いなどにより、日本語の表現と英語の表現は必ずしも一致するわけではないことを伝えている。

⑩ And the same is true for English.

▶ the same「同じこと」は、「(英語を日本語に翻訳するときでも)表現内容が常に正確に対応するとは限らないこと」を表す。直後の文で、この文の内容を具体的に言いかえている。

▶ be true for ～は「～について当てはまる」(≒ be true of ～)。

⑪ As you will see, translation sometimes fails.

▶ as you will seeは「(これで)おわかりのように」、failは「失敗する」。

教科書p.10　Section 2

- □ attractive [ətrǽktɪv]
- □ essence [ésəns]
- □ consult [kənsʌ́lt]
- □ define ~ as ...
- □ elegant [élɪgənt]
- □ simplicity [sɪmplísəti]
- □ detailed [dí:teɪld]
- □ explanation [èksplənéɪʃən]
- □ aesthetic [esθétɪk]
- □ a sense of ~
- □ concept [kánsept]
- □ complex [kàmpléks]
- □ veranda [vərǽndə]
- □ look out at ~
- □ impossible [ɪmpásəbl]
- □ if not impossible
- □ abstract [ǽbstrækt]
- □ equivalent [ɪkwívələnt]

2

①Now, let me tell you about a personal experience. When I was a student in Kyoto, I often visited temples and shrines. ②I was wondering what makes Japanese gardens attractive. ③I remembered being told that the essence of Japanese gardens is *wabi-sabi*. ④I didn't know what exactly this expression meant, so I consulted my dictionary.

⑤*Wabi-sabi* was defined as "elegant simplicity." ⑥And a more detailed explanation followed: "*Wabi* and *sabi* are the highest aesthetic values in traditional Japanese arts. ⑦They refer to a sense of quiet sadness and the encouragement of simplicity." ⑧I felt like I was lost in a deep cloud. ⑨The concept was too complex for me to understand. ⑩But years later, as I sat on the wooden veranda of a temple, looking out at the garden, I thought I finally had a sense of *wabi-sabi*.

⑪This episode shows that it is often very difficult, if not impossible, to translate some concepts from one language into another. ⑫This is true not only for an abstract concept, but also for commonly used expressions in Japanese. How about *mottainai*, *shikataganai*, *otsukaresama*, *itadakimasu*, and *itsumo osewa ni natteimasu*? ⑬See if you can find equivalent expressions in English, or ask your bilingual friends if they are around.

このセクションの内容

辞書で「わびさび」の意味を調べたが、説明が（A.　　　　　）すぎて理解できなかった。しかし数年後、寺で庭を見ながら座っているとき、その（B.　　　　　）がわかった。ある言語から別の言語に翻訳することは難しい。それは、（C.　　　　　）な概念だけでなく一般的な表現についても言える。

① Now, let me tell you about a personal experience.

▶ letは〈許可〉を表す使役動詞。let me *do* 〜で「私に〜させてください」。

② I was wondering what makes Japanese gardens attractive.

▶〈wonder + wh-節〉は「〜だろうかと思う」。

▶〈make + O + 形容詞〉は「Oを〜（の状態）にする」。attractive「魅力的な」

▶ makesと現在形が使われているのは、what以下が現在でも変わらない普遍的な内容になるから。

③ I remembered being told that the essence of Japanese gardens is *wabi-sabi*.

▶ remember being toldは、remember V-ingの受け身で、「〜されたことを思い出す」の意味。 ⇒p.19 G-❸

英文を完成させなさい。

私は天才と呼ばれるのが好きではない。

I don't like (　　　) (　　　) a genius.

④ I didn't know what exactly this expression meant, so I consulted my dictionary.

▶ what exactly this expression meantは間接疑問で、〈疑問詞 + S + V〉の語順。過去形meantが使われているのは〈時制の一致〉のルールによる。

⑤ *Wabi-sabi* was defined as "elegant simplicity."

▶ elegant simplicity「上品[優雅]な簡素さ」は、辞書に載っていた「わびさび」の定義。be defined as 〜は、define A as B「AをBと定義する」の受け身。

⑥ And a more detailed explanation followed: "*Wabi* and *sabi* are the highest aesthetic values in traditional Japanese arts.

▶ follow「後に続く」は自動詞で、⑤の文のelegant simplicityという定義のあとにa more detailed explanation「さらに詳細な説明」が続いていたということ。the highest aesthetic valuesは「もっとも高い美的価値」。

⑦ They refer to a sense of quiet sadness and the encouragement of simplicity."

▶ Theyは*Wabi* and *sabi*を指す。refer to 〜は「〜に言及する、〜を表す」。

▶ a sense of ～は「～の感覚[観念]」（≒ a feeling of ～）、encouragement は「励まし、促進」の意味だが、ここでは「(簡素さを) さらに美的に[豊かに]するもの」と考えればよい。

⑧ I felt like I was lost in a deep cloud.

▶〈feel like + S + V〉は「SがVするように感じる」。

▶ be lostは「道に迷っている」から転じて「途方に暮れた」様子を表す。

⑨ The concept was too complex for me to understand.

▶ The concept「その概念」は、⑦の文のa sense of ... simplicityを指す。

▶〈too + 形容詞 + for + 人 + to *do*〉「とても…なので (人) は～できない、(人) が～するには…すぎる」の構文。≒ The concept was *so* complex *that* I *couldn't* understand it.

⇒p.18 G-❶

✍ 英文を完成させなさい。

このコーヒーは熱すぎて私には飲めない。

This coffee is (　　　) hot for me (　　　) drink.

⑩ But years later, as I sat on the wooden veranda of a temple, looking out at the garden, I thought I finally had a sense of *wabi-sabi*.

▶ asは「～するときに、～する間」。挿入句のlooking out at the gardenは分詞構文で、述語動詞 (sat) と同時に行われている動作を表す。「座って外の～を見ていると」「外の～を見ながら座っているときに」となる。

⑪ This episode shows that it is often very difficult, if not impossible, to translate some concepts from one language into another.

▶ that節内は〈it is + 形容詞 + to *do*〉「～することは…だ」の構文。

▶ 挿入されているif not impossibleは、「不可能ではないとしても」。

⑫ This is true not only for an abstract concept, but also for commonly used expressions in Japanese.

▶ This「このこと」は、⑪の文のthat節の内容を指す。

▶ not only ～ but also ...の構文で、be true for ～「～について当てはまる」の２つのforの前にnot onlyとbut alsoが挿入されている。「～についてだけでなく、…についても当てはまる」となる。

⑬ See if you can find equivalent expressions in English, or ask your bilingual friends if they are around.

▶ see if ～「～かどうか調べ[確かめ]なさい」とask ～「～にたずねなさい」の２つの命令文が並んでいる。

このセクションの内容 の答え→　A. 複雑　B. 感覚　C. 抽象的

- □ go beyond ～
- □ linguist [líŋgwɪst]
- □ sample [sǽmpl]
- □ Swedish [swíːdɪʃ]
- □ as shown ～
- □ slide [sláɪd]
- □ restless [réstləs]
- □ beat [bíːt]
- □ Dutch [dʌ́tʃ]
- □ cozy [kóuzi]
- □ amazing [əméɪzɪŋ]
- □ Finnish [fínɪʃ]
- □ distance [dístəns]
- □ reindeer [réɪndìər]
- □ comfortably [kʌ́mfərtəbli]
- □ take a break
- □ Arabic [ǽrəbɪk]
- □ amount [əmáunt]
- □ conceptualize [kənséptʃuəlàɪz]
- □ in a ～ way

3

①Now, let us go beyond English and Japanese, and look at some of the world's other languages. ②According to some linguists, there are over 7,000 languages in the world, so what I'm going to show is just a tiny sample of words we can't translate easily into English or Japanese.

③Swedish offers an interesting example, as shown on Slide 1. ④This word (*resfeber*) means "the restless beat of a traveler's heart before the journey begins; feelings of being nervous and excited."

Here is an example from the Dutch language. Look at Slide 2. ⑤This word (*gezellig*) means "cozy; a positive warm feeling you have when you are with loved ones." ⑥It's amazing that one word can describe this kind of feeling!

Slide 3 shows an example from Finnish. ⑦This word (*poronkusema*) means "the distance a reindeer can comfortably travel before taking a break."

Slide 4 shows an example from Arabic. ⑧This word (*gurfa*) means "the amount of water that can be held in one hand."

⑨You may find it fascinating how different languages conceptualize the world in different ways. ⑩It seems there is no limit to what you can say in simple words.

このセクションの内容

スウェーデン語、(A.　　　　　　　)語、フィンランド語、アラビア語にも、簡単に翻訳できない単語がいろいろある。それらはさまざまな方法で世界を(B.　　　　　　)していて魅力的だ。簡単な言葉で言えることには(C.　　　　　　)ようだ。

① Now, let us go beyond English and Japanese, and look at some of the world's other languages.

▶ let us *do* は let's *do*「〜しましょう」と同じ。go beyond 〜は「〜(の範囲)を超えて進む」。

② According to some linguists, there are over 7,000 languages in the world, so what I'm going to show is just a tiny sample of words we can't translate easily into English or Japanese.

▶ according to 〜は「〜によれば」、linguist は「言語学者」。

▶ what I'm going to show の what は先行詞を含む関係代名詞(≒ the thing that I'm going to show)で、後半の文の主語になっている。

▶ a tiny sample of words we can't 〜「私たちが〜できない単語のごくわずかな見本[実例]」では、we 以下の節〈S + V 〜〉が直前の名詞 words を後ろから修飾している。このような節を〈接触節〉という。we の前に関係代名詞 that[which] が省略されているとも考えられる。

✍ 次の英文を日本語に直しなさい。

Wabi-sabi was a Japanese word he couldn't understand.

「わびさび」は ______________________________ 日本語の単語だった。

③ Swedish offers an interesting example, as shown on Slide 1.

▶ Swedish は「スウェーデン語」(= the Swedish language)の意味。

▶ as shown 〜は「(〜に)示されているように」(≒ as you can see 〜)。

④ This word (*resfeber*) means "the restless beat of a traveler's heart before the journey begins; feelings of being nervous and excited."

▶" "の中は *resfeber* というスウェーデン語について、２通りの表現で説明をしている。the restless beat は「(旅に出る人の)落ち着かない胸の高鳴り」、feelings of being nervous and excited は「緊張と興奮の気持ち」。

⑤ This word (*gezellig*) means "cozy; a positive warm feeling you have when you are with loved ones."

▶" "の中は *gezellig* というオランダ語(the Dutch language)の説明。セミ

コロン (;) は、「つまり～」という意味で、cozy「居心地のよい」の補足説明をしている。

▶ you have ～は、名詞feelingを後ろから修飾する節。

▶ when you are with ～は「あなたが～といっしょにいるとき」。loved ones は「愛する人たち」で、lovedは「最愛の」という意味の形容詞。

⑥ It's amazing that one word can describe this kind of feeling!

▶〈It is + 形容詞 + that節〉「～ということは…だ」の構文。

▶ this kind of feeling「この種の感情」は、⑤の文の" "内で述べられた複雑な感情のこと。

⑦ This word (*poronkusema*) means "the distance a reindeer can comfortably travel before taking a break."

▶" "の中は*poronkusema*というフィンランド語 (Finnish) の説明。なお、国名の「フィンランド」はFinland。

▶ a reindeer ～は、名詞distance「〔theをつけて〕一定の距離」を後ろから修飾する節。travelは「移動する」という意味の動詞。take a breakは「休息をとる」。

⑧ This word (*gurfa*) means "the amount of water that can be held in one hand."

▶" "の中は*gurfa*というアラビア語 (Arabic) の説明。

▶ thatはwaterを先行詞とする主格の関係代名詞。can be heldはcan hold「持つことができる」の受け身。

✍ 英文を完成させなさい。

今夜は星がたくさん見える。

A lot of stars can (　　　) (　　　) tonight.

⑨ You may find it fascinating how different languages conceptualize the world in different ways.

▶〈find it + 形容詞 + 名詞節〉「～が…だと気づく[わかる]」の構文。itは形式目的語で、後ろのhow節の内容を指す。

例 They made *it* clear *that* they were against the plan.
「彼らはその計画に反対であることを明らかにした」

▶ conceptualizeは「概念化する」、in different waysは「さまざまな方法で」。

⑩ It seems there is no limit to what you can say in simple words.

▶ It seems (that) ～.の構文。Itはthat節の内容を指す形式主語。「～のように思える、～であるようだ」という意味を表す。

▶ there is no limit to ～は「～には限りがない」。whatは先行詞を含む関係代名詞で、what以下は「簡単な言葉で言えること」という意味。

このセクションの内容 の答え→　A. オランダ　B. 概念化　C. 限りがない

教科書p.14　Section 4

- □ conclude [kənklúːd]
- □ stroll [stróul]
- □ breathe [bríːð]
- □ breathe in ～
- □ look up
- □ filter [fíltər]
- □ filter through ～
- □ pile ～ up
- □ non-native [nὰnnéitiv]
- □ allow [əláu]
- □ lastly [lǽstli]
- □ a piece of ～
- □ make sure ～

4

①Before concluding my talk, let me share with you a couple of Japanese words which I find really interesting.

②Imagine that you are strolling in a park on a bright summer day. ③You breathe in the fresh air; you are looking up at the trees; you see the sunlight filtering through the leaves. How do you describe this kind of sunlight? *Komorebi*. ④I find this fascinating.

I buy lots of books. People ask, "⑤Have you read all those books?" ⑥Of course not! ⑦I often leave books unread. ⑧I just pile them up without reading them. ⑨Japanese has a word to describe this kind of "reading": *tsundoku*! I love it.

⑩As speakers of Japanese, you may not find these words unique. Yet, non-native speakers of Japanese often find them unique to Japan.

⑪Learning English is not just about words and rules. ⑫It can allow us to see the world in different ways.

⑬Lastly, may I give you a small piece of advice? ⑭Translation is sometimes used to make sure you have understood the English text you are reading, but remember that there might be something lost in translation.

このセクションの内容

締めくくりに、おもしろい日本語を紹介しよう。「(A.　　　　　)」と「積読」だ。日本語を母語としない人々は、これらをユニークな日本語だと考えるだろう。英語学習は言葉や (B.　　　　　) だけが対象ではなく、学べば、さまざまな方法で世界を見ることができる。最後に助言したい。英文が理解できたかを確かめるために翻訳が使われることがあるが、翻訳によって何かが (C.　　　　　) かもしれないということを忘れないように。

① Before concluding my talk, let me share with you a couple of Japanese words which I find really interesting.

▶ concluding はconclude「～をしめくくる[終える]」の-ing形(動名詞)。

▶ a couple ～interestingが動詞share「～を共有する」の目的語になる。本来はshare ～ with youの語順になるが、目的語が長いためwith youのあとに置いている。a couple of ～は「2つの～、いくつかの～」。

▶ which は目的格の関係代名詞。

② Imagine that you are strolling in a park on a bright summer day.

▶ 命令文。imagine (that) ～は「～ということを想像する」。

③ You breathe in the fresh air; you are looking up at the trees; you see the sunlight filtering through the leaves.

▶ 想像すべき内容が3つ並べられている。breathe in ～は「～を吸い込む」(breathe out ～は「～を吐き出す」)、look upは「見上げる」(≒ raise *one's* eyes「目を上げる」)。

▶ filter through ～は「(水・光・音などが) ～を通してもれる」。the sunlight filtering through ～で「～からもれている日光」で、filteringは現在分詞。

④ I find this fascinating.

▶ 〈find + O + C(形容詞)〉「OがCだと思う[わかる]」の文型。

▶ O(目的語)のthisは、直前の文の*Komorebi*という日本語を指す。

✍ 次の英文を日本語に直しなさい。

I found my smartphone broken.

私は ＿＿＿＿＿＿＿＿＿＿＿＿＿＿＿＿ ことに気づいた。

⑤ Have you read all those books?

▶「読んでしまいましたか」という現在完了(完了)の文。

⑥ Of course not!

▶「もちろん[当然]notだ!」ということ。Of course I haven't read all those books!を短く言ったもの。

⑦ I often leave books unread.

▶〈leave + O + C(形容詞)〉「OをC(の状態)にしておく」の文型。unreadは「(本・新聞などが)まだ読まれていない、未読の」。

例 Don't leave me alone!
「私を一人にして[放って]おかないで！」

⑧ I just pile them up without reading them.

▶justは「ただ(〜する)」、pile 〜 upは「〜を積み上げる」、without V-ingは「〜することなしに、〜しないで」。

⑨ Japanese has a word to describe this kind of "reading": *tsundoku*!

▶to describeは形容詞的用法の不定詞で、後ろからa wordを修飾している。

▶*tsundoku*は「積読」。「積んでおく(＝積んどく)」との語呂(ごろ)合わせ。

⑩ As speakers of Japanese, you may not find these words unique.

▶〈find + O + C(形容詞)〉「OがCだと思う[わかる]」の文型。

▶not find these words uniqueは「これらの単語(＝*komorebi*と*tsundoku*)がユニーク[独特]だとは思わない」という意味。

⑪ Learning English is not just about words and rules.

▶Learning Englishが文の主語。not just about 〜は「単に〜についてだけではない」。「〜について学ぶだけが英語学習ではない」ということ。

⑫ It can allow us to see the world in different ways.

▶Itは⑪のLearning Englishを指す。〈allow + 人 + to *do*〉は「(人)が〜することを可能にする[許す]」→「(人)が〜できるようにする」。

✍ 次の英文を日本語に直しなさい。

Please allow me to ask you a question.
どうか ＿＿＿＿＿＿＿＿＿＿＿＿＿＿＿＿＿＿＿＿。

⑬ Lastly, may I give you a small piece of advice?

▶〈give + 人 + もの〉は「(人)に(もの)を与える」。a (small) piece of 〜は「1つの〜」。adviceは不可算名詞なので、「1つの助言」をこのように表す。

⑭ Translation is sometimes used to make sure you have understood the English text you are reading, but remember that there might be something lost in translation.

▶前半は受け身の文。to make sure (that) you have understood 〜は「あなたが〜を理解しているということを確かめるために」。you are readingは、the English textを後ろから修飾する節。

▶後半は命令文。there might be 〜は「〜があるかもしれない」〈可能性・推量〉。something lost in translationは「翻訳で失われるもの」。

このセクションの内容 の答え→ A. こもれび B. 規則 C. 失われる

Grammar for Communication

1　不定詞の意味上の主語

文の主語と不定詞 (to＋動詞の原形) が表す動作・状態の主体とが異なるときは、不定詞の前に〈for＋人など〉を置けばよい。これを〈不定詞の意味上の主語〉という。〈for＋人など＋to *do*〉で「(人など) が～するための[に]」「(人など) が～すること」などの意味を表す。

---

1. 〈for＋人など＋to *do*〉

◆ Here are a lot of books **for children to read**.
（ここには子どもたちが読むための本がたくさんある）

◆ I'm waiting **for this store to open**.
（私はこの店が開くのを待っている）

◆ It is necessary **for you to eat** breakfast every day.
（あなたは毎日、朝食を食べる必要がある）　＊Itはto eatを指す形式主語

★〈It is＋形容詞＋for＋人＋to *do*.〉の文を、「人」を主語にして書きかえることはできない。
（×）You are necessary to eat breakfast every day.

2. forの代わりにofを用いる場合

kind（親切な）、brave（勇敢な）、careless（不注意な）、polite（礼儀正しい）など、人を評価する[人の性質を表す]形容詞を伴うときは、〈of＋人など＋to *do*〉を使う。「～するとは[～するなんて]（人）は…だ」などの意味になる。

◆ It was *brave* **of him to rescue** the drowning child.
（おぼれている子どもを救うなんて、彼は勇敢だった）
≒ He was brave to rescue the drowning child.

3. 訳し方の工夫

〈for[of]＋人など＋to *do*〉は、次のように訳を工夫してもよい。

◆ We waited **for her to arrive**.
（私たちは彼女が到着するのを待った）

◆ The question was too difficult **for him to understand**.
（その質問は難しすぎて彼には[彼にとって]理解できなかった）

◆ It was kind **of her to help** me with my homework.
（彼女は親切にも私の宿題を手伝ってくれた）

2　不定詞の受け身：to be＋過去分詞

不定詞（to＋動詞の原形）の受け身は〈to be＋過去分詞〉の形で表す。多くの場合、「～されること」の意味になる。

◆ Jim wants **to be elected** as captain.
（ジムは主将に選ばれたいと思っている）

◆ There are lots of famous paintings **to be seen** in the art museum.
（その美術館には見られるべき多くの有名な絵がある）
→（その美術館では多くの有名な絵を見ることができる）

◆ This work needs **to be finished** by 7 o'clock.
（この仕事は7時までに終える必要がある）
≒ This work needs finishing by 7 o'clock.

★〈want[need] to be＋過去分詞〉は〈want[need]＋動名詞〉に書きかえられる場合がある。
This room needs **to be cleaned**. ≒ This room needs **cleaning**.
（この部屋は掃除する必要がある）

3　動名詞の受け身：being＋過去分詞

動名詞（V-ing）の受け身は〈being＋過去分詞〉の形で表す。「～されること」の意味になる。

◆ I like **being given** a T-shirt as a present.
（私はプレゼントとしてTシャツをもらうのが好きだ）

◆ My sister hates **being told** what to do.
（私の妹はすることを指示されるのが大嫌いだ）

◆ He was afraid of **being scolded** by his mother.
（彼は母親から叱られることを恐れていた）

参考

A tall building is **being built** in front of the station.　＊現在進行形の受け身
（駅前に高いビルが建てられている）

Look at the tower **being built** over there.　＊現在分詞の受け身
（あそこに建てられている塔を見てごらん）

確認問題

語彙・表現

1 次の語を（　）内の指示にしたがって書きかえなさい。

(1) lose（名詞形に）　(2) attract（形容詞形に）
(3) simple（名詞形に）　(4) breath（動詞形に）

2 第２音節にアクセント（強勢）のある語を３つ選び、記号で答えなさい。

ア com-plex　イ ab-stract　ウ com-fort-a-ble
エ con-clude　オ al-low　カ cor-re-spond-ing

3 日本語に合うように、（　）内に適切な語を入れなさい。

(1) おもしろい考えが彼の心に浮かんだ。
An interesting idea came (　　　) his (　　　).

(2)「おじ」は「母または父の兄弟」と定義される。
Uncle is (　　　) (　　　) the brother of someone's mother or father.

(3) 私はこの詩を英語に翻訳することができなかった。
I could not (　　　) this poem (　　　) English.

(4) 彼女を説得することは、不可能ではないにしても、難しいだろう。
It will be difficult, (　　　) (　　　) impossible, to persuade her.

(5) ベスは簡単な方法でその問題を解決した。
Beth solved the problem (　　　) a simple (　　　).

文のパターン・文法

1 各組の文がほぼ同じ意味になるように、（　）内に適切な語を入れなさい。

(1) These shoes are so expensive that I can't buy them.
These shoes are too expensive (　　　) me (　　　) buy.

(2) You were careless to do such a thing.
It was careless (　　　) you (　　　) do such a thing.

(3) He speaks Chinese as well as English.
He speaks (　　　) only English (　　　) also Chinese.

(4) I found that having pets in this apartment was difficult.
I found (　　　) difficult (　　　) I had pets in this apartment.

2 (　)内の語句を並べかえて、日本語に合う英文を作りなさい。

(1) あなたはこの日本語の単語が何を意味するか、わかりますか。
Do you know (Japanese word / means / what / this)?
Do you know ______________________________?

(2) その子はできるだけ早く病院に搬送されなければならなかった。
The child had (to / to / be / the hospital / taken) as soon as possible.
The child had ______________________ as soon as possible.

(3) 車で家まで送ってくれてありがとう。
It (of / you / was / to / nice) drive me home.
It ______________________________ drive me home.

(4) 私は祖父にとても愛されていたことを覚えている。
I remember (much / loved / by / very / being) my grandfather.
I remember __________________________ my grandfather.

総合

次の文を読んで、あとの問いに答えなさい。

I buy lots of books. People ask, "Have you read all those books?" ①Of course not! I often leave books unread. I just pile them up (②) reading them. Japanese has a word to describe this kind of "reading": *tsundoku*! I love it.

As speakers of Japanese, you may not find these words unique. Yet, non-native speakers of Japanese often find them unique to Japan.

Learning English is not just about words and rules. ③It can allow us to see the world in different ways.

Lastly, may I give you a small piece of advice? Translation is sometimes used to make sure you have understood the English text you are reading, but remember that there might be something lost in translation.

問1　下線部①を次のように書きかえるとき、(　)内に入る適切な語を書きなさい。
Of course I have (　　　) (　　　) all those books!

問2　(②)に適切な前置詞を入れなさい。

問3　下線部③をItの内容を明らかにして日本語に直しなさい。

問4　筆者はどのようなことを忘れないようにしなさいと助言しているか。日本語で説明しなさい。

Lesson 2 One Book Can Empower a Child

教科書p.24　Section 1

- □ empower [ɪmpáuər]
- □ Shanti Volunteer Association [ʃáːntɪ vὰləntíər əsòusiéɪʃən]
- □ SVA [és víː éɪ]
- □ NGO [én dʒíː óu]
- □ Phea [píə]
- □ Cambodia [kæmbóudiə]
- □ fee [fíː]
- □ quit [kwít]
- □ shyly [ʃáɪli]
- □ decent [díːsənt]
- □ Hak [háːk]
- □ metal [métəl]
- □ fragment [frǽgmənt]
- □ dump [dʌ́mp]
- □ slum [slʌ́m]
- □ Phnom Penh [nὰmpén]
- □ envy [énvi]
- □ It is reported that ～

In many places in the world, children cannot go to school. ①This is the story of those children and of Shanti Volunteer Association (SVA), a Japanese NGO, which is trying to help them.

1

②Phea is a thirteen-year-old girl living in a village in Cambodia. ③Every morning she goes to the river and into the forest to get fish and fruit, which she sells in town. ④She used to go to school. ⑤But when she was in the fourth grade, her family could no longer pay the daily 30-yen fee. ⑥She had to quit school.

Phea says shyly, "⑦I can write my name, but I've forgotten many things. ⑧I wonder if I can get a decent job."

Hak is fourteen. When he was in the second grade, he left school to go to work. ⑨He collects plastic bottles and metal fragments in a dump in the slums of Phnom Penh for about 100 yen a day.

"⑩I envy my friends who attend school," he says. "⑪I wish I could study, too."

⑫It is reported that more than 70 million children around the world cannot go to school. ⑬To help children like Phea and Hak, SVA has been working to give every child an opportunity to learn.

このセクションの内容

世界には学校に行けない子どもが多くいる。ある少女は、家族が1日30円の（A.　　　　）が払えなくなり、学校をやめた。ある少年は2年生のとき退学し、スラム街の（B.　　　　）で働いている。NGO法人のSVAは、すべての子どもたちに学ぶ（C.　　　　）を与えようと活動を続けてきた。

① This is the story of those children and of Shanti Volunteer Association (SVA), a Japanese NGO, which is trying to help them.

▶ andの後ろにthe storyが省略されている。the story of ～ and (the story) of ...で「～と…の話」。

▶ those children「それらの子どもたち」は、世界の多くの地域で学校に行けない子どもたちのこと。

▶ a Japanese NGO, which ～はSVAの補足説明で、〈, which〉は非制限用法の関係代名詞。固有名詞のあとでは、関係代名詞は必ず非制限用法になる。

② Phea is a thirteen-year-old girl living in a village in Cambodia.

▶ thirteen-year-old「13歳の」という意味で、直後のgirlを修飾している。thirteen-years-oldとsをつけないことに注意。

▶ livingは現在分詞で、living以下がgirlを後ろから修飾している。girl living in ～はgirl who lives in ～と言いかえられる。

③ Every morning she goes to the river and into the forest to get fish and fruit, which she sells in town.

▶ andの後ろにgoesが省略されている。

▶ to get ～「～を手に入れるために」は目的を表す副詞的用法の不定詞。

▶〈, which〉は直前のfish and fruitを先行詞とする非制限用法の関係代名詞。

≒ fish and fruit, and she sells *them* in town

例 I bought a pair of sandals, *which* I gave to my mother.
「私はサンダルを1足買い、それを母にあげた」

④ She used to go to school.

▶〈used to *do*〉は「(以前は) よく～したものだ、(以前は) ～した[～だった]」という意味で、今はそうではないという意味を含む。

✍ 次の英文を日本語に直しなさい。

As a child, I used to fish in the nearby river.
子どものころ、＿＿＿＿＿＿＿＿＿＿＿＿＿＿＿＿。

⑤ But when she was in the fourth grade, her family could no longer pay the daily 30-yen fee.

▶ no longer ～は「もはや～ない」。

▶ the daily 30-yen feeは「1日30円の料金[費用]」。feeは「〔単数形で〕料金、手数料」などの意味を表す。ここでは「授業料」のこと。

⑥ She had to quit school.

▶〈had to *do*〉は〈have[has] to *do*〉の過去形で「～しなければならなかった」。quitは「～をやめる」、quite schoolで「退学する」となる。

このセクションの内容 の答え→ A. 学費 B. ごみ捨て場 C. 機会

⑦ I can write my name, but I've forgotten many things.

▶ have forgotten は「忘れてしまった」という現在完了（完了）。

▶ many things は、「学校で習った多くのこと」を表す。

⑧ I wonder if I can get a decent job.

▶ 少女のピアが自分の将来について心配している文。I wonder if ～は「～だろうかと思う」、decent job は「まともな仕事」。

✍ 英文を完成させなさい。

今週末、雨が降るかなあ。

I (　　　) (　　　) it will rain this weekend.

⑨ He collects plastic bottles and metal fragments in a dump in the slums of Phnom Penh for about 100 yen a day.

▶ collects の目的語は、plastic bottles and ～ Phnom Penh。

▶ dump は名詞で「ごみ捨て場、ごみの山」、動詞で「(ごみなど)を捨てる[処分する]」などの意味がある。「ダンプカー」は dump track という。

▶〈for + 金額 + a day〉は「1日につき～（金額）で」。

⑩ I envy my friends who attend school,

▶ envy は「～をうらやましく思う」。

▶ who は主格の関係代名詞で、my friends を後ろから修飾している。

⑪ I wish I could study, too.

▶〈I wish + 仮定法過去〉の文。I wish に〈S + (助) 動詞の過去形〉を続けて、「(今) ～だったら (いいのに) なあ」と、現在の事実に反することや、実現不可能なことへの願望を表す。

例 My father always says, "*I wish* I *were* younger."
「父はいつも、『私がもっと若かったらなあ』と言っている」

⑫ It is reported that more than 70 million children around the world cannot go to school.

▶ It is reported that ～. は「～と報告されている」という受け身の文で、It は that 以下を指す形式主語。more than ～ world が that 節内の主語。

⑬ To help children like Phea and Hak, SVA has been working to give every child an opportunity to learn.

▶ To help と to give はどちらも目的を表す副詞的用法の不定詞。

▶ has been V-ing は現在完了進行形で、動作が継続していることを表す。「ずっと～している」「～することを続けている」という意味になる。

▶〈give + 人 + もの〉は「(人) に (もの) を与える」。opportunity to learn は「学ぶ (べき) 機会」で、to learn は形容詞的用法の不定詞。

教科書p.26　Section 2

- ☐ Afghanistan [æfgǽnəstæ̀n]
- ☐ Myanmar [mjáːnmàːr]
- ☐ Laos [láːous]
- ☐ Nepal [nəpɔ́ːl]
- ☐ cooperate [kouápərèit]
- ☐ Nool [núːl]
- ☐ take ～ out to ...
- ☐ escape [iskéip]
- ☐ escape with *one's* life
- ☐ extremely [ikstríːmli]
- ☐ leaky [líːki]
- ☐ patch [pǽtʃ]
- ☐ patch ～ up
- ☐ lack [lǽk]

2

①SVA works not only in Cambodia but also in Afghanistan, Thailand, Myanmar, Laos, and Nepal. ②It cooperates with local governments and communities to build schools and libraries, and also to send books to children.

③One of those children is Nool, who lives in Afghanistan. ④He used to live with his father in his home village. ⑤His father raised cows, and Nool helped him take the cows out to the field. ⑥Then one day, their village was bombed. ⑦Nool and his father just managed to escape with their lives.

⑧They had to move to a nearby town. Their lives were extremely difficult. ⑨Their house had a leaky roof patched up with pieces of plastic. ⑩They didn't even have blankets to keep themselves warm. They lacked food, so they only had tea for breakfast. ⑪Nool was still afraid of bombing. His daily life was not happy.

⑫Then, one day, Nool had an opportunity to visit an SVA library. ⑬Now he has a purpose in life. He says, "I really enjoy going to the library. ⑭I have lots of fun there. ⑮I will study hard. I promise." ⑯He dreams of being able to read books and study at a school.

このセクションの内容

SVAは地方自治体や（A.　　　　　）と協力して、学校や図書館を建設し、子どもたちに本を送っている。村を（B.　　　　　）され、父とつらい生活を送っていたある少年は、SVA図書館を訪れて以来、人生に（C.　　　　　）ができた。彼は今、学校で読書や勉強をしたいという夢を抱いている。

① SVA works not only in Cambodia but also in Afghanistan, Thailand, Myanmar, Laos, and Nepal.

▶ not only ～ but also ...「～だけでなく…も」の構文。

② It cooperates with local governments and communities to build schools and libraries, and also to send books to children.

▶ ItはSVAを指す。

▶ cooperate with ～は「～と協力する」。

▶ to build ～, and also to send ... は「～を建てるために、そしてまた…を送るために」。どちらも目的を表す副詞的用法の不定詞。

③ One of those children is Nool, who lives in Afghanistan.

▶ those childrenは、②の文の最後にあるchildrenで、「本を送られた子どもたち」のこと。

▶ 固有名詞Noolに続く〈, who〉は、Noolを補足説明する非制限用法の関係代名詞（≒ and he lives in Afghanistan）。

④ He used to live with his father in his home village.

▶ used to *do*は「（以前は）よく～したものだ、（以前は）～した[～だった]」という過去の習慣や状態を表す。

⑤ His father raised cows, and Nool helped him take the cows out to the field.

▶ 〈help + 人 + *do*〉は「（人）が～するのを手伝う」で、〈人〉のあとは原形不定詞になることが多い。〈help + 人 + to *do*〉でもほぼ同じ意味を表す。

✍ 次の英文を日本語に直しなさい。

Could you help us clean the park?

私たちが ________________________________ いただけますか。

▶ take ～ out to ... は「～を…に連れ出す」。

⑥ Then one day, their village was bombed.

▶「爆撃された」という受け身の文。bombは動詞で「～を爆撃する」、名詞で「爆弾」の意味。bombの最後のbは発音しない（＝黙字）ので注意。

⑦ Nool and his father just managed to escape with their lives.

▶ just ～は「ただ～（する）だけ」。

▶ manage to *do*は「～をなんとかやりとげる」、escape with *one's* lifeは「命を伴って逃げる」→「命からがら逃げる」。２人について述べているのでwith their livesとなっている。

⑧ They had to move to a nearby town.

▶ had to ～は「～しなければならなかった」、move to ～は「～に引っ越す[移動する]」。

このセクションの内容 の答え→ A. 地域社会　B. 爆撃　C. 目的

⑨ Their house had a leaky roof patched up with pieces of plastic.

▶ a leaky roof patched up with ～は「～で継ぎを当てられた（水などが）もれる屋根」。過去分詞patched以下がroofを後ろから修飾している。

例 My house has a small garden *taken* care of by my grandparents.
「私の家には祖父母が手入れをしている小さな庭園がある」

▶ patch ～ upは「～に継ぎを当てる、～を一時的に繕う」（≒ repair ～）。

⑩ They didn't even have blankets to keep themselves warm.

▶ evenは「～さえ」。didn't even have ～で「～を持ってさえいなかった、～さえ持っていなかった」の意味になる。

▶ blankets to keep ～は「～を保つための毛布」。

▶〈keep *oneself* + 形容詞〉は「（人）自身を～（の状態）に保つ」。

英文を完成させなさい。

あなたはいつも体を清潔にしておくべきだ。

You should always (　　　) (　　　) clean.

⑪ Nool was still afraid of bombing.

▶ be afraid of ～は「～を恐れている」。

▶ bombingは「爆撃（すること）」。前置詞ofのあとなので、V-ing（動名詞）が使われている。

例 Don't *be afraid of making* mistakes when you speak English.
「英語を話すとき、間違えることを恐れてはいけない」

⑫ Then, one day, Nool had an opportunity to visit an SVA library.

▶ have an opportunity to ～は「～する機会［好機］を持つ［がある］」。to visitは形容詞的用法の不定詞。

⑬ Now he has a purpose in life.

▶ Nowは「今では」、a purpose in lifeは「人生における目標」。

⑭ I have lots of fun there.

▶ lots of ～は「多くの～」（≒ a lot of ～）。

▶ fun「楽しみ、おもしろいこと」は不可算名詞で、複数形にはならない。

⑮ I will study hard.

▶ willは「～するつもりだ」という〈意志〉を表す。直後の文I promise.「私は約束します」は、「私は一生懸命勉強することを約束します」ということ。

⑯ He dreams of being able to read books and study at a school.

▶ dream of V-ingは「～することを夢見（てい）る」。ofのあとにbeing able to ～が続いているので、「～できることを夢見ている」という意味になる。
≒He has a dream that he will be able to read books and study at a school.

- □ Orathai [ərɑ́:tàɪ]
- □ thanks to ～
- □ Bangkok [bǽŋkɑ̀k]
- □ illiterate [ɪlítərət]
- □ pull up
- □ turnip [tə́:rnəp]
- □ granddaughter [grǽndɔ̀:tər]
- □ take part in ～
- □ expand [ɪkspǽnd]
- □ Thai [táɪ]
- □ diplomat [dípləmæ̀t]

3

①Orathai is another child whose life changed for the better thanks to SVA. She lives in Thailand. ②As a child, she lived in a slum area in Bangkok. ③Both parents were illiterate.

④When Orathai was four, an SVA library truck pulled up in her slum. ⑤Kids gathered around, and a volunteer read them a picture book, *The Giant Turnip*. ⑥It is a story about an old couple who grow a turnip so big that they need their granddaughter, a dog, a cat, and a mouse to pull it out of the ground.

⑦Orathai never forgot that moment. She says, "⑧The story taught me that if people want to achieve something big, they have to work together."

When Orathai was eight, SVA built a library near her house. ⑨It became a second home for her. ⑩She read books and took part in activities like singing and dancing. ⑪She still remembers SVA's helping her expand her world.

Orathai is now a successful Thai diplomat.

このセクションの内容

ある少女が４歳のとき、SVAの移動図書館が地元のスラム街にやって来た。そして、（A.　　　　　）が子どもたちに絵本を読んで聞かせた。彼女はその絵本から、大きなことを成し遂げたければ（B.　　　　　）しなければならないことを学んだ。８歳のとき、SVAは少女の家の近所に図書館を建て、彼女はそこでいろいろな活動に参加した。今は成功を収めた（C.　　　　　）である彼女は、SVAが自分の世界を広げてくれたことをまだ覚えている。

① Orathai is another child whose life changed for the better thanks to SVA.

▶ another child whose life changedは「人生が変わったもう１人の子ども」。whoseは所有格の関係代名詞。Orathai is another child.とHer life changed for the better thanks to SVA.の２文がwhoseでつながれている。

✍ 英文を完成させなさい。

私には、母親が弁護士の友人がいる。

I have a friend (　　　) (　　　) is a lawyer.

▶ change for the betterは「より良いものに変わる」(このbetterは名詞)、thanks to ～は「～のおかげで、～のために」(≒ because of ～)。

② As a child, she lived in a slum area in Bangkok.

▶ As a child「子どものころ」はWhen she was a childと同じ意味。

例 As a young woman, she took tea ceremony lessons.
「若かったとき、彼女は茶道を習った」

③ Both parents were illiterate.

▶ Both parents(両方の親、両親)はBoth of her parentsの意味。

▶ 形容詞illiterateはliterate(読み書きができる)の否定形。接頭辞il-は、l(エル)で始まる語の前について「不・非・無」の意味を表す。illegal「不法な、違法の」、illogical「非論理的な」などがある。

④ When Orathai was four, an SVA library truck pulled up in her slum.

▶ library truckは「本を積んだトラック」で、移動図書館のこと。移動図書館とは、近隣に利用できる図書館がない地域に図書を自動車で運ぶサービスのこと。pull upは「(車が)止まる」(≒ stop)。

⑤ Kids gathered around, and a volunteer read them a picture book, *The Giant Turnip*.

▶ gather aroundは「周りに集まる」で、ここでは④の文のlibrary truckの周りに集まったということ。

▶ 〈read + 人 + O〉は「(人)にOを読んで聞かせる」(≒ read + O + to + 人)。

▶ a picture book, *The Giant Turnip*は「『おおきなかぶ』という絵本」の意味。*The Giant Turnip*は、世界中で読まれているロシアの民話。

⑥ It is a story about an old couple who grow a turnip so big that they need their granddaughter, a dog, a cat, and a mouse to pull it out of the ground.

▶ 主語のItは⑤の文の*The Giant Turnip*を指す。a story about an old coupleは「ある老夫婦についての物語」。

このセクションの内容 の答え→ A. ボランティア B. 協力 C. 外交官

▶ an old couple who grow 〜は「〜を育てる老夫婦」で、whoは主格の関係代名詞。who 〜 groundが名詞coupleを後ろから修飾している。

▶ so 〜 that ...は「とても〜なので…」または「…なほど〜」という意味で、程度がはなはだしいことを表す。grow a turnip so big that they need 〜で「彼らが〜を必要とするほど、かぶを大きく育てる」となる。

▶ to pull it out of 〜は「それ(＝かぶ)を〜から引き抜くために」。

⑦ Orathai never forgot that moment.

▶ that momentは、ボランティアが『おおきなかぶ』を読んだ時を指す。momentは「瞬間」だが、一瞬とは限らず、「短い時間、特定の時」の意味でも使われる。

⑧ The story taught me that if people want to achieve something big, they have to work together.

▶ 〈teach + 人 + that節〉は「(人)に〜ということを教える」。if 〜 togetherまでがthat節になる。

▶ achieveは「〜を成し遂げる」、something bigは「何か大きなこと」。

⑨ It became a second home for her.

▶ Itは「SVAが彼女の家の近くに建てた図書館」を指す。

▶ second homeは「第二の故郷」の意味で、生まれ故郷とは別の「心のふるさと」のこと。

⑩ She read books and took part in activities like singing and dancing.

▶ take part in 〜は「(活動など)に参加する」(≒ participate in 〜)。

例 Have you ever *taken part in* volunteer activities?
「あなたはボランティア活動に参加したことがありますか」

⑪ She still remembers SVA's helping her expand her world.

▶ still remembers 〜は「〜を今でも覚えている」。

▶ SVA's helpingは「SVAが助けること」の意味で、SVAがhelping(動名詞)の意味上の主語(助ける主体)になっている。意味上の主語は所有格(SVA's)でも目的格(SVA)でもよいが、口語ではふつう目的格を使う。

⇒p.34 G-❶

次の英文を日本語に直しなさい。

Do you mind us having lunch here?
私たちが ______________________________。

▶ 〈help + 人 + 動詞の原形〉は「(人)が〜するのを助ける[手伝う]、(人)が〜するのに役立つ」。

教科書p.30　Section 4

- □ staff [stǽf]
- □ storytelling [stɔ́ːritèlɪŋ]
- □ session [séʃən]
- □ absorb [əbzɔ́ːrb]
- □ be absorbed in ～
- □ it takes ～
- □ passage [pǽsɪdʒ]
- □ paste [péɪst]
- □ helping hand

4

An SVA staff member in Myanmar says, "①Children seem to have learned thinking skills through reading. ②Kids love storytelling sessions and are absorbed in the world of picture books." ③Her dream is to put a picture book in every child's hand. ④SVA tries to make that dream come true. ⑤It takes a lot of books.

⑥SVA collects about 18,000 books a year in Japan. ⑦The SVA staff translate the books into other Asian languages and print the translated passages on stickers. ⑧Then, volunteers paste the stickers over the Japanese words. ⑨It takes a volunteer about one hour to finish one book. ⑩A lot of helping hands are needed.

One volunteer says, "⑪I was interested in doing some volunteer work, and it was an easy first step forward to make a small change in my life."

Another says, "I used to enjoy reading picture books to my kids. ⑫Now that they have grown up, it gives me joy to imagine kids all over Asia enjoying picture books I help to make."

One picture book can change a life and empower a child. ⑬Just ask Orathai, the Thai diplomat who has never forgotten *The Giant Turnip*.

このセクションの内容

SVAは日本で年間約（A.　　　　　）冊の本を集めている。スタッフは集めた絵本に翻訳文を貼り付けるが、時間がかかるので多くの（B.　　　　　）が必要だ。しかし、スタッフたちは喜びを感じている。1冊の絵本が子どもの（C.　　　　　）を変え、彼らを力づけることができるからだ。

① Children seem to have learned thinking skills through reading.

▶〈seem to have＋過去分詞〉は「～したように思われる」という意味。現在の文で使われる〈to have＋過去分詞〉（不定詞の完了形）は、過去にしたことを表す。 ⇒p.35 G-❷

≒ It seems that children have learned thinking skills through reading.

＊Itはthat節の内容を指す形式主語。

▶learn ～ through ... は「…を通じて～を学ぶ」。thinking skill「考える技術」とは「思考力」のこと。

② Kids love storytelling sessions and are absorbed in the world of picture books.

▶storytelling sessions「物語を話すための集まり［集団活動］」とは、「本の読み聞かせの時間」のこと。

▶be absorbed in ～は「～に夢中になっている」（≒ be very interested in ～「～にとても興味［関心］がある」）。

③ Her dream is to put a picture book in every child's hand.

▶Herは、An SVA staff member in Myanmarを指す。

▶to putは「置くこと」を表す名詞的用法の不定詞。put ～ in ... は「～を…に置く」。「手の中に置く」つまり「手渡す、届ける」ということ。

④ SVA tries to make that dream come true.

▶try to *do*は「～しようと試みる［努力する］」。

▶〈make＋O＋動詞の原形〉は「Oに［を］～させる」（makeは使役動詞）。

✍ 英文を完成させなさい。

そのニュースを聞いて彼女は泣いた。

The news (　　　) her (　　　).

▶that dream「その夢」とは、③の文で述べられている夢で、「すべての子どもに絵本を届ける」こと。

⑤ It takes a lot of books.

▶主語のItは③と④の文にある「すべての子どもに絵本を届けるという夢を実現させること」を表す。takeは「～を必要とする」。

⑥ SVA collects about 18,000 books a year in Japan.

▶18,000はeighteen thousandと読む。a yearは「1年につき」。

⑦ The SVA staff translate the books into other Asian languages and print the translated passages on stickers.

▶translate ～ and print ... と2つの動詞が並列されている。translate ～ into ... は「～を…に翻訳する」、print ～ on ... は「～を…（の上）に印刷する」、translated passagesは「翻訳された文章」。

このセクションの内容 の答え→ A. 18,000 B. 援助（の手） C. 人生

⑧ Then, volunteers paste the stickers over the Japanese words.

▶ paste ～ over ... は「…の上に～を貼る」という意味。over は、覆いかぶさる様子を表す。

⑨ It takes a volunteer about one hour to finish one book.

▶〈It takes + 人 + 時間 + to ～.〉は「(人) が～するのに (時間) がかかる」。

✍ 英文を完成させなさい。

私たちは車で日光に行くのに３時間かかった。

(　　　) took (　　　) three hours to get to Nikko by car.

▶ finish one book「１冊の本を終える」とは、「日本の絵本に、ほかのアジアの言語で印刷されたステッカーを１冊分貼り終える」ことを指す。

⑩ A lot of helping hands are needed.

▶ A lot of helping hands が主語の受け身の文。helping hand は「援助 (の手)」(≒ assistance)。

⑪ I was interested in doing some volunteer work, and it was an easy first step forward to make a small change in my life.

▶ be interested in V-ing は「～することに興味[関心]がある」。

▶ 後半の文の主語 it は doing some volunteer work「ボランティア活動をすること」を指す。

▶ an easy first step forward は「前に進む簡単な第一歩」。to make は形容詞的用法の不定詞で step を修飾する。make a change は「変化を起こす」。

⑫ Now that they have grown up, it gives me joy to imagine kids all over Asia enjoying picture books I help to make.

▶〈Now that + S + 現在完了〉は「S が～してしまった[すでに～した]現在では」という意味。

▶ it gives me joy to *do* は〈give + 人 + もの〉の文型で、it は to 以下 (to imagine ～ make) を指す形式主語。「～することは私に喜びを与える」の意味。

▶〈imagine + O + V-ing〉は「O が～することを想像する」で、O が V-ing (動名詞) の意味上の主語になっている。

▶ I help to make「私が作るのを手伝う」は、直前の picture books を後ろから修飾する節。

⑬ Just ask Orathai, the Thai diplomat who has never forgotten *The Giant Turnip*.

▶「ちょっと[ともかく]たずねてごらんなさい」という命令文。

▶ the Thai diplomat who ～は Orathai の補足説明で、who は主格の関係代名詞。has never forgotten ～は現在完了 (経験) で、「～を決して忘れたことがない」という意味。

Grammar for Communication

1　動名詞の意味上の主語

文の主語と動名詞 (V-ing) が表す動作・状態の主体とが異なるときは、動名詞の前に (代) 名詞の所有格または目的格を置けばよい (目的格のほうが口語的)。これを〈動名詞の意味上の主語〉という。〈(代) 名詞の所有格または目的格＋V-ing〉で「(人など) が～すること」の意味を表す。

---

1. 意味上の主語を持つ動名詞

◆ Do you mind **my[me] sitting** here?
（私がここに座ってもかまいませんか）
≒ Do[Would] you mind if I sit here? / May I sit here?
比較 Do you mind sitting here?
（ここに座ってくれませんか）

◆ He is proud of **his son's[his son] being** honest.
＊ his son'sは所有格、his sonは目的格
（彼は息子が正直であることを誇りに思っている）
≒ He is proud that his son is honest.

◆ I'm sure of **Bill's[Bill] winning** the tennis match.
＊ Bill'sは所有格、Billは目的格
（私はビルがそのテニスの試合に勝つと確信している）
≒ I'm sure that Bill will win the tennis match.

2. 意味上の主語を持つ動名詞の受け身

〈being＋過去分詞〉は動名詞の受け身で、「～されること」という意味になる。beingの前に意味上の主語を置いて、〈人など (意味上の主語) ＋ being ＋過去分詞〉の形で「(人など) が～されること」の意味を表す。

◆ They are afraid of **their town's[their town] being bombed**.
（彼らは、彼らの町が爆撃されることを恐れている）
≒ They are afraid that their town will be bombed.

◆ I was surprised at **our club's[our club] being well known**.
（私は、私たちのクラブがよく知られていることに驚いた）
≒ I was surprised that our club was well known.

2 不定詞の完了形：to have＋過去分詞

〈to have＋過去分詞〉は不定詞の完了形で、主節の動詞が表す時よりも前に行われた動作や状態を表す。〈to have＋過去分詞〉が過去の意味になるか、完了（継続・経験・完了）の意味になるかは、文脈や文中で使われている語句によって決まる。

1.〈seem to have＋過去分詞〉

◆She **seems to have been** sick in bed yesterday.
（彼女は昨日、病気で寝ていたようだ）
★yesterdayがあるので、〈to have＋過去分詞〉は過去の状態を表している。
≒ It seems (that) she *was* sick in bed yesterday.
比較 She seems to be sick in bed.（彼女は病気で寝ているようだ）

◆She **seems to have been** sick in bed for a week.
（彼女は1週間ずっと病気で寝ているようだ）
★for a weekがあるので、〈to have＋過去分詞〉は過去（＝1週間前）から現在まで状態が継続していることを表している。
≒ It seems (that) she *has been* sick in bed for a week.

◆He **seems to have been** absent from school last Friday.　＊過去の状態
（彼はこの前の金曜日、学校を休んだようだ）
≒ It seems (that) he *was* absent from school last Friday.

◆He **seems to have been** abroad three times.　＊過去の経験
（彼は3回、外国に行ったことがあるようだ）
≒ It seems (that) he *has been* abroad three times.

2.〈be said[believed] to have＋過去分詞〉

◆He **is said to have written** the story.　＊過去の動作
（彼がその物語を書いたと言われている［書いたそうだ］）
≒ It is said[They say] (that) he *wrote* the story.

◆The pilot **is said to have seen** UFOs twice.　＊過去の経験
（そのパイロットはUFOを2回見たことがあると言われている）
≒ It is said (that) the pilot *has seen* UFOs twice.

◆About 100 people **are believed to have been killed** in the flood.
（約100人がその洪水で死んだと信じられて［考えられて］いる）
≒ It is believed (that) about 100 people *were killed* in the flood.

確認問題

語彙・表現

1 第2音節にアクセント(強勢)のある語を3つ選び、記号で答えなさい。

ア de-cent　　イ en-vy　　ウ co-op-er-ate
エ il-lit-er-ate　　オ dip-lo-mat　　カ pas-sage
キ es-cape　　ク vol-un-teer　　ケ sto-ry-tell-ing

2 日本語に合うように、(　)内に適切な語を入れなさい。

(1) SVAのおかげで、その少女は学校に通うことができた。
(　) to SVA, the girl was able to (　) school.

(2) 彼らは私たちに協力してくれるかしら。
I wonder (　) they will cooperate (　) us.

(3) あなたはサマーキャンプに参加する予定ですか。
Are you going to take (　) (　) the summer camp?

(4) その奇術師は帽子からウサギを取り出した。
The magician (　) a rabbit (　) of the hat.

(5) あなたのお姉さんのように上手に歌えたらなあ。
I (　) I (　) sing as well as your sister.

(6) ルーシーは日本のアニメを見るのに夢中になっている。
Lucy is (　) (　) watching Japanese anime.

文のパターン・文法

1 各組の文がほぼ同じ意味になるように、(　)内に適切な語を入れなさい。

(1) Look at that house with the blue roof.
Look at that house (　) (　) is blue.

(2) Would you mind if I use this umbrella?
Would you mind (　) (　) this umbrella?

(3) He bought twenty eggs, and he put them into the fridge.
He bought twenty eggs, (　) he put into the fridge.

(4) It seems that she was born in Thailand.
She seems to (　) (　) born in Thailand.

(5) This castle is said to have been built in the 15th century.
It is said that this castle (　) (　) in the 15th century.

2 (　)内の語を並べかえて、日本語に合う英文を作りなさい。

(1) 私は、母が私の日記を読んでも気にしない。
I don't care (my / my / about / reading / mother / diary).
I don't care ＿＿＿＿＿＿＿＿＿＿＿＿＿＿＿＿.

(2) 私たちはその店が閉まっていることに驚いた。
We were surprised (store / closed / being / at / that).
We were surprised ＿＿＿＿＿＿＿＿＿＿＿＿＿＿＿＿.

(3) 彼はもう帰宅したようだ。
He (gone / seems / already / have / to) home.
He ＿＿＿＿＿＿＿＿＿＿＿＿＿＿＿＿ home.

(4) この本は多くの人々に影響を与えたと言われている。
This book (influenced / to / is / said / have) a lot of people.
This book ＿＿＿＿＿＿＿＿＿＿＿＿＿＿＿＿ a lot of people.

総合

次の文を読んで、あとの問いに答えなさい。

SVA collects about 18,000 books a year in Japan. The SVA staff translate the books into other Asian languages and print the ①(translate) passages on stickers. Then, volunteers paste the stickers over the Japanese words. ②(　　　) (　　　) a volunteer about one hour (　　　) finish one book. A lot of helping hands are needed.

One volunteer says, "I was interested in doing some volunteer work, and it was an easy first step forward to make a small change in my life."

Another says, "I used to enjoy reading picture books to my kids. Now that they have grown up, it gives me joy to imagine kids all over Asia ③(help / enjoying / I / make / picture books / to)."

One picture book can change a life and empower a child. Just ask Orathai, the Thai diplomat who has never forgotten *The Giant Turnip*.

問1　①の(　)内の語を適切な形に直しなさい。

問2　下線部②が「1人のボランティアが1冊の本を仕上げるには約1時間かかる」という意味になるように、(　)内に適切な語を入れなさい。

問3　下線部③の(　)内の語句を並べかえて、英文を完成させなさい。

問4　あるボランティアは、ボランティア活動は何をするための簡単な第一歩だったと言っていますか。日本語で答えなさい。

Lesson 3 Accessible Japan

教科書p.42　Section 1

- □ accessible [əksésəbl]
- □ disability [dìsəbíləti]
- □ Josh Grisdale [dʒáʃ grízdèɪl]
- □ diagnose [dàɪəgnóʊs]
- □ be diagnosed with ～
- □ severe [sɪvíər]
- □ cerebral palsy [sérəbrəl pɔ́:lzi]
- □ electric [ɪléktrɪk]
- □ facility [fəsíləti]
- □ nursery [nə́:rsəri]
- □ all the way to ～
- □ despite [dɪspáɪt]
- □ the more ～, the more ...
- □ on *one's* way to ～
- □ employee [ɪmplɔ́ɪi:]

①Is Japan accessible to tourists with disabilities? ②Josh Grisdale, who runs the website Accessible Japan, discusses this question.

1

③When I was six months old, I was diagnosed with severe cerebral palsy. I have used an electric wheelchair since I was four years old.

④I was born in Canada but now live in Tokyo, working at a care facility. ⑤My job is to manage a website for a group that runs nursing homes, kindergartens, and nursery schools.

⑥You may wonder why I came all the way to Japan despite my physical condition. When I was in high school, I took Japanese language classes. ⑦The more I studied about Japan, the more I wanted to see Japan with my own eyes.

In 2000, I received a gift from my father: a one-month trip to Japan! ⑧After doing a tour in Asakusa, my father and I were on our way back to the hotel. We got to the subway entrance but we couldn't find an elevator. ⑨Not knowing what to do, we asked where the elevator was. ⑩To our surprise, six subway employees came and carried me and my 130-kilogram wheelchair down the stairs. I will never forget that experience. ⑪It was then that I dreamed of making Japan my home.

このセクションの内容

4歳のときから電動車いすを使っている筆者は、2000年に父親と（A.　　　　）をした。ある地下鉄の入口で（B.　　　　）が見つからずに困っていると、地下鉄の職員たちが6人で、彼と130キロの車いすを運んで降ろしてくれた。彼にはその経験が忘れられず、日本を自分の（C.　　　　）にしたいと夢見るようになった。

① Is Japan accessible to tourists with disabilities?

▶ be accessible to 〜は「〜にとって行きやすい」、tourists with disabilitiesは「(身体に)障がいのある観光客[旅行者]」。

② Josh Grisdale, who runs the website Accessible Japan, discusses this question.

▶〈, who〉は非制限用法の関係代名詞。挿入されているwho 〜 Japanが先行詞（ここでは固有名詞）を補足説明している。

▶ runはここでは「〜を運営する」、Accessible Japanはwebsiteの名前。

例 My father, *who* runs a cake shop, turned 45 years old today.
「父はケーキ店を経営していて、今日45歳になった」

③ When I was six months old, I was diagnosed with severe cerebral palsy.

▶ be diagnosed with 〜は「〜と診断される」、severe cerebral palsyは「重い脳性麻痺」。cerebralは医学用語で「(大)脳の」という意味。

④ I was born in Canada but now live in Tokyo, working at a care facility.

▶ working 〜は分詞構文で、主語が2つの動作（liveとwork）を同時に行っていることを表す。「介護施設で働きながら東京で暮らしている」「東京に住んで、介護施設で働いている」などの意味になる。

✍ 次の英文を日本語に直しなさい。

I usually do my homework, listening to music.
私はたいてい、＿＿＿＿＿＿＿＿＿＿＿＿＿＿＿＿＿＿＿＿宿題をする。

⑤ My job is to manage a website for a group that runs nursing homes, kindergartens, and nursery schools.

▶ to manageは「〜を管理すること」で、名詞的用法の不定詞。

▶ thatは主格の関係代名詞で、that以下がgroupを後ろから修飾している。

▶ nursing homeは「介護施設、老人ホーム」、nursery schoolは「保育所」の意味。nursingは動詞nurse「〜を看護する」、nurseryは名詞nurse「乳母（うば）」の派生語。

⑥ **You may wonder why I came all the way to Japan despite my physical condition.**

▶ wonder why 〜は「なぜ〜かと不思議に思う」、all the way to 〜は「はるばる〜まで」、despite 〜は「〜にもかかわらず、〜なのに」(≒ in spite of 〜)。

✍ 英文を完成させなさい。

雨なのに、わざわざ家まで来てくれてありがとう。

Thank you for coming (　　　) the (　　　) to my house (　　　) the rain.

⑦ **The more I studied about Japan, the more I wanted to see Japan with my own eyes.**

▶〈The + 比較級〜, the + 比較級 ...〉は「〜すればするほどますます…」の構文。この文のmoreはmuch (副詞) の比較級で、「より多く」の意味。

例 *The older* you grow, *the weaker* your eyesight gets.
「年をとればとるほど視力が低下する」

⑧ **After doing a tour in Asakusa, my father and I were on our way back to the hotel.**

▶ on *one's* way to 〜「(人が) 〜に行く途中で」のtoの前にbackが入っている。on *one's* way back to 〜で「〜に戻る途中で」の意味。

⑨ **Not knowing what to do, we asked where the elevator was.**

▶ Not knowing 〜は否定の分詞構文。ここでは「(私たちは) 何をすべきかわからなかったので」という意味になる。what to doは「何をすべきか」(≒ what we should do)。 ⇒p.50 G-❶

✍ 次の英文を日本語に直しなさい。

Not having enough money, I didn't buy the CD.

______________________________、私はそのCDを買わなかった。

▶ where以下は間接疑問で、〈疑問詞 + 主語 + 動詞〉の語順になっている。

⑩ **To our surprise, six subway employees came and carried me and my 130-kilogram wheelchair down the stairs.**

▶ To *one's* surprise は「(人が) 驚いたことに」(≒ Surprisingly)。

▶ carry 〜 down the stairsは「〜を階下に運ぶ」。

⑪ **It was then that I dreamed of making Japan my home.**

▶ It is 〜 that .... は強調構文で、強調する語句をIt isとthatではさんでいる。It was then that 〜は、then「そのときに」を強調して「〜したのはそのときだった」という意味になる。 ⇒p.51 G-❷

▶ dream of V-ingは「〜することを夢見る[空想する]」、〈make + O + C (名詞)〉は「OをCにする」。

このセクションの内容 の答え→ A. 日本旅行 B. エレベーター C. 故郷

教科書p.44　Section 2

□ adventurer [ədvéntʃərər]
□ at heart
□ have difficulty V-ing
□ location [loukéɪʃən]
□ accessibility [əksèsəbíləti]
□ fortunately [fɔ́:rtʃənətli]
□ touch a life
□ occasion [əkéɪʒən]
□ backrest [bǽkrèst]
□ go right to work
□ be proud to ～

2

①In 2007, I moved permanently to Tokyo. ②Being an adventurer at heart, I visited lots of places in Japan. I learned that Japan was very accessible for people in wheelchairs. ③Yet a lot of visitors from abroad were having difficulty getting information in English. I wanted to do something for them.

④In 2015, I started Accessible Japan, an English website which provides information for visitors with disabilities, like the location of elevators and restrooms as well as the accessibility of tourist sites. ⑤People should not have to give up their dream of visiting Japan just because of a lack of information.

⑥Fortunately, my efforts have touched the lives of many people. ⑦Encouraged by the information on my website, an Australian girl with cerebral palsy and her father realized their dream of coming to Japan. They both loved anime.

⑧On another occasion, having seen my website, staff members of the Nezu Museum asked me to check the accessibility of their facilities. ⑨I noticed a problem with the museum's toilet: it didn't have a backrest. ⑩The staff went right to work. ⑪On my next visit, they were very proud to show me the new backrest on the toilet.

このセクションの内容

筆者は（A.　　　　　）のウェブサイトを立ち上げ、日本を訪れる障がい者に有用な情報を提供した。あるときは（B.　　　　　）から施設の使いやすさを調べてほしいと頼まれ、（C.　　　　　）に問題があることを指摘した。

① In 2007, I moved permanently to Tokyo.

▶ moved permanently to 〜「永久に〜に引っ越した[移転した]」とは、「永住するつもりで〜に引っ越した[移転した]」ということ。

② Being an adventurer at heart, I visited lots of places in Japan.

▶ Being 〜は分詞構文で、主語 (I) の状態を補足説明している。

≒ As I'm an adventurer at heart, I visited ....

例 *Being* 17 years old, I haven't been allowed to drive a car yet.
「17歳なので、私はまだ車の運転を許されていない」

▶ at heartは「心の底では、本当は」。*cf.* by nature「生まれつき」

③ Yet a lot of visitors from abroad were having difficulty getting information in English.

▶ Yetは「けれども、それにもかかわらず」(≒ But)。

▶ have difficulty (in) V-ingは「〜することが困難だ、〜することに苦労する」。

✍ 英文を完成させなさい。

母は毎晩、よく眠れなくて困っている。

My mother is having (　　　) (　　　) well every night.

④ In 2015, I started Accessible Japan, an English website which provides information for visitors with disabilities, like the location of elevators and restrooms as well as the accessibility of tourist sites.

▶ an English website 〜 tourist sitesは、Accessible Japanの説明。主格の関係代名詞which以下がwebsiteを後ろから修飾している。

▶ provide 〜 for ... は「…に〜を提供する」。

▶ like 〜「〜のような」のあとで、提供する情報の内容を挙げている。〜 as well as ... は「…だけでなく〜も」「…はもちろんのこと、〜も」などの意味を表す (≒ not only ... but also 〜)。the location of elevators and restroomsは「エレベーターやトイレの場所」、the accessibility of tourist sitesは「観光地への行きやすさ」。

⑤ People should not have to give up their dream of visiting Japan just because of a lack of information.

▶ should not have to *do*は「〜すべきではない」。just because of 〜は「単に〜という理由だけで」、a lack of 〜は「〜の欠如[不足]」。

⑥ Fortunately, my efforts have touched the lives of many people.

▶ have touchedは「〜した」と〈完了〉を表す現在完了。

▶ touch a lifeは「人生に触れる」→「人生に影響を与える、人生を変える」(≒ change someone in a positive way「(人)をプラス志向に変える」)。

このセクションの内容 の答え→ A. 英語　B. (根津)美術館　C. トイレ

⑦ Encouraged by the information on my website, an Australian girl with cerebral palsy and her father realized their dream of coming to Japan.

▶ Encouraged by ～は、過去分詞で始まる分詞構文。「～に勇気づけられて［励まされて］」と受け身の意味を表す。 ⇒p.50 G-❶

例 *Seen* from here, that mountain looks like a dinosaur.
「ここから見られる［見る］と、あの山は恐竜のように見える」

⑧ On another occasion, having seen my website, staff members of the Nezu Museum asked me to check the accessibility of their facilities.

▶ on another occasionは「別の機会には」。

▶ having seen ～「～を見て」は、完了形で始まる分詞構文。askedが示す時（過去）より前に「見た」ので、完了形が使われている。 ⇒p.50 G-❶

✍ 英文を完成させなさい。

傘をなくしてしまったので、私は新しいものを買った。

(　　　) (　　　) my umbrella, I bought a new one.

▶〈ask + 人 + to *do*〉は「（人）に～するように頼む」。

▶ accessibilityは、④の文では「（観光地への）行きやすさ」の意味だが、ここでは「（施設の）使いやすさ」を表す。形容詞のaccessibleは「（容易に）接近できる、利用可能な」の意味。

⑨ I noticed a problem with the museum's toilet: it didn't have a backrest.

▶コロン (:) は、接続詞と同じ働きをし、ここでは「つまり」の意味を表す。itはthe museum's toiletを指す。

⑩ The staff went right to work.

▶ go right to workは「すぐに仕事に行く」→「すぐに（背もたれをつけるという）仕事を始める」（≒ start working immediately）。

⑪ On my next visit, they were very proud to show me the new backrest on the toilet.

▶文頭のon ～は、ここでは「～のとき［機会］に」の意味。

▶ be proud to *do*は「～することを自慢する［誇りに思う］」（≒ be proud of V-ing）。

✍ 次の英文を日本語に直しなさい。

My brother is proud to work as an elementary school teacher.

私の兄は、＿＿＿＿＿＿＿＿＿＿＿＿＿＿＿＿＿＿＿＿。

▶〈show + 人 + もの〉は「（人）に（もの）を見せる」。

- □ make progress in ～
- □ challenge [tʃǽlɪndʒ]
- □ overcome [òuvərkʌ́m]
- □ divide [dɪváɪd]
- □ divide ～ from ...
- □ barrier [bǽriər]
- □ less than ～
- □ meet a challenge
- □ disabled [dɪséɪbld]
- □ tend [ténd]
- □ tend (not) to ～
- □ set up ～
- □ tourism [túərìzm]
- □ economy [ɪkánəmi]

3

①For the past decade, Japan has been making progress in creating a friendly environment for people with disabilities, but there are still many challenges to overcome. ②For instance, the entrances to restaurants often have steps which divide the building from the outside area. ③It could be a barrier for people like me. Another problem is the accessibility of hotel rooms. ④In fact, less than one percent of hotel rooms are accessible for people in wheelchairs.

⑤I suggest that if we meet these challenges, we will have greater business opportunities. ⑥For example, if you make your restaurant more accessible, then you will have 10 percent more customers because 10 to 15 percent of the world population is disabled. ⑦People with disabilities tend not to travel alone. ⑧They often travel in groups or with families, which would mean many more customers.

⑨Also, I've been working with tour companies, setting up training sessions for tour guides which help them learn how to support people in wheelchairs. ⑩If tourism supports more tourists with disabilities and provides better services, more people will come to Japan, and that will support Japan's economy.

このセクションの内容

日本には、障がい者のために（A.　　　　　　）しなければならない課題がまだたくさんある。それらを解決すれば、障がいを持つ（B.　　　　　　）が増え、それは（C.　　　　　　）にとってもプラスになるだろう。

① For the past decade, Japan has been making progress in creating a friendly environment for people with disabilities, but there are still many challenges to overcome.

▶ For the past decadeは「過去10年間」。

▶ has been makingは現在完了進行形で、動作の〈継続〉を表す。make progress in V-ingは「～することにおいて進歩する」（≒ make advances in V-ing）。

▶ challenge to overcomeは「克服すべき課題」（形容詞的用法の不定詞）。

② For instance, the entrances to restaurants often have steps which divide the building from the outside area.

▶ For instanceは「たとえば」（≒ For example）。

▶ whichは主格の関係代名詞で、which以下がsteps「階段」を後ろから修飾している。divide ～ from ... は「～を…と分ける[仕切る、へだてる]」（≒ separate ～ from ...）。

③ It could be a barrier for people like me.

▶ It「そのこと」とは、②の文で述べられている「レストランの入り口に建物と外をへだてる階段がある」という内容を指す。

▶ could be ～は「～になるかもしれない」と〈可能性〉を表す。可能性の高い順、can be ＞ could be ＞ may beとなる。

④ In fact, less than one percent of hotel rooms are accessible for people in wheelchairs.

▶ In factは「実際は、実のところ」。

▶ lessはlittleの比較級で、less than ～は「～より少ない、～未満」。less ～ roomsが文全体の主語になる。「実際、車いすの人が利用できるホテルの部屋は1パーセントに満たない」ということ。

英文を完成させなさい。

外国に行ったことがあるのは、生徒たちの20パーセントに満たない。

(　　　) (　　　) 20 percent of the students have been abroad.

⑤ I suggest that if we meet these challenges, we will have greater business opportunities.

▶ suggest (that) ～は「～だと提案する[勧める]、～だと思う」。

▶ meet a challengeは「課題に対応する[立ち向かう]」（≒ face a problem）。

▶ business opportunityは「ビジネスの機会」。日本語の「ビジネスチャンス」に近い意味になる。

⑥ For example, if you make your restaurant more accessible, then you will have 10 percent more customers because 10 to 15 percent of the world population is disabled.

このセクションの内容 の答え→ A. 克服 B. 観光客[顧客] C. 日本経済

▶ have 10 percent more customersは「10パーセント多くの顧客を持つ」→「顧客が10パーセント増える」。

▶ disabledは「身体に障がいのある」という意味の形容詞。

⑦ People with disabilities tend not to travel alone.

▶ tend not to *do*はtend to *do*「〜する傾向がある、〜しがちだ」の否定形。tend (not) to *do* ≒ be (not) likely to *do*

✍ 英文を完成させなさい。

彼は太りにくい体質だ。

He tends (　　　) (　　　) gain weight easily.

⑧ They often travel in groups or with families, which would mean many more customers.

▶〈, which〉は非制限用法の関係代名詞。ここでは「そしてそのことは」という意味を表し、直前のThey 〜 familiesまでの内容を指している。and it would mean 〜と言いかえられる。

例 He said he knew my grandmother, which wasn't true.
「彼は私の祖母を知っていると言ったが、それは本当ではなかった」
＊ which wasn't true ≒ but it wasn't true

⑨ Also, I've been working with tour companies, setting up training sessions for tour guides which help them learn how to support people in wheelchairs.

▶ I've been workingは現在完了進行形で、動作の〈継続〉を表す。

▶ set up 〜は「(事業)を始める、〜を開設する」(≒ start (up) 〜)。

▶ setting 〜は分詞構文で、workingと同じ時に行われている動作を表す。「〜を始めながら…と共に(ずっと)働いている」「…と協力して〜を始めている」などの意味になる。

▶ whichは主格の関係代名詞で、which以下がsessionsを後ろから修飾している。training sessionは「研修」。

▶〈help + 人 + *do*〉は「(人)が〜するのを助ける」、learn how to *do*は「〜する方法を学ぶ」。

⑩ If tourism supports more tourists with disabilities and provides better services, more people will come to Japan, and that will support Japan's economy.

▶ If tourism supports 〜 and provides ...は、「もし観光が〜を援助して…を提供すれば」ということ。

▶ and thatのthat「そのこと」は、直前に述べられている内容「より多くの人が日本に来ること」を指す。

教科書p.48　Section 4

- □ firmly [fə́ːrmli]
- □ first-hand [fə̀ːrsthǽnd]
- □ reliable [rɪláɪəbl]
- □ make it a rule to ～
- □ take notes
- □ objective [əbdʒéktɪv]
- □ vary [véəri]
- □ from person to person
- □ citizen [sítəzn]
- □ involve [ɪnválv]
- □ do *one's* part
- □ spirit [spírət]
- □ in the spirit of ～

4

①Going back to the topic of Accessible Japan, I firmly believe in two principles. ②The first principle is to get first-hand information by personally visiting the sites. ③In fact, I've visited 95 percent of the tourist locations listed on my website. ④To make my website more reliable, I make it a rule to take pictures, talk to local people, and take notes.

The second principle is to be honest and objective. ⑤I've been trying to upload detailed information as much as possible, such as information about steps at tourist attractions. ⑥I try not to say, "This place is accessible, so you can go there," because accessibility varies from person to person. ⑦I may find the place accessible, while someone else may not. ⑧What I try to do is to help people make their own decisions based on objective facts.

⑨In 2016, I became a Japanese citizen because I wanted to be involved in all levels of Japanese society. ⑩Now, I want Japan to become the leader in accessibility. ⑪I'd like to do my part to make that happen through my Accessible Japan project. ⑫I will keep working on my website in the spirit of *omotenashi*, which I have learned in this country.

このセクションの内容

筆者は、自分のサイトの情報は自分自身で入手すること、そして正直で（A.　　　　　）であることを（B.　　　　　）にしている。筆者はまた、日本がアクセシビリティの（C.　　　　　）になってほしいと考えている。

① Going back to the topic of Accessible Japan, I firmly believe in two principles.

▶ Going back to 〜は「〜に戻ると」という意味の分詞構文で、慣用的に使われる。ほかにThinking about 〜「〜について考えてみると」、Looking back「振り返ってみると」などがある。

▶ believe in 〜は「〜の存在[価値、正しさ]を信じる」。

② The first principle is to get first-hand information by personally visiting the sites.

▶ to get「手に入れること」は名詞的用法の不定詞。

▶ first-handは「直接の」、personally visiting 〜は「〜を個人的に[自分自身で]訪れること」。

③ In fact, I've visited 95 percent of the tourist locations listed on my website.

▶ I've visitedは現在完了(経験)で、「訪れたことがある」。

▶ tourist locations listed on 〜は「〜に掲載されている観光地」の意味で、listedはthe tourist locationsを修飾する過去分詞。

④ To make my website more reliable, I make it a rule to take pictures, talk to local people, and take notes.

▶ To make 〜は目的を表す副詞的用法の不定詞。

▶〈make + O + 形容詞〉は「Oを〜(の状態)にする」。

▶ make it a rule to *do*は「〜するのが常である、必ず〜するように心がけている」(≒ always *do*)の意味で、itは後ろのto *do*を指す形式目的語。

✍ 英文を完成させなさい。

私は約束を守るように心がけている。

I make (　　　) a rule (　　　) keep my promises.

▶ toのあとに3つの動詞の原形(take、talk、take)が並列している。take notesは「メモをとる[書きとめる]」。

⑤ I've been trying to upload detailed information as much as possible, such as information about steps at tourist attractions.

▶ I've been tryingは現在完了進行形で、動作の〈継続〉を表す。

▶ as much as possibleは「できるだけ多く」(≒ as much as I can)。

▶ such as 〜は「〜のような」の意味で、detailed information「くわしい情報」の具体例を示している。

▶ tourist attractionsは「観光客を引きつける場所」→「観光地」。

⑥ I try not to say, "This place is accessible, so you can go there," because accessibility varies from person to person.

このセクションの内容 の答え→ A. 客観的 B. 原則 C. リーダー

▶ try not to *do* は「〜しないようにしている」。

▶ vary from person to person は「人によって異なる」。vary は「異なる、一致しない」という意味の動詞。

⑦ I may find the place accessible, while someone else may not.

▶〈find + O + 形容詞〉は「Oが〜だとわかる[思う]」。

▶ while 〜は「だが一方では〜」という意味の接続詞。may not のあとに find the place accessible が省略されている。「私はその場所が行きやすいと思うかもしれないが、一方でだれかは(その場所が行きやすいと)思わないかもしれない」ということ。

⑧ What I try to do is to help people make their own decisions based on objective facts.

▶ What I try to do「私がやろうとしていること」が文の主語。what は先行詞を含む関係代名詞(≒ The thing (which [that]) I try to do)。

▶ to help people *do* は「人々が〜することを助ける[手伝う]こと」。

▶ make a decision は「決定を下す」、based on 〜は「〜に基づいて」。

⑨ In 2016, I became a Japanese citizen because I wanted to be involved in all levels of Japanese society.

▶ became a Japanese citizen は「日本の市民になった」→「日本人になった」。

▶ be involved in 〜は「〜に参加する、〜に没頭する」、all levels of Japanese society は「日本社会のあらゆるレベル[階層]」。

⑩ Now, I want Japan to become the leader in accessibility.

▶〈want + O + to *do*〉は「Oに〜してもらいたい」。

✍ 次の英文を日本語に直しなさい。

I want a lot of tourists to visit Japan.

私は ＿＿＿＿＿＿＿＿＿＿＿＿＿＿＿＿＿＿＿＿ もらいたい。

⑪ I'd like to do my part to make that happen through my Accessible Japan project.

▶ do *one's* part は「(人の)役割を果たす」、to make that happen は「それが起こるようにする[それを実現させる]ために」。that は⑩の文に述べられている「日本がアクセシビリティのリーダーになること」を指す。

⑫ I will keep working on my website in the spirit of *omotenashi*, which I have learned in this country.

▶ keep V-ing は「〜し続ける」、in the spirit of 〜は「〜の精神で」。

▶ the spirit of *omotenashi* を非制限用法の関係代名詞〈, which〉を使って、「それを、私はこの国で学びました」と補足説明している。

▶ have learned は現在完了(完了)で、「(すでに)学んだ」。

Grammar for Communication

1　さまざまな分詞構文（受け身・否定・完了）

受け身の分詞構文では、〈Being＋過去分詞～〉のBeingはふつう省略される。否定の分詞構文は〈Not＋分詞～〉で表す。完了の分詞構文は〈Having＋過去分詞～〉で表す。

---

1. 受け身の分詞構文：「～されて（いる［いた］ので）」「～されると」など

◆ **Written** in easy English, the book was good for me to read.
（やさしい英語で書かれていたので、その本は私が読むのに適していた）

◆ **Made** of gold, this ring must be expensive.
（金で作られて［できて］いるので、この指輪は高価に違いない）

2. 否定の分詞構文：「～しない［しなかった］ので」など

◆ **Not knowing** where to go, we stayed there for a while.
（どこに行けばよいかわからなかったので、私たちはしばらくそこにいた）

◆ **Not having** an umbrella, I got wet to the skin.
（傘を持っていなかったので、私はびしょ濡れになった）

3. 完了の分詞構文：「～してから［したあとで］」「～してしまったので」など

◆ **Having** often **met** with her, I know her very well.
（彼女にはよく会ったので、私は彼女をとてもよく知っている）
★知っている時（現在）より前のことを表す。

◆ **Having taken** the wrong train, we were late for the party.
（間違った電車に乗ってしまったので、私たちはパーティーに遅れた）
★遅れた時（過去）より前のことを表す。

2　強調構文：It is ～ that ...

特定の語句をIt is[was]とthatの間に置いて、その語句を強調する修辞法。人にはthatの代わりにwhoを、ものにはwhichを使うこともできる。

---

1. 名詞を強調する

◆ **It was** Kana **that[who]** won first prize in the marathon.

（マラソン大会で１位になったのは佳奈だった）

★*Kana* won first prize in the marathon. のKanaを強調した文。

◆ **It was** ramen **that[which]** I ate for lunch.
（私が昼食に食べたのはラーメンだった）

★I ate *ramen* for lunch. の *ramen* を強調した文。

2. 名詞以外の語（句）を強調する

◆ **It is** seldom **that** he eats breakfast.　＊副詞を強調
（彼が朝食を食べることはめったにない）

★He *seldom* eats breakfast. のseldomを強調した文。

◆ **It was** at the museum **that** I met Ann.　＊副詞句を強調
（私がアンに会ったのは、博物館だった）

★I met Ann *at the museum*. のat the museumを強調した文。

◆ **It was** because he was tired **that** he didn't come.　＊副詞節を強調
（彼が来なかったのは、疲れていたからだった）

★He didn't come *because he was tired*. のbecause he was tiredを強調した文。

3. 形式主語構文との違い

a) 強調構文のIt is ～ that .... は、It isとthatを省いてふつうの語順にすれば文が成り立つ。

b) 形式主語構文のIt is ～ that ....「…ということは～だ」は、It isとthatを省いて語順を変えても文が成り立たない。

It is important **that** we support people with disabilities.
（私たちが障がいを持つ人々を支援することは大切だ）

It is a fact **that** the universe is expanding.
（宇宙が膨張しているというのは事実だ）

4. さまざまな強調表現

◆ What **in the world[on earth]** do you want to do?　＊疑問詞whatを強調
（あなたはいったいぜんたい、何をしたいんだ）

◆ I'm not **in the least** interested in watching soccer games.　＊否定を強調
（私はサッカーの試合を見ることには全然関心がない）

◆ Please **do** come to my house in a few days.　＊動詞を強調
（近いうちにぜひわが家においでください）

確認問題

語彙・表現

1 次の語を（　）内の指示にしたがって書きかえなさい。

(1) fortunately（反意語に）　(2) ability（反意語に）
(3) accessible（名詞形に）　(4) object（形容詞形に）

2 第２音節にアクセント（強勢）のある語を３つ選び、記号で答えなさい。

ア　se-vere　イ　em-ploy-ee　ウ　dec-ade
エ　bar-ri-er　オ　chal-lenge　カ　re-li-a-ble

3 日本語に合うように、（　）内に適切な語を入れなさい。

(1) 私たちは駅までずっと走らなければならなかった。
We had to run (　　　) the (　　　) to the station.
(2) お金を持てば持つほど、もっとほしくなる傾向がある。
The (　　　) money you have, the (　　　) you (　　　) to want.
(3) 私は新しい仕事を見つけるのに苦労している。
I'm having (　　　) (　　　) a new job.
(4) 祖父は健康のために毎日運動するように心がけている。
My grandfather (　　　) (　　　) a rule (　　　) exercise every day for his health.
(5) このエッセイの筆者は今、日本人であることを誇りに思っている。
The writer of this essay is (　　　) (　　　) be a Japanese citizen now.

文のパターン・文法

1 各組の文がほぼ同じ意味になるように、（　）内に適切な語を入れなさい。

(1) When I was walking in the park, I saw a beautiful bird in the tree.
(　　　) (　　　) (　　　) (　　　), I saw a beautiful bird in the tree.
(2) Since she was born in the countryside, she likes insects very much.
(　　　) (　　　) (　　　) (　　　), she likes insects very much.
(3) I wasn't busy, so I went out to walk my dog.
(　　　) (　　　) (　　　), I went out to walk my dog.
(4) She has read the book many times, so she knows the story well.
(　　　) (　　　) (　　　) (　　　) many times, she knows the story well.

2 (　) 内の語句を並べかえて、日本語に合う英文を作りなさい。

(1) 私が好んで食べるのは母のカレーだ。

It (my mother's / that / curry / is / I) like to eat.

It ______________________________ like to eat.

(2) その大地震が起きたのは10年前のことだった。

It (ago / was / that / years / ten) the big earthquake happened.

It ____________________ the big earthquake happened.

(3) 彼の祖母が亡くなったのは、彼が5歳のときだった。

It (that / he / was / was / when / five) his grandmother died.

It ________________________ his grandmother died.

総合

次の文を読んで、あとの問いに答えなさい。

For the past decade, Japan has been making progress in creating a friendly environment for people with disabilities, but there are still many challenges to overcome. ①For instance, the entrances to restaurants often have steps which divide the building from the outside area. It could be a barrier for people (②) me. Another problem is the accessibility of hotel rooms. (③) fact, less than one percent of hotel rooms are accessible for people (④) wheelchairs.

⑤I suggest that if we meet these challenges, we will have greater business opportunities. For example, if you make your restaurant more accessible, then you will have 10 percent more customers ⑥because (the world population / of / disabled / percent / is / 10 to 15). People with disabilities tend not to travel alone. They often travel in groups or with families, ⑦which would mean many more customers.

問1　下線部①、⑤を日本語に直しなさい。

問2　②、③、④の (　) 内に入る最も適切な前置詞を書きなさい。

問3　下線部⑥が「世界の人口の10～15パーセントが障がいを持つ人々なので」という意味になるように、(　) 内の語句を並べかえて、英文を完成させなさい。

問4　下線部⑦のwhichが表す内容を日本語で説明しなさい。

Crossing the Border–*Médecins Sans Frontières*–

教科書p.60　Section 1

- □ border [bɔ́:rdər]
- □ MSF [ém és éf]
- □ in the field
- □ Switzerland [swítsərlənd]
- □ Médecins Sans Frontières [mɛdsɛ̃ sɑ̃ frɔ̃tjɛr]
- □ establish [ɪstǽblɪʃ]
- □ injured [índʒərd]
- □ as a result of ～
- □ regardless [rɪɡɑ́:rdləs]
- □ regardless of ～
- □ religion [rɪlídʒən]
- □ politics [pɑ́lətìks]
- □ organization [ɔ̀:rɡənəzéɪʃən]
- □ Madhu [mɑ́:du]
- □ refugee [rèfjudʒí:]
- □ Sri Lanka [srì:lɑ́:ŋkə]

Dr. Kanto Tomoko joined MSF in 1993. ①She was the first Japanese to work in the field with this international volunteer group. ②Here, she gives a speech to a group of high school students about her experience.

1

③After working for about eight years as a doctor in Japan, I went to Switzerland for further study. ④It was there that I joined *Médecins Sans Frontières* (MSF), “Doctors Without Borders,” an NGO established in France in 1971. ⑤MSF helps people all over the world who are sick or injured as a result of war and disaster, regardless of race, religion, or politics.

⑥I had been thinking about how I might be of some help to others as a doctor. I wanted to see different cultures and places. ⑦I had read about MSF and I had friends who had donated money. ⑧I sent a letter to an MSF office in Paris saying that I wished to join the organization. ⑨They said yes and I was sent to the Madhu refugee camp in Sri Lanka, where fighting was going on.

このセクションの内容

NGOの「(A.　　　　　) なき医師団」は、1971年にフランスで設立され、人種、(B.　　　　　)、政治理念にかかわらず、戦争や災害による病気やけがで苦しむ人々を救援している。スイスで研究していた医師の貫戸朋子さんは、パリの事務局に参加を申し出て了承され、スリランカの (C.　　　　　) キャンプに派遣されることになった。

① She was the first Japanese to work in the field with this international volunteer group.

▶ the first Japanese to work ～「～で働く最初の日本人」のto workは形容詞的用法の不定詞。toの前の名詞(句)が不定詞の動作主になっている。

例 Who was the first woman *to travel* in space?
「宇宙旅行をした最初の女性はだれでしたか」

▶ in the fieldは「現場で[野外で]」(≒ not in an office)という意味。なお、fieldには「分野」の意味もある。*cf.* in the field of ～「～の分野で」

② Here, she gives a speech to a group of high school students about her experience.

▶ give a speech to ～ about ... は「～に向かって…についてスピーチをする」。

③ After working for about eight years as a doctor in Japan, I went to Switzerland for further study.

▶ for further studyは「さらなる勉強[研究]のために」。このfurtherは形容詞farの比較級で「〔心理的に〕それ以上の」を表す。farの比較級にはfarther「〔物理的に〕より遠い」もある。

④ It was there that I joined *Médecins Sans Frontières* (MSF), "Doctors Without Borders," an NGO established in France in 1971.

▶ It was ～ that ... は強調構文。thereを強調して、「私がMSFに参加したのはそこで(＝スイスで)だった」という意味になる。

▶ *Médecins Sans Frontières*はフランス語で、英語では(英語にとっての)外国語をイタリック体[斜体]にして表すことがある。

▶ "Doctors Without Borders"は、*Médecins Sans Frontières*の英語での意味を表す。an NGO以下は「国境なき医師団」の補足説明で、establishedは「(～で)設立された…」とNGOを修飾する過去分詞。

⑤ MSF helps people all over the world who are sick or injured as a result of war and disaster, regardless of race, religion, or politics.

▶ whoは主格の関係代名詞で、who ～ disasterがpeople (all over the world)を後ろから修飾している。injuredは「けがをした」、as a result of ～は「～の結果として」(≒ because of ～)。

▶ regardless of ～は「～に関係なく、～にかかわらず」。文全体は、「MSFは～に関係なく…を助ける」という意味になる。

✍ 英文を完成させなさい。

年齢に関係なく、だれもがそのゲームを楽しんだ。

Everyone, (　　　) (　　　) age, enjoyed the game.

このセクションの内容 の答え→ A. 国境　B. 宗教　C. 難民

⑥ I had been thinking about how I might be of some help to others as a doctor.

▶ had been V-ingは過去完了進行形で、「それ以前から（ずっと）～し続けていた」という意味。ここでは、筆者が1971年にMSFに参加したとき以前から（ずっと）考えていたということ。

✍ 英文を完成させなさい。

彼が到着するまで、私たちは30分待ち続けていた。

We (　　　) (　　　) (　　　) for 30 minutes before he arrived.

▶ think about how ～は「どのように～かについて考える」の意味で、how以下は間接疑問。mightは〈可能性・推量〉を表す。

▶ how I might be of some help to othersで「どうすれば私はほかの人々の助けになるだろうか」。〈of＋抽象名詞〉で形容詞の働きをし、of helpは「役立つ、助けになる」（≒ helpful）の意味。

例 His advice was *of* no *use*.　（≒ His advice was not *useful*.）
「彼の助言は役に立たなかった」

⑦ I had read about MSF and I had friends who had donated money.

▶ had readとhad donatedはどちらも過去完了（経験）で、「（それ以前に）～したことがあった」という意味。筆者がMSFに参加した時が基準になっている。

▶ whoは主格の関係代名詞で、who以下がfriendsを後ろから修飾している。

⑧ I sent a letter to an MSF office in Paris saying that I wished to join the organization.

▶ a letter ... saying that ～は「～と述べている［～と書いてある］手紙」。

✍ 次の英文を日本語に直しなさい。

I got an email from Jim saying that he would arrive in Japan soon.
私はジムから ＿＿＿＿＿＿＿＿＿＿＿＿＿＿＿＿＿＿＿＿ 受け取った。

▶ wish to joinは「参加することを願う」。手紙を送ったのが過去（sent）なので、wishedと過去形になっている（時制の一致）。

⑨ They said yes and I was sent to the Madhu refugee camp in Sri Lanka, where fighting was going on.

▶ said yes「はいと言った」とは、「参加してよいと言った」ということ。

▶ was sent to ～は「～に送られた」という受け身。

▶〈, where〉は非制限用法の関係副詞。場所を表す固有名詞のあとに置いて、「そしてそこで（は）」と補足説明している。 ⇒p.66 G-❶

◆go onは「続く」（≒ continue）。

教科書p.62　Section 2

- □ Tamil [tǽmɪl]
- □ interpreter [ɪntə́ːrprətər]
- □ health worker
- □ equipment [ɪkwípmənt]
- □ patient [péɪʃənt]
- □ malaria [məléəriə]
- □ asthma [ǽzmə]
- □ pneumonia [njumóuniə]
- □ diarrhea [dàɪəríːə]
- □ soldier [sóuldʒər]
- □ weapon [wépən]
- □ put away ～
- □ find out ～

2

①At Madhu there were 28,000 refugees, and yet there was only one small hospital, where we had only two nurses, two Tamil doctors, interpreters, and health workers. ②We had only the simplest medical equipment to work with. ③There were times when we felt sad because we had to treat so many patients with old equipment.

④We started at 9 a.m. and treated about 150 people each day. They spoke Tamil. ⑤We asked them simple questions and decided what to do. In the afternoon, we treated people in our eight beds, usually pregnant women and babies. ⑥Sometimes we went to a small camp eight kilometers away from Madhu. We worked from morning till night.

⑦Malaria, asthma, pneumonia—these diseases were the most common. Poor food and water were also serious problems. ⑧When the rainy season came in October, diarrhea increased and we lost some of our children. ⑨We treated everyone who came to us, even soldiers carrying weapons, but only after they put their weapons away.

⑩We were told we would be safe. ⑪However, there were times when we were ordered not to go out at night. ⑫We listened to the radio to find out whether it was safe to go outside or not.

このセクションの内容

マドゥでは、簡単な（A.　　　　　）と少数のスタッフで朝から晩まで働いた。乏しい食料と（B.　　　　　）も深刻な問題で、10月に（C.　　　　　）になると子どもの患者が下痢で亡くなった。夜の外出を禁じられたこともあった。

① At Madhu there were 28,000 refugees, and yet there was only one small hospital, where we had only two nurses, two Tamil doctors, interpreters, and health workers.

▶ and yetは「それにもかかわらず」の意味で、〈接続詞＋副詞〉のひとまとまりで使われる。

▶〈, where〉は非制限用法の関係副詞で、where ～ workersがhospitalという場所を補足説明している。「そしてそこには[そこでは]」という意味になる。interpreterは「通訳」、health workerは「医療従事者」。

② We had only the simplest medical equipment to work with.

▶ simplestはsimple「簡単な」の最上級。

▶ equipment to work withは「(それを使って)作業するための機器」で、to workは形容詞的用法の不定詞。equipmentはwithの目的語になるので、withは省略できない。 ⇒p.67 G-❷

③ There were times when we felt sad because we had to treat so many patients with old equipment.

▶ whenは関係副詞で、when以下がtimesを後ろから修飾している。「私たちが悲しく感じた時が(何度か)あった」ということ。

✍ 英文を完成させなさい。

私は留学したいと思ったこともある。

There were (　　　) (　　　) I wanted to study abroad.

▶ because ～は悲しかった理由を表す。had to ～はhave to ～「～しなければならない」の過去形、treatは「～を治療する」。

④ We started at 9 a.m. and treated about 150 people each day.

▶ each dayは「どの日も(毎日)」という意味。every dayよりもそれぞれの日を強調する言い方。

⑤ We asked them simple questions and decided what to do.

▶〈ask＋人＋もの〉は「(人)に(もの)をたずねる」、decide what to doは「何をすべきか[どうすればよいか]を決める」(≒ decide what we should do)。

⑥ Sometimes we went to a small camp eight kilometers away from Madhu.

▶ campは「難民の収容施設[難民キャンプ]」、eight kilometers away from Madhuは「マドゥから８キロ離れた」。

⑦ Malaria, asthma, pneumonia—these diseases were the most common.

▶ ダッシュ(―)に続けて文や語句などを挿入したり説明を加えたりすることができる。ここでは、malaria「マラリア」、asthma「ぜん息」、pneumonia

このセクションの内容 の答え→ A. 医療機器 B. 水 C. 雨季

「肺炎」の病気について、these diseasesで始まる文で説明している。

⑧ When the rainy season came in October, diarrhea increased and we lost some of our children.

▶ the rainy seasonは「雨季」、diarrheaは「下痢」。lost some of our children「子ども(の患者)の何人かを失った」とは、「子どもの何人かが死んでしまった」ということ。

⑨ We treated everyone who came to us, even soldiers carrying weapons, but only after they put their weapons away.

▶ whoは主格の関係代名詞で、who以下がeveryoneを後ろから修飾している。「私たちのところに来たすべての人々」という意味になる。

▶ even soldiers carrying ～は「～を持って[携帯して]いる兵士たちさえ」の意味で、carryingは進行中の動作を表す現在分詞。

▶ but only after ～「しかし～したあとでだけ[～して初めて]」は、but we treated them only after ～ということ。

▶ put ～ awayは「～を片づける[しまう]」。

⑩ We were told we would be safe.

▶ were told (that) ～は「～と言われた」という受け身。時制の一致によりwouldと過去形になっている。≒ They said to us, "You will be safe."

⑪ However, there were times when we were ordered not to go out at night.

▶ whenは、timesを後ろから修飾する関係副詞。「～ような時が(何度か)あった」ということ。

▶ were ordered not to *do*は「～しないように命じられた」という受け身。不定詞の否定はnot to *do*の形で表す。

✍ 英文を完成させなさい。

私はそのケーキを食べないように言われた。

I was told (　　　) (　　　) (　　　) the cake.

⑫ We listened to the radio to find out whether it was safe to go outside or not.

▶ to find outは、目的を表す副詞的用法の不定詞。find out ～は、ここでは「～を調べる」(≒ get information about ～)。

▶ whether ～ or notは「～かどうか」。whetherのあとは〈it is ～ to ...〉の文で、itはto goを指す形式主語。「屋外に出る[外出する]ことが安全かどうか」という意味になる。口語ではor notが省略されることもある。

例 I don't know *whether* Nancy will join us *or not*.
「ナンシーが私たちに加わるかどうか、私にはわからない」

教科書p.64　Section 3

□ be beyond help
□ oxygen [ɑ́ksɪdʒən]
□ pale [péɪl]
□ improve [ɪmprúːv]
□ tank [tǽŋk]
□ make a sign
□ turn off ～
□ leave ～ in the hands of God

3

①The most difficult thing about our work at Madhu was making decisions. ②We had to think about the local situation, because looking at the situation through Western or Japanese eyes could lead us to make wrong decisions. ③Since our medicine as well as our medical equipment was very limited, we had to look at each situation as it happened and choose the best thing to do.

④I clearly remember the day when a woman brought her five-year-old boy to our hospital. ⑤I saw immediately that he was beyond help. ⑥We gave him oxygen, but he was pale, his breathing was difficult, and the oxygen mask made him uncomfortable. He was not improving. We were using our last tank of oxygen. ⑦We didn't know when the next tank was coming. ⑧If another person needing oxygen arrived, maybe this tank could save his or her life. ⑨I made my decision and made a sign to the nurse who was working with me to turn off the oxygen. ⑩The nurse simply couldn't do it. I waited five seconds and then turned it off myself. ⑪I did it because I thought it best to leave the child in the hands of God. Was that the right decision? I still don't know.

このセクションの内容

もっとも難しかったのは、（A.　　　　　）を下すことだった。ある日、5歳の男の子が来院し、1つしかない（B.　　　　　）を使ったが、治る見込みはなかった。貫戸さんはほかの患者用に取っておこうと思い、（C.　　　　　）に酸素を止めるように合図したが、どうしてもできなかった。貫戸さんは、男の子を神の手にゆだねるべきだと考えて、自分で酸素を止めた。

① The most difficult thing about our work at Madhu was making decisions.

▶The ～ Madhuが文の主語。making decisionsは「決定を下すこと」の意味で、makingは動名詞。

② We had to think about the local situation, because looking at the situation through Western or Japanese eyes could lead us to make wrong decisions.

▶looking at the situation through Western or Japanese eyes「西洋や日本の見方[視点]で状況を見ること」とは、「(医療機器が少ない現地の状況を考えずに)西洋諸国や日本の医療環境を前提にすること」を表す。

▶couldは「～する可能性がある」、〈lead + 人 + to *do*〉は「(人)に～するように仕向ける、(人)に～させる」。

✍ 英文を完成させなさい。

あなたはどうしてその結論を下すに至ったのですか。

What (　　　) you (　　　) make the decision?

③ Since our medicine as well as our medical equipment was very limited, we had to look at each situation as it happened and choose the best thing to do.

▶Since ～は「～なので」(≒ Because, As)、～ as well as ... は「…だけでなく～も」(≒ not only ... but also ～)。「医療機器だけでなく薬剤も非常に限られているので」という意味。

▶look at each situation as it happenedは「それぞれの状況を、それが起こるごとに[そのつど]検討する」。itはeach situationを指す。

▶the best thing to doのto doは、形容詞的用法の不定詞。

④ I clearly remember the day when a woman brought her five-year-old boy to our hospital.

▶whenは関係副詞で、the dayがどのような日かを説明している。関係副詞のwhenは省略されることがある。

例 I remember *the day* I met Cathy for the first time.
「私はキャシーに初めて会った日(のこと)を覚えている」

▶five-year-oldは「5歳の」という意味で、直後のboyを修飾している。

⑤ I saw immediately that he was beyond help.

▶seeには「(見て)わかる」の意味がある。saw immediately that ～は「～ということが(見て)すぐにわかった」ということ。

▶be beyond help「助けを超えている」とは、「助かる見込みがない」ということ(≒ cannot be helped)。

このセクションの内容 の答え→ A. 決断 B. 酸素タンク C. 看護師

✍ 次の英文を日本語に直しなさい。

His idea was beyond my understanding.

彼の考えは、＿＿＿＿＿＿＿＿＿＿＿＿＿＿＿＿＿できなかった。

⑥ We gave him oxygen, but he was pale, his breathing was difficult, and the oxygen mask made him uncomfortable.

▶butのあとに3文が並列している。

▶paleは「(顔色が) 青白い、青ざめた」、breathingは「呼吸」。

▶〈make＋人＋形容詞〉は「(人) を～(の状態) にする」。

⑦ We didn't know when the next tank was coming.

▶knowの目的語はwhenで始まる節 (間接疑問)。was comingは近い未来の予定を表し、「次の (酸素) タンクがいつ届く (予定) か」の意味になる。

⑧ If another person needing oxygen arrived, maybe this tank could save his or her life.

▶仮定法過去の文ではなく、過去における条件と帰結を表す直説法の文。another person needing oxygenは「酸素を必要としているもう一人 (の患者)」。needingはpersonを修飾する現在分詞。≒ I said to myself, "If another person needing oxygen arrives, maybe this tank can save his or her life."

▶this tankは、5歳の男の子に使っている最後の酸素タンクのこと。

⑨ I made my decision and made a sign to the nurse who was working with me to turn off the oxygen.

▶make a sign to ～ to *do*は「～に、…するように合図する」(≒ sign)。

▶the nurse who was working with meのwhoは主格の関係代名詞。

▶turn off ～またはturn ～ offは「(水・ガスなど) を止める」(≒ stop ～)。

⑩ The nurse simply couldn't do it.

▶否定語の前に置かれたsimplyは、「まったく、どうしても」などの意味。

▶itは「酸素を止めること」を指す。

⑪ I did it because I thought it best to leave the child in the hands of God.

▶think it best to *do*は「～することが最善だと思う」。itはto以下を指す形式目的語。

✍ ほぼ同じ意味を表すように、英文を完成させなさい。

I thought it was best to say nothing.

I thought (　　　) best (　　　) say nothing.

▶leave ～ in the hands of Godは「～を神の手にゆだねる」(≒ leave ～ to chance「～を成り行きにまかせる」)。

教科書p.66　Section 4

- □ volunteer for ～
- □ compassion [kəmpǽʃən]
- □ necessary [nésəsèri]
- □ countless [káʊntləs]
- □ follow your heart
- □ minority [mənɔ́:rəti]
- □ confidence [kánfɪdəns]
- □ have confidence in ～
- □ put ～ into action
- □ belief [bɪlí:f]

4

①My six months at Madhu passed quickly, but they were very important to me as they gave true meaning to my life and work.

②The work of NGOs like MSF is helping solve many of the world's problems, but there is so much more to do. ③It is my hope that many more Japanese will volunteer for such work, go and see more of the world, and begin to have a sense of compassion for people who need help. ④Such volunteers will find that they get as much as they give. ⑤In my own case, the experience not only gave direction to my life but also gave me an opportunity to think about what it is to live as a human being. ⑥I plan to join MSF again and continue working with them until MSF is no longer necessary. There are still countless sick and injured people all over the world.

⑦Crossing the border takes courage—your family and friends may object—but if it seems to you the right thing to do, follow your heart. ⑧You might find yourself in the minority, but have confidence in yourself and have the courage to put your beliefs into action.

このセクションの内容

貫戸さんは、より多くの（A.　　　　　）がMSFのようなNGOの活動に志願することを望んでいる。彼女はその活動を通じて、（B.　　　　　）として生きることの意味を考える機会を得た。国境を越えることには（C.　　　　　）が必要だが、それが正しいと思えるなら自分の心に従うべきだ、と述べて、彼女はスピーチを締めくくった。

① **My six months at Madhu passed quickly, but they were very important to me as they gave true meaning to my life and work.**

▶ 2つのtheyは、どちらもMy six months at Madhuを指す。

▶ as ～は「～なので」と理由を表す(≒ because)。

▶ give ～ to ... は「～を…に与える」。

② **The work of NGOs like MSF is helping solve many of the world's problems, but there is so much more to do.**

▶ The work of NGOsは「NGOの仕事」「NGOの活動」などの意味。like ～は前置詞で「～のような」。

▶ help *do*は「～するのに役立つ」という意味で、物などを主語にして、その機能を表すことがある。

✍ 次の英文を日本語に直しなさい。

This tool helps repair a broken door.

この道具は ＿＿＿＿＿＿＿＿＿＿＿＿＿＿＿＿＿＿＿＿ 。

▶ there is so much more to doのso much moreは「もっと多くのこと」、to doは「すべき…」で、形容詞的用法の不定詞。

③ **It is my hope that many more Japanese will volunteer for such work, go and see more of the world, and begin to have a sense of compassion for people who need help.**

▶〈It is ... that ～.〉「～ということは…だ」の構文。

▶ that節内の主語はmany more Japanese「ずっと多くの日本人」、willのあとにvolunteer ～、go and see ～、begin ～が並列している。

▶ volunteer for ～は「～を進んで引き受ける、～を自発的に申し出る」(≒ offer help for ～「～に援助を申し出る」)。such workとは、②の文のMSFのようなNGOの仕事のこと。

▶ go and see more of ～は「～をもっと見に行く」、a sense of compassionは「思いやりの感覚[気持ち]」。

▶ people who need helpは「助けを必要とする人々」の意味で、whoは主格の関係代名詞。

④ **Such volunteers will find that they get as much as they give.**

▶ Such volunteers「そのようなボランティアたち」とは、③の文で貫戸さんが望むボランティアたちのこと。

▶ get as much as they giveは「彼らが与えるのと同じくらい多くを得る」。

✍ 英文を完成させなさい。

驚いたことに、彼は私の2倍食べた。

To my surprise, he ate twice as (　　　) (　　　) I ate.

このセクションの内容 の答え→ A. 日本人　B. 人間　C. 勇気

⑤ In my own case, the experience not only gave direction to my life but also gave me an opportunity to think about what it is to live as a human being.

▶ In my own caseは「私自身の場合は」。主語のthe experienceとは、貫戸さんがMSFで経験したこと。

▶ not only ～ but also ...「～だけでなく…も」の構文で、２つのgaveが並列している。directionはここでは「目標」の意味。

▶〈give＋人＋もの〉は「(人)に(もの)を与える」。opportunity to thinkは「考える(ための)機会」で、to thinkは形容詞的用法の不定詞。

▶ what it is to live as ～は間接疑問で、「～として生きることはどういうことか」の意味。〈it is ～ to ...〉の構文で、itはto liveを指す形式主語。

⑥ I plan to join MSF again and continue working with them until MSF is no longer necessary.

▶ continue V-ingは「～し続ける」(≒continue to *do*)。

▶ no longer ～は「もはや～ない」。until MSF is no longer necessaryで、「MSFが不要になるまで」の意味を表す。

例 I'm afraid these oranges are *no longer* fresh.
「これらのオレンジはもう新鮮ではないようだ」

⑦ Crossing the border takes courage—your family and friends may object—but if it seems to you the right thing to do, follow your heart.

▶ Crossing ～は「～を越えること」(動名詞)、take courageは「勇気がいる」。

▶２つのダッシュ(—)に挟まれた文は、take courageについて説明を加えている。objectは「反対する」。

▶ it seems to you ～は「それがあなたにとって～だと思える」、itはCrossing the borderを指す。the right thing to doは「すべき正しいこと」。

▶ follow your heart「あなたの心に従う」とは「あなたがしたいと思うことをする」(≒do what you really want to do)ということ。

⑧ You might find yourself in the minority, but have confidence in yourself and have the courage to put your beliefs into action.

▶ mightは「かもしれない」、find yourself in the minorityは「あなた(自身)が少数派の中にいることを見出す」→「自分が少数派だと気づく」。

▶ but以下はhaveで始まる２つの命令文が並列している。have confidence in yourselfは「あなた自身の中に自信を持っている」→「自分を信じる」(≒trust yourself)。have the courage to ～は「～する勇気がある」、put ～ into actionは「～を行動に移す」。

Grammar for Communication

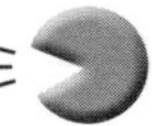

1 関係副詞の非制限用法

〈先行詞＋コンマ (,) ＋関係詞〉の形で、先行詞に説明を加える用法を「非制限用法」と呼ぶ。非制限用法で用いることができる関係副詞にはwhereとwhenがあり、それぞれ「そしてそこで[に]～」「そしてそのとき～」のように、先行詞について補足説明をする。

◆ She went to Singapore**, where** she met her old friend.
（彼女はシンガポールに行き、そしてそこで旧友に出会った）
≒ She went to Singapore, *and* she met her old friend *there.*

◆ The war ended in 1945**, when** Sally was born in Tokyo.
（戦争は1945年に終わり、そしてそのときサリーは東京で生まれた）
≒ The war ended in 1945, *and* Sally was born in Tokyo *at that time.*

---

1. 関係副詞の制限用法：where、when、why、how

◆ This is the school **where** my mother teaches math.
（これは私の母が数学を教えている学校だ）

◆ I remember the day **when** the big earthquake struck.
（私はその大地震が起こった日のことを覚えている）
≒ I remember the day the big earthquake struck.
≒ I remember **when** the big earthquake struck.　＊疑問詞whenの間接疑問
★関係副詞のwhenは省略することができる。またはthe dayを省略して「いつ～したか」（間接疑問）と表すこともできる。

◆ This is the reason **why** I didn't go there yesterday.
（これが、私が昨日そこに行かなかった理由だ）

◆ This is **how** the car accident occurred.
（このようにしてその交通事故は起こった）
★関係副詞のhowは先行詞のthe wayを含む。
≒ This is the way (in which) the car accident occurred.

2. 関係副詞の非制限用法：where、when

関係副詞の内でwhereとwhenのみ非制限用法で用いることができる。非制限用法では関係副詞は省略することはできない。

◆ Last summer we went to Okinawa**, where** we spent two weeks.
（私たちは去年の夏に沖縄に行き、そこで２週間過ごした）
◆ He visited the town**, where** his grandparents used to live.
（彼はその町を訪れたが、そこには祖父母が以前住んでいた）
◆ I was taking a shower around ten**, when** the lights went out.
（私が10時ごろシャワーを浴びていると、そのとき明かりが消えた）
◆ I want to get home by six**, when** the soccer game starts.
（私は６時までに帰宅したいが、それはサッカーの試合が始まるからだ）
◆ The park**, where** I used to play, is now closed.
（その公園は、そこで私は以前よく遊んだものだが、今は閉鎖されている）
★非制限用法の関係副詞節は、文中に挿入されることがある。

2 不定詞＋前置詞

「ペンで手紙を書く」はwrite a letter *with* a penと言うので、「手紙を書くためのペン」はa pen to write a letter *with*となる。この前置詞は省略することができないので注意すること。

◆ I think everyone needs someone **to talk to**.
（私はだれでも話し相手が必要だと思う） *cf.* talk to someone
◆ This is the box **to put** my CDs **in**.
（これは私のCDを入れる箱だ） *cf.* put my CDs in the box
◆ I have no friends **to play with** today.
（今日はいっしょに遊ぶ友達がいない） *cf.* play with friends
◆ They are looking for a cottage **to live in** during the summer.
（彼らは夏の間暮らす小さな別荘を探している） *cf.* live in a cottage
◆ There is nothing **to worry about**.
（心配することは何もありません） *cf.* worry about something

「何か書くものを持って来てください」と言うとき、次の２通りの英文が考えられる。意図するものに応じて前置詞が異なる。
（筆記用具の場合）
◆ Please bring me something **to write with**. *cf.* write with a pen
（用紙などの場合）
◆ Please bring me something **to write on**. *cf.* write on a notebook

確認問題

語彙・表現

1 次の語を（　）内の指示にしたがって書きかえなさい。

(1) organize（名詞形に）　(2) decide（名詞形に）
(3) object（反意語〔動詞〕に）　(4) believe（名詞形に）

2 第２音節にアクセント（強勢）のある語を２つ選び、記号で答えなさい。

ア　in-jured　イ　re-li-gion　ウ　pol-i-tics
エ　ref-u-gee　オ　in-ter-pret-er　カ　nec-es-sary

3 日本語に合うように、（　）内に適切な語を入れなさい。

(1) 大雨の結果、洪水が発生した。
A flood occurred (　　　) a (　　　) of a heavy rain.

(2) 読み終わったらその雑誌をかたづけなさい。
(　　　) the magazine (　　　) when you finish reading it.

(3) 父は天気に関係なく、川に釣りに行く。
My father goes fishing in the river (　　　) (　　　) the weather.

(4) よいことはすぐに実行に移すことが大切だ。
It is important to (　　　) good things into (　　　) immediately.

(5) マイクは自分の料理の技術に自信を持っている。
Mike has (　　　) (　　　) his skills in cooking.

(6) 鈴木医師は、その患者は助かる見込みがないと私に話した。
Dr. Suzuki told me that the patient was (　　　) (　　　).

文のパターン・文法

1 日本語に合うように、（　）内に適切な語を入れなさい。

(1) 私たちはこの前の土曜日に泳ぎに行ったが、そのときはとても寒かった。
We went swimming last Saturday, (　　　) it was very cold.

(2) 私が銀座のデパートに行ったら、そこで先生を見かけた。
I went to the department store in Ginza, (　　　) I saw my teacher.

(3) 彼は2000年に生まれたが、その年に彼の祖母が亡くなった。
He was born in 2000, (　　　) his grandmother passed away.

2 (　)内の語句を並べかえて、日本語に合う英文を作りなさい。

(1) 彼女は、どうすれば病気の人々の助けになれるかを考えた。
She thought about (of / be / how / she / help / could) to sick people.
She thought about ________________________ to sick people.

(2) 私たちは、授業中は日本語を話さないように命じられた。
We (speak / were / not / ordered / to) Japanese during class.
We ________________________ Japanese during class.

(3) 私が座ってよいいすはどれか、教えてください。
Please tell (I / which / can / chair / sit on / me).
Please tell ________________________.

(4) その少年にはいっしょにサッカーをする友達が大勢いる。
The boy has a lot of (play / to / friends / with / soccer).
The boy has a lot of ________________________.

総合

次の文を読んで、あとの問いに答えなさい。

At Madhu there were ①<u>28,000</u> refugees, and yet ②<u>there was only one small hospital, where we had only two nurses, two Tamil doctors, interpreters, and health workers</u>. We had only the simplest medical equipment to work (　③　). There were times when we felt sad because we had to treat so many patients (　③　) old equipment.

We started at 9 a.m. and treated about 150 people each day. They spoke Tamil. ④<u>We asked (and / questions / do / decided / what / them / simple / to)</u>. In the afternoon, we treated people in our eight beds, usually pregnant women and babies. Sometimes we went to a small camp eight kilometers away from Madhu. We worked from morning till night.

問1　下線部①の読み方を英語で書きなさい。

問2　下線部②を日本語に直しなさい。

問3　2つの(　③　)に共通して入る最も適切な語を書きなさい。

問4　下線部④が「私たちは彼らに簡単な質問をし、何をすべきかを決めました」という意味になるように、(　)内の語を並べかえて、英文を完成させなさい。

Lesson 5 Mental Toughness

教科書p.80 Section 1

- □ toughness [tʌ́fnəs]
- □ perform [pərfɔ́ːrm]
- □ perform up to ～
- □ potential [pəténʃəl]
- □ tough [tʌ́f]
- □ calm [kɑ́ːm]
- □ at the moment
- □ come naturally
- □ require [rɪkwáɪər]
- □ be ahead of the crowd in V-ing
- □ technique [tekníːk]
- □ upcoming [ʌ́pkʌ̀mɪŋ]

Yumi is in the volleyball club. ①She often gets nervous before a game. ②She found a magazine article that shows how successful athletes develop the mental toughness to perform up to their full potential.

1 Let's get tough!

③Mental toughness is the ability to use the full power of your mind and your will. ④It will help you in any situation in which you have to remain calm in the face of difficulty. ⑤Mental toughness means focusing all of your attention on the challenge that you are facing at the moment.

⑥Mental toughness does not come naturally. ⑦It must be learned. ⑧Just as physical toughness requires long, hard training, mental toughness requires lots of practice.

⑨Athletes are ahead of the crowd in developing mental toughness, but almost anyone—artists, musicians, actors, scholars, teachers, and students—can learn the techniques that athletes use.

⑩If you are facing a difficult tennis match, an upcoming concert, or a challenging examination, mental toughness will increase your chances of success.

⑪Here are your mental toughness key words: *Stay focused. Relax. Talk to yourself. Use imaging. Practice for failure.*

このセクションの内容

由美は、成功した（A.　　　　　）がどのように精神的な強さを磨いているのかを紹介した雑誌記事を読んだ。精神的な強さとは、心と（B.　　　　　）の力を最大限に活用する能力だが、学ばなければ身につかず、多くの修練を必要とする。記事では、彼らが使うさまざまな（C.　　　　　）を、キーワードを挙げて紹介している。

① **She often gets nervous before a game.**

▶ getは「～(の状態)になる」、nervousは「不安で、緊張して」。

② **She found a magazine article that shows how successful athletes develop the mental toughness to perform up to their full potential.**

▶ a magazine article that shows ～は「～を示している雑誌記事」で、thatは主格の関係代名詞。記事の内容はhow以下に書かれている。

▶ how以下はshowの目的語で、間接疑問。successful athletesは「成功した運動選手たち」、developは「～を発達[発展]させる、～を伸ばす」、the mental toughnessは「精神的な強さ」。

▶ to performは副詞的用法の不定詞。perform up to ～は「～まで達する[高める]」(≒ reach ～)、their full potentialは「彼らの最大の可能性」。

③ **Mental toughness is the ability to use the full power of your mind and your will.**

▶ the ability to use ～は「～を使う[活用する]ための能力」(形容詞的用法の不定詞)。willは「意志」。

④ **It will help you in any situation in which you have to remain calm in the face of difficulty.**

▶ Itは、③の文で述べた能力を指す。in which ～は〈前置詞＋関係代名詞節〉で、situationを後ろから修飾している。関係詞節内で、先行詞situationが前置詞inの目的語になる。 ⇒p.82 G-❶

✍ 英文を完成させなさい。

あれは私のおばが住んでいる家だ。

That is the house (　　　) (　　　) my aunt lives.

▶ remain calmは「ずっと冷静でいる」、in the face of ～は「～に直面して」。

⑤ **Mental toughness means focusing all of your attention on the challenge that you are facing at the moment.**

▶ focusは「～に焦点を当てる、～に集中する」。focusing ～ on ... で「～を…に向けること」の意味を表す。focusingは動名詞。

▶ thatは目的格の関係代名詞で、that以下がchallengeを後ろから修飾している。face at ～は「～に直面する」、at the momentは「現在、そのとき」(≒ right now)。

⑥ Mental toughness does not come naturally.

▶ come naturally「自然に来る」とは、「自然に生じる」ということ(≒ develop by itself「ひとりでに発達する」)。

⑦ It must be learned.

▶ Itは⑥の文のMental toughness「精神的な強さ」を指す。

▶ must be learnedは助動詞を含む受け身。精神的な強さは、(自然に生じるものではなく)学んで習得しなければならないということ。

⑧ Just as physical toughness requires long, hard training, mental toughness requires lots of practice.

▶ Just as ～は「～とまったく同じように」、physical toughnessは「肉体の強さ」。

⑨ Athletes are ahead of the crowd in developing mental toughness, but almost anyone—artists, musicians, actors, scholars, teachers, and students—can learn the techniques that athletes use.

▶ be ahead of the crowd in V-ingは「～することにおいて群衆[多くの人]の先を行っている」(≒ be the first to ～「～する最初の人だ」)。

▶ almost anyone ... can ～は「ほとんどだれもが～できる」。

▶ the technique that athletes useは「運動選手が使うテクニック」で、thatは目的格の関係代名詞。

⑩ If you are facing a difficult tennis match, an upcoming concert, or a challenging examination, mental toughness will increase your chances of success.

▶ examinationまでがif節の内容。upcoming concertは「近づいている(出演する)コンサート」、challenging examinationは「難しい試験」。

▶ 主節は「精神的な強さは～を増やすだろう」という、無生物を主語にした文。increaseは「～を増やす」という他動詞。 ⇒p.83 G-❷

⑪ Here are your mental toughness key words: *Stay focused. Relax. Talk to yourself. Use imaging. Practice for failure.*

▶ Here are ～.は「ここに～がある」。コロン(:)のあとにkey wordsの内容を挙げている。それぞれのキーワードは、Section 2以降の文章で説明されている。

このセクションの内容 の答え→ A. 運動選手 B. 意志 C. 技術[テクニック]

教科書p.82　Section 2

- □ Roger Federer [rádʒər fédərər]
- □ of all time
- □ Grand Slam [grǽnd slǽm]
- □ keep up ～
- □ self-confidence [sèlfkánfidəns]
- □ plague [pléig]
- □ be plagued with ～
- □ perfectly [pə́:rfiktli]
- □ when asked
- □ negativity [nègətívəti]
- □ Usain Bolt [jú:sein bóult]
- □ Jamaican [dʒəméikən]
- □ sprinter [spríntər]
- □ consider [kənsídər]

2　Stay focused. Relax.

①You might be surprised that even world-class athletes get nervous and lose confidence. ②Roger Federer is one of the greatest tennis players of all time. ③He is the winner of 20 Grand Slam tournaments. ④You might think that he would have no problems keeping up his self-confidence. ⑤You would be wrong.

⑥Roger Federer is sometimes plagued with negative thoughts. ⑦He was playing a match which he had perfectly prepared for, yet somehow he was losing. ⑧When asked how he felt, he said, "No matter how positive you are, you just see negativity flying all around you." So what is his advice? ⑨Accept all the difficult thoughts and feelings and just stay focused on the game.

⑩Usain Bolt, the Jamaican sprinter who is considered the fastest man in the world, knows the key to staying focused: Just relax. Bolt says, "⑪I try to be myself, just be relaxed, and be a fun person. ⑫I try to find somebody who I know, try to talk and laugh and just relax and not think about anything else."

このセクションの内容

世界ランクの運動選手でさえ、試合中には緊張し、（A.　　　　　）を失うことがある。時々否定的な考えに悩まされるテニス選手のロジャー・フェデラーは、そうした考えや感情を受け入れて、（B.　　　　　）に集中し続けるべきだと助言している。世界最速とみなされている短距離走者のウサイン・ボルトは、集中力を維持する鍵は、（C.　　　　　）らしさを失わないこと、リラックスすること、楽しい人間でいることだと述べた。

① You might be surprised that even world-class athletes get nervous and lose confidence.

▶ might be surprised that ～は「～ということに驚くかもしれない」。might は推量を表す。

▶ even world-class athletes は「世界レベルの運動選手でさえ」。get nervous「緊張する」と lose confidence「自信を失う」が並列している。

② Roger Federer is one of the greatest tennis players of all time.

▶ Roger Federer はテニス選手。

▶〈one of the ＋最上級＋複数名詞〉は「最も～の中の1人[1つ]」、of all time は「これまでで、史上」。

③ He is the winner of 20 Grand Slam tournaments.

▶ Grand Slam「グランドスラム」とは、国際テニス連盟が定めた4大大会で、「全豪オープン」、「全仏オープン」、「ウィンブルドン選手権」、「全米オープン」のこと。

④ You might think that he would have no problems keeping up his self-confidence.

▶ 主節の might と that 節内の would はどちらも推量を表す。would は might よりも強く確信しているときに使われ、ここでは「彼(のような優れた選手)なら～だろう」という意味になる。

▶ have no problems V-ing は「～することに問題はない」(V-ing の代わりに to *do* は使えない)、keep up ～は「～を維持する」(≒ maintain ～)。

✍ 英文を完成させなさい。

あなたをここで待つことには何の問題もない。

I have no (　　　) (　　　) for you here.

⑤ You would be wrong.

▶④の文のようにあなたが考えるなら、間違っているだろうということ。

⑥ Roger Federer is sometimes plagued with negative thoughts.

▶ be plagued with ～は「～で悩まされる」という意味の受け身(≒ be troubled by ～)。negative thoughts は「否定的な[ネガティブな]考え」。

⑦ He was playing a match which he had perfectly prepared for, yet somehow he was losing.

▶ which は関係代名詞で、which ～ for が match を後ろから修飾している。「試合の準備をする」は prepare *for* a match なので、前置詞の for が必要。

⇒p.82 G-❶

▶ had perfectly prepared は「すでに完璧に準備しておいた」の意味で、過去完了(完了)。yet somehow は「しかしどういうわけか」。

このセクションの内容 の答え→ A. 自信　B. 試合　C. 自分

⑧ When asked how he felt, he said, “No matter how positive you are, you just see negativity flying all around you.”

▶ when asked ～は、when he was asked ～を簡潔に表したもの。

▶ no matter how ～は「どんなに～でも」（≒ however ～）。no matter how positive you areで、「どんなに肯定的[楽観的]な人であっても」という意味になる。positiveはnegativeの反意語。

✍ 次の英文を日本語に直しなさい。

No matter how long it takes, we need to finish the work.

____________________________、私たちはその仕事を終える必要がある。

▶ justは「ただ～だけ」。negativityは形容詞negativeの名詞形。「あなたの周りに否定性（＝否定的な考え）が飛び回っているのをただ見てしまうだけだ」とはつまり、「あなたが否定的な考えに陥ってしまうことはどうにも避けられない」ということ。

⑨ Accept all the difficult thoughts and feelings and just stay focused on the game.

▶ Accept ～ feelingsとjust stay ～ gameの２つの命令文が並列している。

▶ stay focusedのstayは「(ある状態)のままでいる」の意味。focusedは「集中した」。stay focusedは、精神的な強さのキーワードの１つ。

⑩ Usain Bolt, the Jamaican sprinter who is considered the fastest man in the world, knows the key to staying focused: Just relax.

▶ コンマにはさまれた部分（the Jamaican ～ world）は、Usain Boltについて補足説明をしている。whoは主格の関係代名詞。be considered (to be) ～は受け身で「～とみなされている」の意味。

▶ the key to staying focusedは「集中力を保つための鍵[秘訣]」。コロン (:) は「それはつまり」という意味。

⑪ I try to be myself, just be relaxed, and be a fun person.

▶ この文と次の⑫の文は、集中力を保つためにボルトが行っている方法を述べたもの。I try to be ～, just (try to) be relaxed, and (try to) be a fun personということ。try to be myselfは「自分らしくしようと努める」、(try to) be a fun personは「楽しい人であろうと努める」。

⑫ I try to find somebody who I know, try to talk and laugh and just relax and not think about anything else.

▶ whoは関係代名詞で、who I knowがsomebodyを後ろから修飾している。whomを使うこともできるが、口語ではwhoが使われることが多い。

▶ and not think about ～は、and *try* not *to* think about ～「～について考えないように努める」を簡略化した形。

- □ emotion [ɪmóʊʃən]
- □ muscle [mʌ́sl]
- □ performance [pərfɔ́ːrməns]
- □ champion [tʃǽmpiən]
- □ cue [kjúː]
- □ whenever [(h)wenévər]
- □ mad [mǽd]
- □ scared [skéərd]
- □ be down 20 to nothing
- □ whatever [(h)wʌtévər]
- □ switch [swítʃ]
- □ switch off ～
- □ turn on ～
- □ golfer [gɑ́lfər]
- □ putt [pʌ́t]
- □ downhill [dàʊnhíl]
- □ tip [típ]
- □ make a shot
- □ Chris [krís]
- □ Sally [sǽli]
- □ in the world
- □ double-fault [dʌ́blfɔ́ːlt]
- □ in the long run

3 Talk to yourself.

Stay focused. Relax. Great advice. But how do you do that? ①One way is self-talk.

Your mind, emotions, and your muscles all work together. ②If you tell yourself you'll fail, your performance will suffer. Champions use positive self-talk to stay focused under pressure.

③Develop positive cue words to encourage yourself. ④Use these words whenever you are feeling mad, sad, or scared. ⑤Here are examples of negative and positive self-talk:

⑥*It's just too tough! / I love new challenges!*

⑦*We're down 20 to nothing! / It's not over till it's over.*

I've never done this before! / Here's a chance to learn something new.

⑧Whatever your game is, switch off the negative and turn on the positive. ⑨If you're a basketball player shooting a free-throw, tell yourself: "That basket is as big as Lake Biwa! I can't miss!" ⑩If you're a golfer trying to make a putt, talk to yourself: "It's all downhill now, right into the hole!"

One more tip: ⑪Talk to yourself in the second person. ⑫Instead of saying, "I'm going to make that shot," say, "Chris, you're going to make that shot." "⑬Sally, there's no way in the world you can double-fault!"

⑭It may not work every time, but in the long run, it will.

このセクションの内容

集中し、リラックスする方法の1つは、自分に対して（A.　　　　　）的に話しかけることだ。さらに、自分に対して（B.　　　　　）で話しかけることも有効である。この方法は毎回うまくいくとは限らないが、（C.　　　　　）にはうまくいくだろう。

① One way is self-talk.

▶ One wayとは、ここでは「集中し、リラックスする方法の1つ」のこと。self-talkは「自分自身に話しかけること、ひとりごと」。

② If you tell yourself you'll fail, your performance will suffer.

▶ tell yourself (that) ～は「～と自分に言う［言い聞かせる］」、failは「失敗する」。sufferは、ここでは「（活動能力が）低下する」の意味。

③ Develop positive cue words to encourage yourself.

▶ 動詞Developで始まる命令文。positive cue wordsは「肯定的［前向き］な合図の言葉」→「自分を肯定するような合言葉」。

▶ ... to encourage ～「～を励ますための…」は形容詞的用法の不定詞。

④ Use these words whenever you are feeling mad, sad, or scared.

▶ these wordsは、③の文のpositive cue wordsを指す。

▶ whenever ～は「いつ～しようとも」（≒ no matter when ～）。

✍ 次の英文を日本語に直しなさい。

Whenever I visit my aunt, she welcomes me.

＿＿＿＿＿＿＿＿＿＿＿＿＿＿＿＿＿＿＿、彼女は私を歓迎してくれる。

▶ feel madは「腹立たしく思う」、(feel) scaredは「恐ろしく思う」。

⑤ Here are examples of negative and positive self-talk:

▶ Here are ～. は「ここに～がある」、examples of negative and positive self-talkは「否定的なひとりごとと肯定的なひとりごとの例」。コロン(:)は、あとに例の内容が続くことを示している。

⑥ It's just too tough! / I love new challenges!

▶ スラッシュ（/）の前がnegative self-talkの例、あとがpositive self-talkの例になる。too toughは「難しすぎる」、new challengesは「新しい挑戦」。

⑦ We're down 20 to nothing! / It's not over till it's over.

▶ be down 20 to nothingは「20対0でリードされて［負けて］いる」（≒ be losing 0-20）。

▶ be overは「終わって」の意味。「終わるまでは終わらない」とは、「まだ終わったわけではない、最後まであきらめてはだめだ」ということ。

⑧ Whatever your game is, switch off the negative and turn on the positive.

▶ Whatever ～は「～が何[どう]であっても」(≒ No matter what ～)。

✍ 次の英文を日本語に直しなさい。

Whatever they say, I will not give up.

＿＿＿＿＿＿＿＿＿＿＿＿＿＿＿＿＿＿＿、私はあきらめないでしょう。

▶ switch off ～は「～をオフにする[切る]」(≒ turn off ～)、turn on ～は「～をオンにする[つける]」(≒ switch on ～)。

▶ the negativeは「否定的な考え」、the positiveは「肯定的な考え」の意味。〈the＋形容詞〉で「～なもの[こと]」を表す。

例 The child was afraid of *the dark*.「その子どもは暗闇を怖がった」

⑨ If you're a basketball player shooting a free-throw, tell yourself: "That basket is as big as Lake Biwa! I can't miss!"

▶ shootingは現在分詞で、「(フリースローのシュート)を投げている」の意味。

▶ That basketはバスケットボールのゴールのこと。〈as＋形容詞＋as ～〉は「～と同じくらい…」。

▶ can'tは「～するはずがない」。miss「失敗する」は、シュートを外すこと。

⑩ If you're a golfer trying to make a putt, talk to yourself: "It's all downhill now, right into the hole!"

▶ make a puttは「(ゴルフの)パットを入れる[決める]」。

▶ downhillは「下り坂」、(and it's) right into ～は「まっすぐ～の中だ」。

⑪ Talk to yourself in the second person.

▶ in the second personは「二人称で」。「二人称で自分に話しかける」とは、「自分に向かって『おまえは～だ』などと話しかける」ということ。

⑫ Instead of saying, "I'm going to make that shot," say, "Chris, you're going to make that shot."

▶ Instead of V-ingは「～する代わりに」、make a shotは「(球技の)ショットを打つ」。

⑬ Sally, there's no way in the world you can double-fault!

▶ there is no way (that) ～は「～する方法はない」→「～するはずはない」。in the worldは否定を強調する語句で「絶対に(～ない)」の意味。double-faultは「(テニスの)サーブを２本続けて失敗すること」。

⑭ It may not work every time, but in the long run, it will.

▶ Itは「自分に対して二人称で話しかけること」を指す。workは「うまくいく」、in the long runは「長い目で見れば、結局は」(≒ in the end「最後には」)。it willのあとにworkが省略されている。

このセクションの内容 の答え→ A. 肯定 B. 二人称 C. 最後[最終的]

教科書p.86　Section 4

- □ visualize [víʒuəlàɪz]
- □ shoot a basket
- □ in *one's* mind
- □ Emily Cook [éməli kúk]
- □ skier [skíːər]
- □ roar [rɔ́ːr]
- □ Nicole W. Forrester [nikóul dʌ́blju: fɔ́ːrəstər]
- □ scenario [sənǽriòu]
- □ occur [əkə́ːr]
- □ Serena Williams [səríːnə wíljəmz]
- □ serve [sə́ːrv]
- □ alleviate [əlíːvièɪt]
- □ nervousness [nə́ːrvəsnəs]
- □ work for ～
- □ Win or lose, ～
- □ be ready for ～

4 Use Imaging. Practice for failure.

Many champions use imaging. ①Imaging means visualizing the action you are going to take: shooting a basket or passing a football. ②Imaging is not just making pictures in your mind. ③It also involves hearing, feeling, and thinking.

Emily Cook, an Olympic skier, used imaging. ④By imagining the smell of the snow, the wind on her neck, and the roar of the crowd, Cook increased her focus and confidence. She says, "You have to hear it. You have to feel it, everything."

⑤Nicole W. Forrester, an Olympian and eight-time Canadian high jump champion, spent hours imaging what she wanted to do. ⑥She would even create bad scenarios that could occur, and then image a successful response.

Tennis great Serena Williams also images failure. ⑦She will imagine she's down 15 to 30 and hitting her second serve; she simply can't double-fault! ⑧Feeling pressure during practice helps her alleviate nervousness on game day.

Stay focused. Relax. Talk to yourself. Use imaging. Practice for failure. ⑨These techniques work for world-class athletes. ⑩They can also help you develop the mental toughness you'll need to meet new challenges. ⑪Win or lose, with mental toughness you will be ready for whatever comes next.

このセクションの内容

多くの運動選手は、イメージトレーニングを積んで、（A.　　　　　）と自信を高めている。たとえば、（B.　　　　　）をイメージして練習すれば、（C.　　　　　）当日の緊張を和らげることができる。

① Imaging means visualizing the action you are going to take: shooting a basket or passing a football.

▶ visualizing ～は「～を視覚化すること」（動名詞）。

▶ you are going to take「実行しようとしている」は、直前のthe action「動作」を後ろから修飾する節。

▶ コロン (:) のあとはactionの具体例。shooting a basketは「バスケットボールでシュートをすること」（≒ try to score in a basketball game）、passing a footballは「フットボールでボールをパスすること」。

② Imaging is not just making pictures in your mind.

▶ not just[only] V-ingは、「～することだけではない」、in *one's* mindは「心の中で」（≒ in *one's* imagination「想像力を働かせて」）。

③ It also involves hearing, feeling, and thinking.

▶ ②の文を受けて、「それ（= imaging）はまた～」という文。involveは「～を含む」。（見ることだけでなく）聞くこと、感じること、考えることもイメージすることだということ。

④ By imagining the smell of the snow, the wind on her neck, and the roar of the crowd, Cook increased her focus and confidence.

▶ By V-ingは「～することによって」。imaginingの目的語にthe smell ～、the wind ～、the roar ～が並列している。the roar of the crowdは「群衆[観衆]のざわめき」。

⑤ Nicole W. Forrester, an Olympian and eight-time Canadian high jump champion, spent hours imaging what she wanted to do.

▶ コンマではさまれた語句はNicole W. Forresterの補足説明。Olympianは名詞で、「オリンピック選手」。

▶ 〈spend＋所要時間＋V-ing〉は「～することに（時間）を費やす」。

✍ 英文を完成させなさい。

彼は図書館で、何時間も本を読んで過ごした。

He (　　　) (　　　) (　　　) a book in the library.

▶ what she wanted to doは「彼女がしたいこと」の意味で、whatは先行詞を含む関係代名詞。

⑥ She would even create bad scenarios that could occur, and

then image a successful response.

▶ wouldは「～しようとした」という過去の意志を表す。

▶ bad scenarios that could occurは「起こりうる悪い事態[シナリオ]」の意味で、thatは主格の関係代名詞。

▶ imageは「イメージする」という意味の動詞。successful responseは「(悪い事態に対する)うまい対応」のこと。

⑦ She will imagine she's down 15 to 30 and hitting her second serve; she simply can't double-fault!

▶ imagine (that) ～は、「～ということをイメージする」、be down 15 to 30は「(テニスで)15対30で負けている」。

▶ セミコロン(;)は接続詞の働きをする。ここでは「だから」などの意味。

▶ simplyは、否定語の前に置いて「絶対に[どうしても](～ない)」の意味を表す。

⑧ Feeling pressure during practice helps her alleviate nervousness on game day.

▶ Feeling ～ practiceが文の主語で、Feelingは動名詞。

▶〈help＋人＋動詞の原形〉は「(人)が～するのを助ける、(人)が～するのに役立つ」。alleviate nervousnessは「緊張を和らげる」。

⑨ These techniques work for world-class athletes.

▶ These techniquesとは、直前にイタリック体[斜体]で書かれている5つの技術を指す。work for ～は「～の役に立つ」(≒ be useful for ～)。

⑩ They can also help you develop the mental toughness you'll need to meet new challenges.

▶ Theyは⑨の文のThese techniquesを指す。you'll need ～ challengesは、mental toughnessを後ろから修飾する節。

▶ to meet a challengeは「難問に対処するために」。

⑪ Win or lose, with mental toughness you will be ready for whatever comes next.

▶ Win or lose, ～は「(たとえ)勝っても負けても～」という意味の慣用表現(≒ Whether you win or lose, ～)。with mental toughnessは「精神的な強さがあれば」(≒ if you have mental toughness)

▶ be ready for ～は「～の準備ができている」(≒ be prepared for ～)。whatever ～は、ここでは「～するものは何でも」の意味で、名詞節をつくる。whatever comes nextは「次に起こるどんなことでも」。

例 You can buy *whatever* you need.
「あなたが必要なものは何でも買っていいですよ」

このセクションの内容 の答え→ A. 集中力 B. 失敗 C. 試合

Grammar for Communication

1　前置詞＋関係代名詞

前置詞を関係代名詞の前に置くことがある。たとえば、the city *in which* I was bornは「私が生まれた都市」の意味で、〈前置詞＋関係代名詞節〉がthe cityを後ろから修飾している。話し言葉では、前置詞を関係代名詞節の後ろに置いて、the city *which* I was born *in*とすることがある。この場合、the city I was born *in*のように、whichを省略することができる。

1. 先行詞が「人以外」の場合

◆ Yokohama is the city **in which** I was born.

I was born in the city.

（横浜は私が生まれた都市だ）

≒Yokohama is the city (**which[that]**) I was born **in**.

★前置詞を後ろに置くときは、関係代名詞のthatも使える。ただし、〈前置詞＋that〉の形はない。

★この文は次のように、関係副詞whereを使って表すことができる。

Yokohama is the city **where** I was born.

◆ June 13 is the day **on which** the novelist died.

The novelist died on the day.

≒June 13 is the day (**which[that]**) the novelist died **on**.

≒June 13 is the day **when** the novelist died.

（6月13日はその小説家が死んだ日だ）

◆ This is the book **about which** she spoke last week.

≒This is the book (**which[that]**) she spoke **about** last week.

（これは先週、彼女が話していた本だ）

2. 先行詞が「人」の場合

◆ The girl **with whom** your mother is talking is Mary.

Your mother is talking with the girl.

≒The girl (**whom[who, that]**) your mother is talking **with** is Mary.

（あなたのお母さんが話している少女はメアリーだ）

3. 句動詞を使う場合

take care of ～（～の世話をする）のように２語以上で１つの動詞のように扱うものを〈句動詞〉と呼ぶ。句動詞はふつう、切り離して関係代名詞の前に置くことはできない。

◆ This is the bonsai **which[that]** my grandfather **takes care of**.
（これは祖父が世話をしている[手入れをしている]盆栽だ）
（×）This is the bonsai **of which** my grandfather **takes care**.

◆ It is an event **which[that]** anime fans are **looking forward to**.
（それはアニメファンが楽しみにしているイベントだ）
（×）It is an event **to which** anime fans are **looking forward**.

2 無生物主語の他動詞構文

〈無生物〉を主語とし、他動詞を使って「(人) に～させる」などの意味を表すものを〈無生物主語構文〉という。実際に動作を行わない〈無生物〉が、人の行動の原因や手段などになる場合、〈無生物主語構文〉で表すことがある。

◆ This sweater *will keep* you warm.
cf. If you wear this sweater, you will be kept warm.
（このセーターを着ればあなたは暖かくしていられる）

◆ This song *reminded* me of my grandmother.
cf. I remembered my grandmother when I heard this song.
（この歌を聞いて、私は祖母を思い出した）

◆ The sudden pain *caused* the runner to stop running.
cf. Because of the sudden pain, the runner stopped running.
（突然の痛みのために、ランナーは走るのをやめた）

◆ A short walk *gave* me an idea.
cf. When I had a short walk, I got an idea.
（少し歩いたら[散歩したら]、私にある考えが浮かんだ）

◆ Illness *prevented* me from going swimming in the sea.
cf. Because of illness, I could not go swimming in the sea.
（病気のために、私は海に泳ぎに行くことができなかった）

◆ What *made* him get angry?　＊疑問詞が主語の文
cf. Why did he get angry?
（彼はなぜ怒ったのですか）

確認問題

語彙・表現

1 次の語を（　）内の指示にしたがって書きかえなさい。

(1) tough（名詞形に）　(2) courage（動詞形に）
(3) shot（動詞形に）　(4) negative（反意語に）

2 第１音節にアクセント（強勢）のある語を２つ選び、記号で答えなさい。

ア　ath-lete　イ　up-coming　ウ　tech-nique
エ　sce-nar-i-o　オ　oc-cur　カ　pre-pare

3 日本語に合うように、（　）内に適切な語を入れなさい。

(1) 長い目で見れば、彼の事業は成功するだろう。
His business will be successful in the (　　　) (　　　).

(2) 多くの人々が、正体不明の病気に悩まされた。
Many people (　　　) (　　　) with the unknown disease.

(3) 私は、彼は史上最も価値のあるバスケットボール選手だと思う。
I think he is the most valuable basketball player of (　　　) (　　　).

(4) パーティーの準備はできていますか。
(　　　) you ready (　　　) the party?

(5) 私の母はちょうど今、病気で寝ている。
My mother is sick in bed at (　　　) (　　　).

文のパターン・文法

1 各組の文がほぼ同じ意味になるように、（　）内に適切な語を入れなさい。

(1) The village where my uncle lives is near the sea.
The village (　　　) (　　　) my uncle lives is near the sea.

(2) August is the month when we have a long vacation.
August is the month (　　　) (　　　) we have a long vacation.

(3) The man I write letters to every month is my grandfather.
The man (　　　) (　　　) I write letters every month is my grandfather.

2 日本語に合うように、（　）内に適切な語を入れなさい。

(1) 私がいつ彼に電話をかけても、彼は電話に出なかった。
(　　　) I called him, he did not pick up the phone.

(2) 価格がどうであれ、私はその車を買うだろう。
( ) the price is, I will buy the car.
(3) あなたが何歳になっても、ご両親はあなたのことが心配だ。
( ) ( ) ( ) old you get, your parents worry about you.

3 ( )内の語句を並べかえて、日本語に合う英文を作りなさい。

(1) これらは妹が世話をしているネコたちだ。
These are the cats (of / that / care / takes / my sister).
These are the cats ________________________.
(2) 嵐のせいで、私たちは外出できなかった。
The storm (going / us / out / stopped / from).
The storm ________________________.
(3) 彼女が突然帰ってきたので、私たちは驚いた。
Her (us / made / return / surprised / sudden).
Her ________________________.

総合

次の文を読んで、あとの問いに答えなさい。

Nicole W. Forrester, an Olympian and eight-time Canadian high jump champion, ①(she / to / spent / do / hours / what / wanted / imaging). She would even create bad scenarios that could occur, and then image a successful response.

Tennis great Serena Williams also images (②). She will imagine ③she's ( ) 15 ( ) 30 and hitting her second serve; she simply can't double-fault! ④Feeling pressure during practice helps her alleviate nervousness on game day.

問1 下線部①が「自分がしたいことをイメージするのに何時間も費やした」という意味になるように、( )内の語を並べかえなさい。

問2 ②の( )内に入る最も適切な語を選びなさい。
ア practice　イ success　ウ confidence　エ failure

問3 下線部③が「15対30で負けている」という意味になるように、( )内に入る最も適切な語を書きなさい。

問4 下線部④を日本語に直しなさい。

Reading 1 The Day We Planted Hope

教科書p.94〜p.95 *l*.6　I

- □ apartment [əpɑ́:rtmənt]
- □ unpack [ʌ̀npǽk]
- □ Claire [kléər]
- □ leaf through 〜
- □ drawing [drɔ́:iŋ]
- □ cross out 〜
- □ daddy [dǽdi]
- □ well-worn [wèlwɔ́:rn]
- □ Nebraska [nəbrǽskə]
- □ Vicky [víki]
- □ grandad [grǽndæ̀d]
- □ farmland [fɑ́:rmlæ̀nd]
- □ acre [éikər]
- □ barn [bɑ́:rn]
- □ hayloft [héilɔ̀:ft]
- □ moo [mú:]
- □ collapse [kəlǽps]
- □ laughter [lǽftər]
- □ collapse in laughter

①We had just moved to a new apartment, and my wife and I were unpacking our things. ②Our three-year-old daughter, Claire, was leafing through old books.

"Please read me this," she said.

③Claire pointed to a page with drawings and the words of an old children's song: "Do you know how to plant cabbages?" ④Someone had crossed out "cabbages" and written "watermelons!"

"Daddy! ⑤Did *you* do that?" Claire asked. ⑥I told her my grandfather had written in the book.

⑦"Daddy, why did your grandfather *do* that?" ⑧As I sat down to tell the story, my thoughts traveled a well-worn road back to Nebraska.

⑨When I was a boy, my sister Vicky and I spent summers with our grandfather in Nebraska. ⑩Grandad had been a farmer. ⑪He had sold most of his farmland, but he still kept eighty acres and a barn. ⑫Our happiest times were when Grandad took us out to "the eighty." Vicky and I loved to play in the hayloft of the old barn. ⑬Grandad would make mooing noises like a cow, and we'd collapse in laughter.

このセクションの内容

引っ越しの荷物をほどいていると、娘が古い本を見つけ、ある（A.　　　　）を指さした。だれかが「キャベツ」という文字を「（B.　　　　）」に書きかえていた。だれがなぜそうしたのかとたずねられた私は、昔、ネブラスカで祖父と過ごした（C.　　　　）の日々を思い出した。祖父は私と妹を売り残した土地に連れて行き、私たちはそこで楽しく過ごしたのだった。

① We had just moved to a new apartment, and my wife and I were unpacking our things.

▶ had just moved to ～は「～に引っ越したばかりだった」という過去完了の文。荷物を開けていたとき（過去）より以前に完了した動作を表す。

✍ 英文を完成させなさい。

電車はすでに出てしまい、私はどうしてよいかわからなかった。

The train (　　　) already (　　　), and I didn't know what to do.

② Our three-year-old daughter, Claire, was leafing through old books.

▶ leaf through ～は「（本・雑誌など）にざっと目を通す」（≒ look through ～）。

③ Claire pointed to a page with drawings and the words of an old children's song: "Do you know how to plant cabbages?"

▶ point to ～は「～を指さす」、withは「～が載っている」。

例 Alice didn't like reading books *with* no pictures or conversations.
「アリスは絵や会話の載っていない本を読むのが好きではなかった」

▶ wordsはここでは「歌詞」の意味。コロン（:）のあとは、子ども向けの古い歌（an old children's song）の題名。how to ～は「～する仕方[方法]」。

④ Someone had crossed out "cabbages" and written "watermelons!"

▶ had crossed out ～は「線を引いて～を消していた」（≒ had put a line through ～）、(had) written ～は「～と書いていた」で、どちらも過去完了。本を見たとき（過去）より以前の動作を表す。

⑤ Did *you* do that?

▶ youがイタリック体[斜体]になっているのは、強調のため。「～したのはあなた（= Daddy）なの？」ということ。

▶ do that「そのことをする」とは、④の文の行為を指す。

⑥ I told her my grandfather had written in the book.

▶ herは娘のClaireを指す。herのあとに接続詞のthatが省略されている。

▶ had writtenは過去完了で、話した（told）ときよりも過去の動作を表す。

⑦ "Daddy, why did your grandfather *do* that?"

▶ この文の*do* thatも、④の文に書かれている行為を指す。doのイタリック体[斜体]は強調のため。実際にdoが大きく発音され、「どうしてそんなことをしたの？」のような意味になる。

⑧ As I sat down to tell the story, my thoughts traveled a well-worn road back to Nebraska.

▶ As ～は「～すると（同時に）」、to tell ～は「～を話すために」。

このセクションの内容 の答え→ A. ページ B. スイカ C. 夏

▶ thoughtsは「さまざまな思い」、well-wornは「古ぼけた」。「さまざまな思いが古い道を旅してネブラスカに戻った」とは、「ネブラスカでの遠く懐かしい思い出がよみがえってきた」ということ。

⑨ When I was a boy, my sister Vicky and I spent summers with our grandfather in Nebraska.

▶ この文から、「私」(= Claireの父親)の回想が始まる。

▶ spentはspend「～を過ごす」の過去形。summersと複数形になっているのは、毎年夏休みを利用して祖父の家に滞在していたということ。

⑩ Grandad had been a farmer.

▶ had been a famerは過去完了で、祖父と夏を過ごしていたときを基準にして、「そのときまでずっと農夫だった」という意味。

✍ 英文を完成させなさい。

結婚したとき、彼らは知り合って10年だった。

They (　　　) (　　　) each other for ten years when they got married.

⑪ He had sold most of his farmland, but he still kept eighty acres and a barn.

▶ had soldは過去完了で、「売ってしまっていた」という意味。most of ～は「～のほとんど、たいていの～」。

▶ stillは「まだ、依然として」、keepは「～を保つ[持ち続ける]」。acreは面積の単位で、1エーカーは約4,000平方メートル。

⑫ Our happiest times were when Grandad took us out to “the eighty.”

▶ Our happiest timesは「私たち(=「私」と妹)がいちばんうれしかったとき」。whenは先行詞(the times)を含む関係副詞で、名詞節をつくる。

✍ 次の英文を日本語に直しなさい。

The scariest thing for me was when lightening struck nearby.

私がいちばん怖かったのは、＿＿＿＿＿＿＿＿＿＿＿＿＿＿＿＿＿＿。

▶ take ～ out to ... は「～を…に連れ出す」。the eightyとは、売らずに残しておいた80エーカーの農地を指す。引用符(“ ”)が付いているのは、その農地をそう呼んでいたと考えられる。

⑬ Grandad would make mooing noises like a cow, and we’d collapse in laughter.

▶ would (often) ～は「よく～したものだった」と、過去の習慣を表す。

▶ make mooing noises like a cowは「牛のようなモーという鳴き声を出す」。we’dはwe wouldの短縮形。collapse in laughterは「笑いで崩壊する」→「笑い転げる」ということ(≒ laugh very hard)。

教科書p.95 *ll*.7〜26　Ⅱ

- □ announce [ənáuns]
- □ pastime [pǽstàim]
- □ spit [spít]
- □ seed [síːd]
- □ hmm [m]
- □ sparkle [spáːrkl]
- □ Better 〜
- □ quick [kwík]
- □ mid- [míd]
- □ shiver [ʃívər]
- □ jump out of 〜
- □ slice [sláis]
- □ refrigerator [rifrídʒərèitər]
- □ lawn [lɔ́ːn]
- □ flash [flǽʃ]
- □ in a flash
- □ spot [spát]

①"I'm going to be a farmer too," I announced.

②"What are you going to grow?" asked Grandad.

③Suddenly I thought of a favorite pastime—spitting watermelon seeds as far as possible. ④"How about watermelons?" I asked.

⑤"Hmm, that's something I haven't tried to grow!" ⑥With his brown eyes sparkling, Grandad said, "Better get your seeds in the ground quick, though."

⑦It was mid-August and soon Vicky and I would go home and back to school. ⑧I shivered, feeling the first chill of autumn.

⑨"Let's do it now!" I said. ⑩I was so excited that I nearly jumped out of my seat. "First," Grandad said, "we need seeds."

⑪Remembering the slice of watermelon I'd seen in my aunt's refrigerator, I raced across the lawn to her house. ⑫In a flash I was back with five black seeds in my hand. ⑬Grandad suggested a sunny spot behind the house to plant the seeds. ⑭But I wanted a place where I could easily watch my plants grow.

このセクションの内容

スイカの種を吐いて飛ばすのが好きだった私は、（A.　　　　　）にスイカを育てたいと言うと、彼は「それなら早く種をまかないと」と答えた。私は芝生の向こうの（B.　　　　　）の家に行き、冷蔵庫からスイカの種を取ってきた。祖父は家の後ろの（C.　　　　　）のよい場所がいいと言ったが、私は、育つ様子がよく観察できる場所に種をまきたかった。

① "I'm going to be a farmer too," I announced.

▶ be going to be ～は「～になるつもりだ」、announceは「表明する」。

② "What are you going to grow?" asked Grandad.

▶ asked GrandadはGrandad askedと同じ意味。倒置が起きている。

③ Suddenly I thought of a favorite pastime—spitting watermelon seeds as far as possible.

▶ think of ～は「～を思い出す[思いつく]」。ダッシュ(—)以下は、a favorite pastime「大好きな娯楽」の具体的な説明。spitは「～を吐き出す」。

▶ as ～ as possibleは「できるだけ～に」(≒ as ～ as S can)。

✍ほぼ同じ意味を表すように、英文を完成させなさい。

I practiced as hard as I could during summer vacation.

I practiced as hard (　　　)(　　　) during summer vacation.

④ "How about watermelons?" I asked.

▶ 祖父の質問(What are you going to grow?)に対する答え。How about growing watermelons?を短くしたもの。

⑤ "Hmm, that's something I haven't tried to grow!"

▶ 祖父の発言。主語のthatは「スイカ」のこと。I haven't tried to grow「私が育てようとしたことがない」は、somethingを後ろから修飾している。haven't triedは現在完了(経験)。

⑥ With his brown eyes sparkling, Grandad said, "Better get your seeds in the ground quick, though."

▶〈with + O + V-ing〉は、「Oが～している状態で、Oを～しながら」と〈付帯状況〉を表す。sparkleは「輝く」。*cf.*〈with + O + 過去分詞〉「Oが～されている状態で」

例 The girl ran to me *with her hair waving.*
「その少女は髪をなびかせて私にかけ寄った」
He sat *with his legs crossed.*
「彼は脚を組んだまま座っていた」

▶〈Better + 動詞の原形〉は、You had better *do*「あなたは～するほうがいい」を短く言ったもの。

▶ get ～ in ...は「～を…に入れる」、quick「すぐに、ただちに」は副詞。

▶ 文末のthoughは「けれども、しかし」という意味の副詞で、先に述べたこととは対照的な内容を述べるときに使う。ここでは、「(スイカを育てたいなら)すぐに種をまくほうがいいけれど」という意味。

例 She was my classmate. I haven't seen her for years, *though.*
「彼女は私の同級生だった。もう何年も会っていないけどね」

このセクションの内容 の答え→ A. 祖父 B. おば C. 日当たり

⑦ It was mid-August and soon Vicky and I would go home and back to school.

▶ Itは時や時間を表す。mid-Augustは「8月中旬」。

▶ wouldは過去の時点における未来のことを述べた文。go home and back to school「家に帰って学校に戻る」とは、夏休みが終わって本来の家に帰り、また学校が始まるということ。

⑧ I shivered, feeling the first chill of autumn.

▶ shiverは動詞で「(寒さなどで)身震いする」の意味。feeling ～は分詞構文で、身震いした理由を表す。chillは「冷気、冷たさ」。

⑨ "Let's do it now!" I said.

▶ do itとは、ここではスイカの種をまくことを表す。

⑩ I was so excited that I nearly jumped out of my seat.

▶ so ～ that ...「とても～なので…」の構文。nearlyは「ほとんど、もう少しで」。「(興奮のあまり)いすから飛び降りそうになった」ということ。

⑪ Remembering the slice of watermelon I'd seen in my aunt's refrigerator, I raced across the lawn to her house.

▶ Remembering ～ refrigeratorは〈付帯状況〉を表す分詞構文で、「～を思い出しながら」の意味。slice of ～は「～のスライス、薄切りにした～」。

▶ I'd (= I had) seen in my aunt's refrigeratorは、the slice of watermelonを後ろから修飾している。過去完了になっているのは、思い出したときよりも以前に(薄切りのスイカを)見たから。

▶ race across ～ to ...は「～を横切って…に向かって急ぐ」、her houseは、おばの家のこと。

⑫ In a flash I was back with five black seeds in my hand.

▶ In a flashは「あっという間に」(≒ very quickly)、with ～は「～を持って」。

⑬ Grandad suggested a sunny spot behind the house to plant the seeds.

▶ suggestは「～を提案する」。祖父はa sunny spot「日当たりのよい場所」を提案している。to plant ～は「～を植えるために」。

⑭ But I wanted a place where I could easily watch my plants grow.

▶ 関係副詞where以下が、a placeを後ろから修飾している。

▶ 〈watch + O + 動詞の原形〉は「Oが～するのを観察する」。my plants「私の植物」とはスイカのこと。他の知覚動詞にはseeやhearなどがある。

✍ 次の英文を日本語に直しなさい。

I heard someone knock on the door.

私は、だれかが＿＿＿＿＿＿＿＿＿＿＿＿＿＿＿＿＿＿。

Reading 1

教科書p.95 *l*.27～p.96 *l*.13　Ⅲ

□ shade [ʃéɪd]
□ oak [óʊk]
□ hoe [hóʊ]
□ reaction [riǽkʃən]
□ Now what ?
□ Now comes ～
□ check on ～
□ sprout [spráʊt]
□ suppertime [sʌ́pərtàɪm]
□ plot [plát]
□ muddy [mʌ́di]
□ mess [més]

①We walked into the shade of a huge oak. ②"Right here, Grandad," I said. ③I could sit with my back against the tree, reading comic books as the watermelons grew. It was perfect.

④"Go to the garage and get the hoe," was Grandad's only reaction. ⑤Then he showed me how to prepare the ground and plant the seeds. ⑥"Don't crowd them," he said. ⑦"Give them plenty of room to grow."

⑧"Now what, Grandad?"

⑨"Now comes the hard part," he said. "You wait."

⑩And for a whole afternoon, I did. ⑪Every hour I checked on my watermelons, each time watering the seeds again. ⑫For some reason, they had still not sprouted by suppertime, although my plot was a muddy mess. ⑬At the dinner table I asked Grandad how long it would take.

⑭"Maybe next month," he said, laughing. ⑮"Maybe sooner."

このセクションの内容

私が巨大な樫の（A.　　　　　）をスイカの栽培場所に選ぶと、祖父はていねいに種のまき方を教えてくれた。そして、待つように言った。私は午後の間ずっと、スイカを調べては水をやったが、（B.　　　　）になっても（C.　　　　）が出なかった。祖父にあとどれくらいかかるかたずねると、祖父は「たぶん来月。いや、もっと早くかもしれないぞ」と答えた。

① We walked into the shade of a huge oak.

▶ shadeは「日の当たらない日陰や物陰」。類義語のshadowは「物や人が作る影（法師）」。

② "Right here, Grandad," I said.

▶ Right hereは「まさにここ」→「（スイカを育てるには）この場所が最適だ」。

③ I could sit with my back against the tree, reading comic books as the watermelons grew.

▶ sit with *one's* back against ～は「～を背にして座る」。reading ～は〈付帯状況〉を表す分詞構文で、「～を読みながら」。

▶ 接続詞のasは、ここでは「～しているとき」（≒ while）を表す。

④ "Go to the garage and get the hoe," was Grandad's only reaction.

▶ hoeは「（農具の）くわ」で、田畑を耕すときに使う。

▶ 引用符（" "）の祖父の発言が文全体の主語になっている。「～が唯一の反応だった」は、「～とだけ言った」ということ。

⑤ Then he showed me how to prepare the ground and plant the seeds.

▶ heはGrandadを指す。〈show + 人 + how to *do*〉は「（人）に～する方法を示す」。

▶ prepare the groundは「地面を準備する」→「地面を整える［耕す］」。

⑥ "Don't crowd them," he said.

▶ crowdは動詞で、「～を（ぎゅうぎゅうに）詰め込む」という意味。themはseedsを指す。つまり、「種をまばらにまきなさい」ということ。

⑦ "Give them plenty of room to grow."

▶ themはseedsを指す。

▶ 〈give + O_1 + O_2〉は「O_1にO_2を与える」、plenty of roomは「十分な間隔［スペース］」、to growは「（スイカが）育つために」。

⑧ "Now what, Grandad?"

▶ Now what? は「さて次は何を？」（≒ What should I do next?）。

⑨ "Now comes the hard part," he said.

▶ Now comes ～は「それから～が来る」（≒ The next part is ～）。副詞nowを文頭に置いて、主語のthe hard partと動詞のcomesの語順が入れ替わっている（倒置）。

　例 Here *comes the bus*! 「あっ、バスが来たよ！」

⑩ And for a whole afternoon, I did.

▶ wholeは「全体の、すべての」。for a whole afternoonで「午後の間ずっと」

このセクションの内容 の答え→ A. 木陰　B. 夕食時　C. 芽

の意味を表す。

▶ I did はI waited ということ。直前に祖父が言った "You wait."「待つんだ」を受けている。

⑪ **Every hour I checked on my watermelons, each time watering the seeds again.**

▶ every hour は「毎時」、check on ～は「～を調べる、チェックする」(≒ look at the condition of ～「～の状態を見る」)。

▶ each time は「～するたびに」(≒ every time) の意味で、後ろにI checked on my watermelons が省略されている。

▶ watering ～は分詞構文で、同時に起こる動作を表す。water は動詞で、「～に水やりをする」の意味。毎時間スイカの状態をチェックするたびに水やりをしたということ。

⑫ **For some reason, they had still not sprouted by suppertime, although my plot was a muddy mess.**

▶ For some reason は「なんらかの理由で」→「なぜだかわからないが」。

▶ they はまいたスイカの種を指す。had still not sprouted は「まだ発芽しなかった」の意味で、否定の過去完了。suppertime「夕食時」(過去) の時点より以前のことを表す。

▶ although ～は「しかし～、とはいえ～」(≒ but) の意味。

▶ plot は「構想、筋書」のほかに、「土地、区画 (ここでは耕作地)」の意味があり、my plot was a muddy mess も 2 通りの意味を持つ。1 つ目は、スイカの種をまいた区画の様子が muddy mess「泥だらけでめちゃくちゃな状態」だったということ。木陰になる場所に種をまいて、毎時間水やりをした結果を表している。2 つ目は比喩表現として、すぐにスイカの芽が出るという「『私』の構想」は muddy mess「台なし」だったということ。

⑬ **At the dinner table I asked Grandad how long it would take.**

▶ how (long) 以下は間接疑問。how long it would take で「(発芽するには) どれくらいの時間がかかるか」の意味。

✍ 英文を完成させなさい。

私は彼女に、駅までどれくらいかかるかたずねた。

I asked her how long (　　　) (　　　) (　　　) to get to the station.

⑭ **"Maybe next month," he said, laughing.**

▶「たぶん来月に (芽が出る)」ということ。laughing は〈付帯状況〉を表す分詞構文で「笑いながら」の意味。

⑮ **"Maybe sooner."**

▶ sooner のあとに than next month が省略されている。

教科書p.96 *l*.14〜p.97 *l*.12 Ⅳ

- □ lazily [léɪzɪli]
- □ melon
- □ chuckle [tʃʌ́kl]
- □ play a joke on 〜
- □ midnight [mídnàɪt]
- □ miracle [mírəkl]
- □ grandson [grǽnsʌ̀n]
- □ head home

①The next morning, I lay lazily in bed, reading a comic book. ②Suddenly, I remembered: *the seeds!* I ran outside.

What's that? I wondered. Then I realized—*it's a watermelon!* ③A huge, perfectly shaped melon was lying there, under the tree. I couldn't believe it. ④*Wow! I'm a farmer!* ⑤It was the biggest melon I'd ever seen, and I'd grown it.

⑥Suddenly, I realized that I hadn't really grown it at all. Grandad came out of the house. ⑦"You picked a great spot," he chuckled.

⑧"Oh, Grandad!" I said. ⑨Then we decided to play the joke on others. ⑩After breakfast we loaded the melon into the trunk of Grandad's car and took it to town. ⑪He showed his friends the "midnight miracle" his grandson had grown—and they let me believe they believed it.

⑫Later that month, when Vicky and I headed home, Grandad gave us a book. ⑬"For school," he said seriously. ⑭I opened it to where he'd written "watermelons"—and laughed at another of Grandad's jokes.

このセクションの内容

種をまいた翌朝、私が外に出ると、（A.　　　　）に巨大なスイカがあった。最初は自分が育てたものだと喜んだが、実は祖父がそこに置いたのだった。祖父はそのスイカを町に持って行き、友人たちに「これは（B.　　　　）が一晩で育てたものだ」と（C.　　　　）を言った。8月の後半、私と妹が家に帰るとき、祖父は1冊の本をくれた。あるページを開くと、cabbagesの文字が消されてwatermelonsと書かれていた。

① The next morning, I lay lazily in bed, reading a comic book.

▶ layはlie「横たわる、横になっている」(自動詞)の過去形。lie-lay-lainと活用する。lazily「くつろいで、だらけて」は、形容詞lazyの副詞形。
cf. lay「〜を横たえる」(他動詞)　＊活用はlay-laid-laid

▶ reading 〜は〈付帯状況〉を表す分詞構文で、「〜を読みながら」の意味。

② Suddenly, I remembered: *the seeds!*

▶コロン(:)のあとの*the seeds!*「(そうだ、)種だ！」は、「私」が思い出したこと。イタリック体[斜体]になっているのは、心の中でこのように叫んだことを表している。

③ A huge, perfectly shaped melon was lying there, under the tree.

▶ A huge perfectly shaped melonは「大きくて完璧な形をしたスイカ」。shapedは「〜な形をした」の意味で過去分詞。melonは、ここではwatermelonのこと。

▶ lyingはlie「横たわる」のV-ing形。

▶ under the treeは、thereの具体的な説明(同格)。the treeは、その下にスイカの種をまいたhuge oak「巨大な樫の木」のこと。

④ *Wow! I'm a farmer!*

▶「私」の心の中の叫び。「やった！　ぼくは一人前の農夫だ！」ということ。

⑤ It was the biggest melon I'd ever seen, and I'd grown it.

▶ Itは木の下に横たわっていたスイカを指す。

▶ I'd (= I had) ever seenは、the biggest melonを後ろから修飾する節。「それまでに見たなかで最も大きなスイカ」という意味になる。

▶ I'd grown itは「それ(= the biggest melon)を私が育てた」の意味。

▶ I'd ever seenとI'd grown itはどちらも過去完了で、巨大なスイカを見た時点(過去)より以前のことを表す。

✍ 英文を完成させなさい。

それは私がそれまでに食べたなかでいちばんおいしいケーキだった。

It was the (　　　) delicious cake I (　　　) (　　　) had.

⑥ Suddenly, I realized that I hadn't really grown it at all.

▶ hadn't really grownは過去完了で、気づいた(realized)時点(過去)よりも以前のことを表す。itは木の下の巨大なスイカを指す。

▶ not 〜 at allは「まったく〜ない」。

⑦ "You picked a great spot," he chuckled.

▶ pickは「〜を選ぶ」、spotは「地点、場所」、chuckleは「くすくす笑う」。「おまえはすばらしい場所を選んだね」というのは、「だから、まいた種がもう実になったよ」という祖父の冗談(冷やかし)。

このセクションの内容 の答え→　A. 木の下　B. 孫　C. 冗談

⑧ "Oh, Grandad!" I said.

▶巨大なスイカを木の下に置くという祖父のいたずらと、⑦の文の冗談に対する「私」の反応。「もう、おじいちゃん(やめてよ)!」のような意味。

⑨ Then we decided to play the joke on others.

▶decide to *do*は「～することに決める」、play a joke on ～は「～に冗談を言う、～をからかう」。othersはother peopleのこと。

例 My grandad would often *play jokes on* us.
「おじいちゃんはよく私たちをからかったものだった」

⑩ After breakfast we loaded the melon into the trunk of Grandad's car and took it to town.

▶load ～ into ... は「～(荷物)を…の中に載せる」、townは地域の中心になっている商業地区や繁華街を表す。

⑪ He showed his friends the "midnight miracle" his grandson had grown—and they let me believe they believed it.

▶〈show + 人 + もの〉は「(人)に(もの)を見せる」。

▶his grandson had grownはthe "midnight miracle"を後ろから修飾する節。"midnight miracle"「真夜中の奇跡」とは、巨大なスイカが一晩で育ったことをユーモラスに表現したもの。

▶theyはhis friendsを指す。〈let + 人 + 動詞の原形〉は、「(人)に～させてやる」。let me believe (that) they believed itで、「彼らは自分たちが『真夜中の奇跡』を信じていると私に思い込ませた」という意味になる。

▶ダッシュ(—)は、結末への導入を示すために使われている(⑭も同じ)。

⑫ Later that month, when Vicky and I headed home, Grandad gave us a book.

▶later that monthは「その月(=8月)の後半」、head homeは「家に向かう、帰宅の途につく」(≒ go home)。

⑬ "For school," he said seriously.

▶For school「学校のために」とは、「読んで勉強しなさい」ということ。

⑭ I opened it to where he'd written "watermelons"—and laughed at another of Grandad's jokes.

▶itは⑫の文のa bookを指す。whereは先行詞(the place)を含む関係副詞で、名詞節をつくる。whereの節がtoの目的語になっている。open ～ to ...で「(本など)～の…(の場所)を開く」。

例 Open your textbooks *to page* 30.「教科書の30ページを開きなさい」

▶another of Grandad's jokes「祖父のもう1つの冗談」は、祖父が本のcabbagesの文字を消してwatermelonsと書いたこと。

教科書p.97 *l*.13〜p.98 V

- □ be about to 〜
- □ take off for 〜
- □ soil [sɔ́ɪl]
- □ pointless [pɔ́ɪntləs]
- □ charge up 〜
- □ a flight of stairs
- □ fill 〜 with ...
- □ sprinkle [spríŋkl]
- □ take pains
- □ steal into 〜
- □ Done.
- □ sill [síl]
- □ from side to side
- □ command [kəmǽnd]
- □ mommy [mámi]
- □ prank [prǽŋk]
- □ take away 〜
- □ enthusiastic [ɪnθjùːziǽstɪk]
- □ acceptance [əkséptəns]
- □ refusal [rɪfjúːzl]
- □ get in the way
- □ zest [zést]
- □ take root in 〜

Claire listened quietly to the story. Then she asked, "Daddy, can I plant seeds too?" ①Looking at all the boxes waiting to be unpacked, I was about to say, "We'll do it tomorrow." ②Then I realized Grandad never said that.

③We took off for the market. ④At a small shop that sold seeds, Claire picked some that promised bright red flowers, and I added a bag of potting soil.

⑤On the walk home, I thought about those seeds I'd planted. ⑥Why didn't Grandad just tell me that watermelons don't grow well in Nebraska, that it was too late to plant them anyway, that it was pointless to try growing them in the deep shade? ⑦Instead of boring me with the "how" of growing things, which I would soon forget, Grandad made sure I first experienced the "wow."

⑧Claire charged up the three flights of stairs to our apartment, and in a few minutes she was filling a pot with soil. ⑨As I sprinkled the seeds into her open palm, I felt for the first time the pains Grandad had taken. ⑩He had stolen back into town that August afternoon and bought the biggest melon in the market. That night, after I was asleep, he had placed it exactly above my seeds.

⑪"Done, Daddy," Claire said. ⑫I opened the window over the sink, and she put her pot outside on the sill, moving it from side to side until she found the perfect spot. "Now grow!" she commanded.

⑬A few days later, shouts of "They're growing!"

woke us. ⑭Claire led us to the kitchen to show a pot of small green shoots. "Mommy," she said, "I'm a farmer!"

⑮I had always thought the midnight miracle was just another of Grandad's pranks. Now I realized it was one of his many gifts to me. ⑯He had planted something that could never be taken away: an enthusiastic acceptance of the happiness life offers—and a refusal to allow anything to get in the way.

⑰As Claire jumped with joy, I watched my grandfather's zest for living take fresh root in her life. And that was the biggest miracle of all.

このセクションの内容

私の話を聞いた娘は、自分も種をまきたいと言い、（A.　　　　　）な花が咲く種を選んだ。数日後、娘は「芽が出ている！」と叫んだ。私は娘が喜ぶ様子を見て、あのとき祖父が巨大なスイカを置いたのは、単なる（B.　　　　　）ではなく、祖父が私にくれたたくさんの贈り物の１つで、希望を持って生きてゆく（C.　　　　　）を私に教えてくれたのだと気づいた。

① Looking at all the boxes waiting to be unpacked, I was about to say, "We'll do it tomorrow."

▶ Looking at ～は分詞構文で、「～を見て、～を見たとき」の意味。

▶〈look at + O + V-ing〉は「Oが～しているのを見る」、to be unpackedは不定詞の受け身で、「荷物が取り出される［荷ほどきされる］こと」。

▶ be about to *do*は「（今にも）～しようとしている」（≒ be just ready to ～）。

▶ do itはplant seedsのこと。

② Then I realized Grandad never said that.

▶ thatは①の文の"We'll do it tomorrow."という言葉を指す。つまり、祖父は大事なことを先に延ばさなかったということ。

③ We took off for the market.

▶ take off for ～は「～に向かって出発する」（≒ leave for ～）。

④ At a small shop that sold seeds, Claire picked some that promised bright red flowers, and I added a bag of potting soil.

▶ ２つのthatは関係代名詞。someはsome seedsのこと。promised bright

red flowersは「鮮やかな赤い花をつける(ことが約束された)」の意味。

⑤ On the walk home, I thought about those seeds I'd planted.

▶ I'd (= I had) plantedがthose seedsを後ろから修飾している。「私が植えたあの種」とは、「私」が祖父のところで植えたスイカの種のこと。

⑥ Why didn't Grandad just tell me that watermelons don't grow well in Nebraska, that it was too late to plant them anyway, that it was pointless to try growing them in the deep shade?

▶ 3つのthat節が並列している。全体で「なぜ祖父は、～ということや、～ということや、～ということを私に言わなかったのだろう」の意味。

▶ too late to *do*は「～するには遅すぎる」、it is pointless to *do*は「～することはむだだ」。

⑦ Instead of boring me with the "how" of growing things, which I would soon forget, Grandad made sure I first experienced the "wow."

▶ instead of ～は「～の代わりに」。boreは動詞で「～を退屈させる」の意味。

▶ with the "how" of growing thingsは「栽培のしかた(を説明すること)で」。〈, which〉以下はthe "how" of growing thingsを補足説明している。

▶ make sure (that) ～は「～であることを確実にする」、I first experienced the "wow"は「私がまず"wow"を体験する」。

▶ "how"と"wow"は対照的に使われている。"how"は「理にかなった(ときに子どもには退屈な)方法」、"wow"は「体験による驚きや感動」を表している。

⑧ Claire charged up the three flights of stairs to our apartment, and in a few minutes she was filling a pot with soil.

▶ charge up ～は「～をかけ上がる」(≒ run up ～)。

▶ three flights of stairsは「三続きの階段」。踊り場から踊り場までの一続きの階段をa flight of stairsと表す。

▶ fill ～ with ...は「～を…で満たす」(≒ make ～ full of ...)。

⑨ As I sprinkled the seeds into her open palm, I felt for the first time the pains Grandad had taken.

▶ As ～は「～したとき」(≒ When ～)、sprinkleは「～をふりかける」、into her open palmは「彼女(＝娘)の広げた手のひらに」。

▶ the pains Grandad had takenは「かつて祖父がした苦労」で、take painsは「苦労する」(≒ make efforts)の意味。

⑩ He had stolen back into town that August afternoon and bought the biggest melon in the market.

▶ steal into ～は「こっそり～に移動する」(≒ go secretly to ～)。had stolen

このセクションの内容 の答え→ A. 真っ赤 B. いたずら[冗談] C. 熱意[情熱]

と (had) boughtは過去完了で、「私」が思い出しているとき（過去）よりも以前（「私」が子どものころ）の祖父の行為を表している。

⑪ “Done, Daddy,” Claire said.

▶ Doneは、I'm done「できた、終わった」で、種をまき終えたということ。

⑫ I opened the window over the sink, and she put her pot outside on the sill, moving it from side to side until she found the perfect spot.

▶ sillは「窓敷居」のこと。教科書p.98の挿絵で確認できる。

▶ moving ～は動作の連続を表す分詞構文。and movedと書きかえられる。

▶ from side to sideは「左右に」（≒ back and forth）。

⑬ A few days later, shouts of “They're growing!” woke us.

▶ 無生物主語構文。「～という叫びが私たちを目覚めさせた」→「～という叫びで私たちは目覚めた」ということ。TheyはClaireがまいた種を指す。

⑭ Claire led us to the kitchen to show a pot of small green shoots.

▶ 〈lead + 人 + to ～〉は「（人）を～に連れて行く」、to show ～は「～を見せるために」。

⑮ I had always thought the midnight miracle was just another of Grandad's pranks.

▶ had always thought（過去完了）は、Claireの種が芽を出すまでずっと考えてきたということ。justは「単なる」、prankは「いたずら」（≒ joke）。

⑯ He had planted something that could never be taken away: an enthusiastic acceptance of the happiness life offers—and a refusal to allow anything to get in the way.

▶ something that could never be taken away「決して取り去れない何か」→「深く心に残ること」。take away ～は「～を取り去る」（≒ remove ～）。

▶ コロン (:) 以下はsomethingの補足説明。さらにダッシュ (—) のあとに対照的な内容が続く。enthusiastic acceptance of ～は「～を熱狂的に[熱心に]受け入れること」、the happiness life offersは「人生が提供する幸福」。

▶ refusal to *do*は「～することを拒否すること」、〈allow + O + to *do*〉は「Oを～させておく」、get in the wayは「妨げになる」（≒ be a barrier）。

⑰ As Claire jumped with joy, I watched my grandfather's zest for living take fresh root in her life.

▶ as ～は「～したとき」、jump with joyは「喜んで飛び跳ねる」。

▶ 〈watch + O + 動詞の原形〉は「Oが～するのを見る」。take root in ～は「～に根づく」（≒ begin to grow in ～）。

確認問題

語彙・表現

1 次の語を（　）内の指示にしたがって書きかえなさい。

(1) accept（名詞形に）　　(2) mud（形容詞形に）
(3) refuse（名詞形に）　　(4) sleep（形容詞形に）

2 第２音節にアクセント（強勢）のある語を２つ選び、記号で答えなさい。

ア　gran-dad　　イ　pas-time　　ウ　re-frig-er-a-tor
エ　com-mand　　オ　mid-night　　カ　en-thu-si-as-tic

3 日本語に合うように、（　）内に適切な語を入れなさい。ただし、最初の文字が指定されているときは、その文字で書き始めなさい。

(1) 火はあっという間に燃え広がった。
The fire spread in (　　　) (f　　　).

(2) 私が到着したとき、パーティーはちょうど始まるところだった。
The party (　　　) just (a　　　) to start when I arrived.

(3) 飛行機はあと30分でハワイに向かって離陸する。
The plane will (　　　) (　　　) for Hawaii in 30 minutes.

(4) 祖母はその花びんを水で満たした。
My grandmother (　　　) the vase (　　　) water.

文のパターン・文法

1 各組の文がほぼ同じ意味になるように、（　）内に適切な語を入れなさい。

(1) The TV was so loud that I couldn't sleep.
The TV was (　　　) loud (　　　) me (　　　) sleep.

(2) He said to me, "I have been a farmer for a long time."
He (　　　) me that he (　　　) (　　　) a farmer for a long time.

(3) I was awakened by my mother's shout at five a.m.
My mother's shout (　　　) (　　　) at five a.m.

(4) Since I didn't have anything to do, I went to bed earlier than usual.
(　　　) (　　　) to do, I went to bed earlier than usual.

(5) The boy stood leaning against the wall.
The boy stood (　　　) his (　　　) against the wall.

2 (　) 内の語句を並べかえて、日本語に合う英文を作りなさい。

(1) 彼女がいちばん幸せだったのは、カナダで暮らしたときだった。
Her (she / when / lived / happiest / was / time) in Canada.
Her ________________________________ in Canada.

(2) 私は彼に、空港までどれくらい時間がかかるか尋ねた。
I asked him (long / would / to / it / how / take) get to the airport.
I asked him ________________________ get to the airport.

(3) 彼女は自分が描いた絵を私に見せたがった。
She wanted (the picture / to / she / drawn / me / had / show).
She wanted ________________________________.

(4) 私はその本の、しおりを挟んだところを開いた。
I opened the book (where / I / left / to / had) a bookmark
I opened the book ______________________ a bookmark.

総合

次の文を読んで、あとの問いに答えなさい。

The next morning, I ①(lie) lazily in bed, reading a comic book. Suddenly, I remembered: *the seeds!* I ran outside.

What's that? I wondered. Then I realized—*it's a watermelon!* A huge, perfectly shaped melon was ②(lie) there, under the tree. I couldn't believe it. *Wow! I'm a farmer!* ③It was the biggest melon I'd ever seen, and I'd grown it.

Suddenly, I realized that I hadn't really grown it at all. Grandad came out of the house. "You picked a great spot," he chuckled.

"Oh, Grandad!" I said. Then we decided to play the joke on others. After breakfast we loaded the melon into the trunk of Grandad's car and took it to town. He showed his friends the "midnight miracle" his grandson had grown—and ④(they / they / believe / believed / me / let) it.

問1　①、②の (　) 内の語を適切な形に直しなさい。

問2　下線部③とほぼ同じ意味を表すように、次の (　) 内に適切な語を書きなさい。
I (　　　) (　　　) seen such a (　　　) melon

問3　下線部④が「彼らは、自分たちがそれを信じていると私に思い込ませた」という意味になるように、(　) 内の語を並べかえなさい。

問4　祖父は友人たちにどのような冗談を言ったのか、日本語で説明しなさい。

Lesson 6 Walking in Gaudí's Footsteps

教科書p.102　Section 1

- □ footstep [fʊ́tstèp]
- □ Antoni Gaudí [æntóuni gáudi]
- □ devote [dɪvóut]
- □ devote ～ to ...
- □ Sagrada Família [sɑːgrɑ́ːdə fɑːmíːljə]
- □ chief [tʃíːf]
- □ sculptor [skʌ́lptər]
- □ major in ～
- □ sculpture [skʌ́lptʃər]
- □ a pile of ～
- □ construction [kənstrʌ́kʃən]
- □ inner [ínər]
- □ carve [kɑ́ːrv]
- □ What if ～ ?
- □ work out
- □ Barcelona [bɑ̀ːrsəlóunə]
- □ solidly [sɑ́lədli]
- □ hop [hɑ́p]
- □ hop onto ～
- □ bar [bɑ́ːr]
- □ sardine [sɑ̀ːrdíːn]
- □ wine [wáɪn]
- □ hardly [hɑ́ːrdli]
- □ Catalan [kǽtələn]
- □ atmosphere [ǽtməsfìər]
- □ feel at home

①Antoni Gaudí (1852-1926) devoted his life to the Sagrada Família. In the following interview, Sotoo Etsuro, the chief sculptor, talks about his experiences.

1

②**You are now a world-famous sculptor, but did you want to become one when you were young?**

③I graduated from an art school majoring in sculpture, and became an art teacher. ④In those days, I didn't know what I really wanted to do. ⑤One day, I was driving and saw a pile of construction stones. ⑥It may sound strange, but I heard my inner voice say, "I want to carve stones."

I quit my job and decided to go to Europe. ⑦I had only a little money with me, but I never asked, "What if this doesn't work out?"

Did you go straight to Barcelona?

⑧No, I went to Paris first, but I felt there was no place for me. ⑨The whole city was so solidly built. ⑩It was as if you couldn't touch anything. ⑪I hopped onto a train for Barcelona.

I arrived late in the evening. ⑫I walked out of the station, and found myself on a street lined with bars. ⑬I still remember the taste of the sardines, tomatoes, and wine I had that night. ⑭Although I hardly understood Spanish or Catalan, the simple food and warm atmosphere made me feel at home.

このセクションの内容

美術学校の（A.　　　　　）科を卒業して美術教師になった外尾さんは、ある日、建築用の石の山を見て「石を彫りたい」と思った。そこで職を辞して（B.　　　　　）に渡ったが、そこには自分のための場所がなさそうだった。次いでバルセロナに行き、バーで食事をした。その夜に食べた質素な料理と温かい雰囲気で、彼は（C.　　　　　）気分になった。

① Antoni Gaudí (1852-1926) devoted his life to the Sagrada Família.

▶ devote ～ to ... は「～を…にささげる」。the Sagrada Família「サグラダ・ファミリア」はスペインのバルセロナにある建設中の教会。

② You are now a world-famous sculptor, but did you want to become one when you were young?

▶外尾さんへの最初の質問。oneは不特定の１人［１つ］を指す代名詞。ここでは、a sculptor「彫刻家」。

③ I graduated from an art school majoring in sculpture, and became an art teacher.

▶ schoolは大学の「学部」や「学科」を表す。major in ～ は「～を専攻する」（≒ study ～ as *one's* main subject）。

④ In those days, I didn't know what I really wanted to do.

▶ In those daysは「その当時、あの頃」で、ここでは外尾さんが大学を卒業して先生になった頃のこと。*cf.* these days「この頃」

⑤ One day, I was driving and saw a pile of construction stones.

▶ a pile of ～は「たくさんの～、山ほどの」（≒ a whole lot of ～）の意味で、ものなどが山積みにされた様子を表す。constructionは「建築」。

⑥ It may sound strange, but I heard my inner voice say, "I want to carve stones."

▶ It may sound strangeは「奇妙に聞こえるかもしれないが」。主語のItは、but以下の内容を指す。

▶〈hear + O + 動詞の原形〉は「Oが～するのを聞く」。inner voiceは「内なる声、心のささやき」。

⑦ I had only a little money with me, but I never asked, "What if this doesn't work out?"

▶ What if ～?は「～したらどうなるだろうか」という問いかけや不安を表し、What will[would] happen if ～?を短くしたもの。thisは前文の、仕事をやめてヨーロッパに行くこと。work outは「うまくいく」（≒ turn out well）。

✍ 英文を完成させなさい。

彼が試験に合格しなかったらどうなるだろうか。

(　　　) (　　　) he doesn't pass the exam?

⑧ No, I went to Paris first, but I felt there was no place for me.

▶ there was no place for me「私のための場所がない」とは、石を彫刻する場が見当たらないということ。

⑨ The whole city was so solidly built.

▶ The whole cityはパリの市街地のこと。so solidlyは「とても堅固に」。

⑩ It was as if you couldn't touch anything.

▶ It was as if 〜は「〜であるかのようだった」。youは一般の人を指す。「何も触れられないようだった」→「(パリはすっかり完成していて) 手を加える余地がないようだった」ということ。as ifのあとは仮定法で表すことが多いが、ここでは話し手 (＝外尾さん) が事実でないと感じているのではなく、実際に感じたパリの様子を伝えている。実際の様子を伝えるときは、as ifのあとで直説法の動詞が使われることがある。

✍ 次の英文を日本語に直しなさい。

It looks as if it is going to snow tonight

今夜は＿＿＿＿＿＿＿＿＿＿＿＿＿＿＿＿＿＿＿＿。

⑪ I hopped onto a train for Barcelona.

▶ hop onto 〜は「(ひょいと) 〜に跳び乗る」(≒ jump onto 〜)、train for 〜は「〜行きの列車」の意味。

⑫ I walked out of the station, and found myself on a street lined with bars.

▶ find *oneself*は「自分を見つける」→「気がつくと〜にいる」という意味。

▶ linedは過去分詞でa street lined with 〜は「〜が立ち並ぶ通り」(≒ a street which is lined with 〜)。

⑬ I still remember the taste of the sardines, tomatoes, and wine I had that night.

▶ the taste of 〜「〜の味」のあとに3つの飲食物が並んでいる。I had that nightは、sardines、tomatoes、wineを修飾する節。

⑭ Although I hardly understood Spanish or Catalan, the simple food and warm atmosphere made me feel at home.

▶ Although 〜は「〜だけれども」、hardlyは「ほとんど〜しない」。

例 I *hardly* knew him. 「私は彼とほとんど面識がなかった」

▶〈make＋人＋動詞の原形〉は「(人) に〜させる」、feel at homeは「くつろいだ気分になる」(≒ feel relaxed)。

 このセクションの内容 の答え→ A. 彫刻 B. パリ C. くつろいだ

教科書p.104　Section 2

□ chance upon ～
□ underway [ʌ̀ndərwéɪ]
□ instinct [ínstɪŋkt]
□ architect [ɑ́:rkɪtèkt]
□ turn away ～
□ in *one's* eyes
□ outsider [àutsáɪdər]
□ discourage [dɪskə́:rɪdʒ]
□ expectation [èkspektéɪʃən]
□ meet *one's* expectations
□ overjoyed [òuvərdʒɔ́ɪd]
□ congratulation [kəngrætʃəléɪʃən]

2

What did you think when you first saw the Sagrada Família?

①I was strolling around Barcelona and chanced upon a building site where there was a mountain of stones. ②In fact, it was the construction site of the Sagrada Família. ③Although construction had been underway since 1882, there was still a lot of work to be done. ④My instinct told me that those stones were waiting for me.

You got a job as a stone-cutter. ⑤How did you manage that?

⑥I went to see the chief architect, but I was turned away at the door. ⑦Nobody knew me, and in their eyes, I was simply an outsider. ⑧Their refusal, however, didn't discourage me. ⑨I kept going back. ⑩A month later, with the help of a Barcelona sculptor, I finally met the chief architect. ⑪He gave me a chance to take a test as a stone-cutter. ⑫The question was whether I could meet his expectations. ⑬You can't imagine how nervous I was while waiting for the result, or how overjoyed I was when somebody said, "Congratulations!" ⑭That was how I became a sculptor for the Sagrada Família. It's now my life's work.

このセクションの内容

外尾さんは、サグラダ・ファミリアの建設現場に山積みにされた（A.　　　　）を見かけたとき、直感的にそこで彫刻がしたいと思った。（B.　　　　）のところに何度も通い、ある彫刻家の助けでようやく会うことができた。外尾さんは石工の（C.　　　　）を受けて合格し、彫刻家として参加することになった。

① I was strolling around Barcelona and chanced upon a building site where there was a mountain of stones.

▶ stroll around ～は「～をぶらつく[散歩する]」、chance upon[on] ～は「～を偶然見つける、～に偶然出会う」。

▶ whereは関係副詞で、where以下がa building site「建築現場」を後ろから修飾している。a mountain of stonesは「山積みの石」。

✍ 英文を完成させなさい。

私はたくさんの花が咲いている公園を偶然見つけた。

I chanced (　　　) a park (　　　) there were a lot of flowers.

② In fact, it was the construction site of the Sagrada Família.

▶ In factは「事実、実際」、itはa building siteのこと。construction siteはbuilding siteと同じ意味だが、建物以外の建設現場も表す。

③ Although construction had been underway since 1882, there was still a lot of work to be done.

▶ Although ～は「～だけれども」。had been underway「ずっと進行していた」は過去完了で、外尾さんが建設現場を見つけたとき（過去）より以前のことを表す。

▶ a lot of work to be doneは「されるべき多くの仕事」。

④ My instinct told me that those stones were waiting for me.

▶ instinctは「本能、直感」の意味で、「私の直感が私に～ということを告げた」とは、「私は直感的に～だと思った」ということ。

⑤ How did you manage that?

▶ manageは「～を（なんとか）成し遂げる」。thatは、直前の文にある「石工としての仕事を得たこと」を指す。

⑥ I went to see the chief architect, but I was turned away at the door.

▶ the chief architectは、サグラダ・ファミリアの主任建築家のこと。

▶ but以下は受け身の文。turn away ～は「～を追い払う」（≒ not let ～ enter）の意味で、主任建築家に会わせてもらえなかったということ。

⑦ Nobody knew me, and in their eyes, I was simply an outsider.

▶ and 以下は、and I was simply an outsider in their eyes「そして彼らの目には、私は単なる部外者だった」の語順を入れかえたもの。their は、サグラダ・ファミリアの建設に関わっている人々を指す。in *one's* eyes は「(人)の目には、(人)の見地からは」(≒ in *one's* view)。

⑧ Their refusal, however, didn't discourage me.

▶ 無生物主語構文。「しかし、彼らの拒絶は私を落胆させなかった」→「しかし、彼らに拒絶されても私は落胆しなかった」ということ。

⑨ I kept going back.

▶ keep V-ing は「〜し続ける」、go back は「戻る」→「再挑戦する」。

⑩ A month later, with the help of a Barcelona sculptor, I finally met the chief architect.

▶ with the help of 〜は「〜の助け[協力]で」、finally は「ついに」。

⑪ He gave me a chance to take a test as a stone-cutter.

▶〈give + 人 + もの〉は「(人)に(もの)を与える」、a chance to *do* は「〜する機会」、as a stone-cutter は「石工としての」。

⑫ The question was whether I could meet his expectations.

▶ The question was whether 〜は「〜かどうかが問題だった」。whether のあと、または文末に or not をつけることもある。 ⇒p.117 G-❷

✍ 英文を完成させなさい。

彼らにそれができるかどうかが問題だ。

The question (　　　) (　　　) or (　　　) they can do it.

▶ meet *one's* expectations は「(人)の期待にこたえる」(≒ answer *one's* needs)。

⑬ You can't imagine how nervous I was while waiting for the result, or how overjoyed I was when somebody said, "Congratulations!"

▶ You can't imagine 〜は「あなたには〜が想像できないだろう」の意味。

▶ imagine の目的語に2つの how で始まる節(間接疑問)が並列している。how nervous I was while 〜は「〜の間にどれほど緊張したか」、how overjoyed I was when 〜は「〜のときにどれほど大喜びしたか」。

▶ while waiting は while I was waiting を短くしたもの。

⑭ That was how I became a sculptor for the Sagrada Família.

▶ That は、これまで述べてきたことを指す。

▶ how は関係副詞で、先行詞の the way を含む。That was how 〜で「このようにして〜した」の意味。⑤の文の How did you 〜?の質問に対する答えのまとめとなる文。

このセクションの内容 の答え→ A. 石 B. 主任建築家 C. 試験

☐ practically [prǽktɪkəli]
☐ suspicion [səspíʃən]
☐ japonés [xaponés]
☐ ordeal [ɔːrdíːl]
☐ for a drink
☐ win (*one's*) acceptance
☐ prove [prúːv]
☐ prove *oneself*
☐ angel [éɪndʒəl]
☐ harp [hɑ́ːrp]
☐ misunderstanding [mìsʌndərstǽndɪŋ]
☐ definitely [défənətli]
☐ come around
☐ nerve [nə́ːrv]
☐ get on *one's* nerves
☐ hammer [hǽmər]
☐ for *one's* part
☐ annoy [ənɔ́ɪ]

3

①You were practically just out of art school. ②The other stone-cutters had been working for years. ③It must have been hard to fit in.

④At first, the other stone-cutters treated me with suspicion. ⑤They called me *japonés*, meaning "Japanese."

Mornings began with an ordeal. ⑥At 7 a.m., all of us stone-cutters would get together for a drink. I had to drink to fit in. ⑦But it was not by drinking that I won their acceptance; it was by proving myself. ⑧I impressed them with my first sculpture, a statue of an angel playing a harp. ⑨It was then they started to call me "Sotoo."

⑩Did you experience any misunderstandings due to cultural differences?

⑪Definitely. There were misunderstandings almost every day. ⑫For instance, when I was working, the other stone-cutters would come around to chat. ⑬That got on my nerves, so I said, "Let me work!" ⑭That made them talk even more. ⑮In the end, I got so angry that I threw my hammer to make them go away. After that, they left me alone. ⑯For my part, I had no idea why they kept annoying me. ⑰I should have known that they were just trying to be friendly. ⑱They wanted me to feel relaxed.

このセクションの内容

経験の浅い外尾さんは同僚から「（A.　　　　　）」を意味するjaponésと呼ばれたが、実力を示して受け入れられ、「外尾」と呼ばれるようになった。彼は毎日、（B.　　　　　）の違いに戸惑った。くつろがせるつもりで同僚が彼に話しかけたときも、仕事のじゃまになると感じて（C.　　　　　）した。

① You were practically just out of art school.

▶ be just out of 〜は「〜を出た（＝卒業した）ばかりだ」。

② The other stone-cutters had been working for years.

▶ had been workingは過去完了進行形。「（それ以前に）ずっと働いていた」。

③ It must have been hard to fit in.

▶ Itはto fit in「うまく調和する」を指す形式主語。

▶〈助動詞＋have＋過去分詞〉は、過去にしたことへの推量、可能性、能力などを表す。〈must have＋過去分詞〉は「〜した［だった］に違いない」と〈推量〉を表す。

⇒p.116 G-❶

④ At first, the other stone-cutters treated me with suspicion.

▶〈treat＋人＋with 〜〉は「（人）を〜で扱う」、suspicionは「疑い、疑うこと」。つまり「（仕事ができるかどうか）私を疑った」ということ。

⑤ They called me *japonés*, meaning "Japanese."

▶〈call＋O＋C〉は「OをCと呼ぶ」、meaning 〜は「〜を意味する」（≒ which means 〜）。

⑥ At 7 a.m., all of us stone-cutters would get together for a drink.

▶ usとstone-cuttersは同格で「私たち石工」という意味。

▶ would *do*は「〜したものだった」の意味で、過去の習慣を表す。drinkは名詞で、「（一杯の）酒」を表す。

⑦ But it was not by drinking that I won their acceptance; it was by proving myself.

▶ itはthat以下を指す形式主語。win (*one's*) acceptanceは「（人）に受け入れられる」（≒ become part of the group）。

▶ セミコロン（;）は接続詞と同じ働きをし、ここではnotに対応して「〜ではなくて」（≒ but）の意味。prove *oneself*は「自分自身［自分の力量］を証明する」（≒ show *one's* ability）。

⑧ I impressed them with my first sculpture, a statue of an angel playing a harp.

▶〈impress＋人＋with＋もの〉は「（もの）で（人）に感銘を与える」。

▶ コンマのあとは、my first sculptureの具体的な説明。

⑨ It was then they started to call me "Sotoo."

▶ It is ... (that) ～. の強調構文で、thatが省略されている。「彼らが～したのはそのときだった」と、thenを強調した文。

⑩ Did you experience any misunderstandings due to cultural differences?

▶ misunderstandingは「誤解」、due to ～は「～のせいで、～が原因で」(≒ because of ～, owing to ～)。

⑪ Definitely.

▶ ⑩の質問への答え。≒ Definitely yes.「もちろん(誤解を)経験しました。」

⑫ For instance, when I was working, the other stone-cutters would come around to chat.

▶ For instanceは「例えば」(≒ For example)、would *do*は過去の習慣、come around to chatは「おしゃべりをしに立ち寄る」(come around ≒ stop by)。

⑬ That got on my nerves, so I said, "Let me work!"

▶ Thatは⑫の文の「ほかの石工がおしゃべりをしに来ること」を指す。get on *one's* nervesは「(人)をいらいらさせる」(≒ make ～ angry)。

✍ 英文を完成させなさい。

彼女の態度で、私はいらいらした。

Her attitude (　　　) on my (　　　).

⑭ That made them talk even more.

▶ Thatは、"Let me work!"「私を働かせてくれ！」という言葉を指す。

▶ 〈make＋人＋動詞の原形〉は「(人)に～させる」、evenは「さらに」。

⑮ In the end, I got so angry that I threw my hammer to make them go away.

▶ so ～ that ...「とても～なので…」の構文。to make them go awayは「彼ら(＝同僚)を追い払うために」。

⑯ For my part, I had no idea why they kept annoying me.

▶ For my partは「私としては」(≒ As for me)。

▶ I had no idea why ～は「なぜ～なのか、私にはわからなかった」(≒ I didn't know why ～)ということ。keep V-ingは「～し続ける」。

⑰ I should have known that they were just trying to be friendly.

▶ 〈should＋have＋過去分詞〉は「～すべきだった(のにしなかった)」という後悔を表す。

⑱ They wanted me to feel relaxed.

▶ 〈want＋人＋to *do*〉は「(人)に～してもらいたい」、feel relaxedは「くつろぐ」。

このセクションの内容 の答え→　A. 日本人　B. 文化　C. いらいら

教科書p.108　Section 4

☐ dedicate [dédɪkèɪt]
☐ dedicate *oneself* to ～
☐ inspiration [ìnspəréɪʃən]
☐ sketch [skétʃ]
☐ consider ～ as ...
☐ absolutely [ǽbsəlù:tli]
☐ struggle [strʌ́gl]
☐ fit into ～
☐ tomb [tú:m]
☐ path [pǽθ]
☐ from that day on
☐ philosophy [fəlásəfi]
☐ walk in *one's* footsteps
☐ motto [mátou]
☐ encounter [enkáuntər]
☐ take up
☐ passion [pǽʃən]
☐ optimistic [àptɪmístɪk]
☐ loose [lú:s]
☐ cut loose
☐ once in a while

4

①**You've dedicated yourself to the Sagrada Família for over 40 years.** ②**What keeps you going?**

③Gaudí is my inspiration. ④He started working on this project, knowing that he wouldn't be able to complete it. ⑤When he died, he didn't leave detailed plans; he left only some sketches, models, and followers. ⑥I consider myself as one of his followers.

⑦**Working without detailed plans must have been hard, right?**

⑧Absolutely. ⑨I really had to struggle to find how to make sculptures that would fit into Gaudí's work. One day, when I was visiting Gaudí's tomb, I heard his voice: ⑩"Don't look at what I have done; look at what I was looking at." ⑪I thought, "This is a path I can follow."

⑫From that day on, I have been trying to understand Gaudí's philosophy, his respect for nature, and the inspiration he received from it. ⑬In short, I am walking in Gaudí's footsteps.

One last question: ⑭**Do you have mottos you live by?**

Life is full of encounters and challenges. ⑮Be ready to take up any challenges with passion and courage. ⑯Have good friends who make you optimistic. ⑰And one more thing: Cut loose once in a while.

このセクションの内容

ガウディは詳細な（A.　　　　　）を残さなかったので、外尾さんはガウディの哲学や（B.　　　　　）への敬意、そしてそこから受けた霊感を理解しようと努めた。彼は最後に、「人生は（C.　　　　　）と挑戦に満ちている」と述べ、自分のモットーを紹介している。

① You've dedicated yourself to the Sagrada Família for over 40 years.

▶ dedicate *oneself* to ～は「自分自身を～にささげる、～に専念する」(≒ devote *oneself* to ～)。

② What keeps you going?

▶無生物主語構文。〈keep + 人 + V-ing〉は「(人) に～させ続ける」で、ここでは理由をたずねている。≒ Why do you keep going?

③ Gaudí is my inspiration.

▶「ガウディは私に霊感を与えてくれる存在だ」ということ。

④ He started working on this project, knowing that he wouldn't be able to complete it.

▶ He は Gaudí を指す。this project「この事業」とは、サグラダ・ファミリアの建築のこと。

▶ knowing ～は〈付帯状況〉を表す分詞構文で「～を知りながら」の意味。

✍ 次の英文を日本語に直しなさい。

He swam in the river, knowing it was dangerous.

彼は、＿＿＿＿＿＿＿＿＿＿＿＿＿＿＿＿その川で泳いだ。

⑤ When he died, he didn't leave detailed plans; he left only some sketches, models, and followers.

▶ detailed plans「詳細な計画」は、サグラダ・ファミリアの建設計画のこと。

▶ガウディが残さなかったものと残したものの対比がわかるように、セミコロン (;) で２文がつながれている。followers は「(ガウディの) 信奉者」。

⑥ I consider myself as one of his followers.

▶ consider ～ as ... は「～を…とみなす」(≒ think of ～ as ...)。

⑦ Working without detailed plans must have been hard, right?

▶ Working without ～は「～なしで働くこと」。

▶ must have been hard は「大変だったに違いない」と、過去のことへの〈推量〉を表す。文末の right? は「～ですよね」と、念を押す表現。

⑧ Absolutely.

▶⑦の質問への答えで「まったくその通り」の意味。≒ Absolutely yes.

⑨ I really had to struggle to find how to make sculptures that would fit into Gaudí's work.

▶ struggle to ～は「～しようと努める[奮闘する]」、find how to make ～は「～の作り方を見つける」。

▶ thatは主格の関係代名詞で、that以下がsculpturesを後ろから修飾している。fit into ～は「～とぴったりと合う、調和する」(≒ match ～)。

⑩ "Don't look at what I have done; look at what I was looking at."

▶ 2つの命令文が並んでいる。what I have doneは「私が(すでに)したこと」、what I was looking atは「私が見て[目を向けて]いたこと」の意味。

✍ 英文を完成させなさい。

あなたは自分がしたことに満足していますか。

Are you satisfied with (　　　) you (　　　) (　　　)?

⑪ I thought, "This is a path I can follow."

▶ Thisは、⑩の文の内容を指す。I can follow「私が従うことができる」は、path「進路、方向」を後ろから修飾する節。

⑫ From that day on, I have been trying to understand Gaudí's philosophy, his respect for nature, and the inspiration he received from it.

▶ From that day onは「その日から、その日以来」、have been trying to ～は「(ずっと) ～するように努めている」という現在完了進行形。

▶ understandの目的語が3つ並列している。the inspiration he received from itは「彼がそれ(=自然)から受け取った霊感」の意味。

⑬ In short, I am walking in Gaudí's footsteps.

▶ In shortは「要するに」、walk in *one's* footstepsは「(人)の足跡を歩く」→「(人)の志を継ぐ」(≒ follow *one's* example)。

⑭ Do you have mottos you live by?

▶ you live byは、mottos「座右の銘、モットー」を後ろから修飾する節。live by ～は「～を生活の指針とする」。

⑮ Be ready to take up any challenges with passion and courage.

▶ ⑮、⑯、⑰の文は外尾さんのモットーで、すべて命令文になっている。take up ～は「～を受け入れる」(≒ accept)、with ～は「～を持って」。

⑯ Have good friends who make you optimistic.

▶ whoは主格の関係代名詞。make you optimisticは「あなたを楽観的にする」。

⑰ And one more thing: Cut loose once in a while.

▶ cut looseは「思い切り楽しむ」(≒ relax)、once in a whileは「時々、たまには」(≒ sometimes)。「はめをはずすことも時には必要だ」ということ。

このセクションの内容 の答え→ A. 計画　B. 自然　C. 出会い

Grammar for Communication

1 助動詞＋have＋過去分詞

〈助動詞＋have＋過去分詞〉を使って、過去のことがらに対する現在の〈推量〉、〈推量・後悔・非難〉、〈可能性・能力〉などを表すことができる。

---

1. must＋have＋過去分詞：「〜した[だった]に違いない」〈推量〉

◆ She **must have been** sad to hear the news.
（その知らせを聞いて、彼女は悲しかったに違いない）

◆ He **must have seen** the car accident.
（彼はその自動車事故を見たに違いない）

2. should＋have＋過去分詞

① 「〜すべきだった（のに）」〈後悔・非難〉

◆ It's going to rain. I **should have brought** an umbrella. ＊後悔
（雨が降りそうだ。私は傘を持ってくるべきだった）
★実際には持ってこなかったことを表している。

◆ You **shouldn't have said** such a thing to him. ＊非難
（あなたは彼にそんなことを言うべきではなかった）
★実際には言ったことを表している。

② 「当然〜した[だった]はずだ」〈推量〉

◆ He **should have returned** home before eight.
（彼は８時前には家に戻ったはずだ）

3. might[may]＋have＋過去分詞：「もしかしたら〜した[だった]かもしれない」〈推量〉

◆ I cannot find my watch. I **might have left** it at the office.
（腕時計が見つからない。事務所に置いてきたかもしれない）

4. could＋have＋過去分詞：「〜した[できた]かもしれない」〈可能性・能力〉

◆ Your drunk driving **could have caused** an accident.
（あなたは飲酒運転で事故を起こしていたかもしれない）
★実際には起こらなかったことでも、起こる可能性があったと相手の行動を非難している。

疑問文や否定文では、強い疑いや否定を表すことがある。

◆ Who **could have imagined** this would happen?
（こんなことが起こるとだれが想像できただろうか）
≒ No one **could have imagined** this would happen.

◆ I saw her at school yesterday. She **couldn't have been** in Okinawa yesterday.
（私は昨日学校で彼女を見た。彼女が昨日、沖縄にいたはずがない）

5. would＋have＋過去分詞：「～した[だった]だろう」〈推量〉

◆ Mike left home three hours ago. He **would have arrived** there by now.
（マイクは3時間前に家を出た。今はそこに到着しているだろう）
★話し手はマイクが到着したかどうかは知らない。

〈would[could] + have + 過去分詞〉は仮定法過去完了の文で、過去の事実に反する仮定を表すときに使う。

◆ If you had been there, I **would have spoken** to you.
（もしあなたがそこにいたら、私はあなたに話しかけただろうに）

2 S is C (C＝whether節)

〈S＋V＋C〉のCの位置にwhetherで始まる節がくることがある。whether節は「～かどうかということ」を表す名詞節で、whether or not ～またはwhether ～ or notのように表すこともある。

◆ **The question is whether** he will agree with us.
（問題は、彼が私たちに同意するかどうかだ）

◆ **What I want to know is whether or not** these products will sell well.
（私が知りたいのは、これらの製品がよく売れるかどうかだ）

◆ **Whether** they will help us is not clear.
（彼らが私たちを手伝ってくれるかどうか、はっきりしない）

◆ She asked me **whether** I had a brother.
（彼女は、私に兄弟がいるかどうかたずねた）

whether節には、副詞節としての用法もある。

◆ **Whether she wins or loses**, she never changes her facial expression.
（勝っても負けても、彼女は決して表情を変えない）

◆ You should go there **whether you like it or not**.
（好むと好まざるとにかかわらず、あなたはそこに行くべきだ）

確認問題

語彙・表現

1 第２音節にアクセント（強勢）のある語を２つ選び、記号で答えなさい。

ア dis-cour-age　　イ in-stinct　　ウ ar-chi-tect
エ out-sid-er　　オ at-mo-sphere　　カ def-i-nite-ly

2 日本語に合うように、（　）内に適切な語を入れなさい。

(1) 彼女は大学で経済学を専攻した。
She (　　) (　　) economics in college.

(2) 母は、ホテルではくつろげないと言っている。
My mother says that she can't (　　) (　　) (　　) in a hotel.

(3) 彼は数学の研究に生涯をささげた。
He (　　) his life (　　) studying mathematics.

(4) 大雨でこの電車が止まったらどうしよう。
(　　) (　　) this train stops due to the heavy rain?

(5) 私は懸命に努力したが、うまくいかなかった。
I tried hard, but it did not (　　) (　　).

文のパターン・文法

1 各組の文がほぼ同じ意味になるように、（　）内に適切な語を入れなさい。

(1) I regret that I didn't bring my camera today.
I (　　) (　　) brought my camera today.

(2) The rainy weather may be a problem tomorrow.
The question is (　　) or (　　) it will be rainy tomorrow.

2 日本語に合うように、（　）内に適切な語を入れなさい。

(1) 彼はめがねをかけないで出かけたに違いない。
He (　　) (　　) (　　) out without wearing his glasses.

(2) その話は聞いたかもしれないが、私はそれを覚えていない。
I (　　) (　　) (　　) the story, but I don't remember it.

(3) 私はそのイベントに参加できたのだが、参加しなかった。
I (　　) (　　) attended the event, but I didn't.

3 (　) 内の語句を並べかえて、日本語に合う英文を作りなさい。

(1) あの男性はきっと、若いとき足が速かっただろう。

That man (been / must / a fast / have / runner) when he was young.

That man ______________________________ when he was young.

(2) どうして私がそれを信じることができただろうか。

How (believed / have / I / could / it)?

How ______________________________?

(3) 私が知りたかったのは、彼が真実を話しているかどうかだ。

What I wanted to know (he / whether / the truth / telling / was / was).

What I wanted to know ______________________________.

総合

次の文を読んで、あとの問いに答えなさい。

Working without detailed plans must have been hard, right?

Absolutely. ①I really had to struggle to find how to make sculptures that would fit into Gaudí's work. One day, when I was visiting Gaudí's tomb, I heard his voice: "Don't look at what I have done; look at what I was looking at." I thought, "This is a path I can follow."

From that day (②), I have been trying to understand Gaudí's philosophy, his respect for nature, and the inspiration he received from it. In short, I am walking in ③Gaudí's footsteps.

One last question: Do you have mottos you live by?

Life is full of encounters and challenges. Be ready to take up any challenges with passion and courage. Have good friends who make you optimistic. And one more thing: Cut loose once in a while.

問１　下線部①を日本語に直しなさい。

問２　②の (　) 内に入る最も適切な語を選びなさい。

ア on　イ at　ウ of　エ in

問３　下線部③の具体的な内容を本文中の英語で３つ答えなさい。

問４　「私」が座右の銘としているのはどのようなことか。１つ選んで日本語で説明しなさい。

Lesson 7 Why Biomimicry?

教科書p.122　Section 1

- □ biomimicry [bàɪəmímɪkri]
- □ Janine Benyus [dʒəníːn bénjəs]
- □ conform [kənfɔ́ːrm]
- □ No other living thing ～
- □ accomplish [əkámplɪʃ]
- □ pesticide [péstɪsàɪd]
- □ institution [ìnstɪtjúːʃən]
- □ exist [ɪgzíst]
- □ far and wide
- □ educate [édʒəkèɪt]
- □ harmful [háːrmfl]
- □ poison [pɔ́ɪzən]
- □ CO_2 [síː óu túː]
- □ global warming [glóubəl wɔ́ːrmɪŋ]
- □ harmony [háːrməni]
- □ in harmony with ～
- □ maintain [meɪntéɪn]
- □ in other words
- □ sustainable [səstéɪnəbl]

①Science and technology have given us a comfortable life. But sometimes our technology damages the natural world. ②Janine Benyus, a science writer, suggests a way to make our technology conform to nature: "biomimicry."

1

③No other living thing on earth has accomplished more than human beings. ④We have created many useful things such as airplanes, trains, computers, cell phones, medicines and pesticides, as well as institutions such as schools, universities, hospitals and banks. ⑤Without them, the modern world would not exist.

⑥These things let us travel far and wide, gather information quickly, educate ourselves, and treat diseases. ⑦However, things we have created can be harmful. ⑧Pesticides kill insects but can poison the soil. ⑨We need cars, but CO_2 may be one of the main causes of global warming.

Now we must ask this question: ⑩If we were to live in harmony with nature, could we maintain our comfortable way of living? ⑪In other words, how is it possible for us to live a sustainable life?

このセクションの内容

地球上で人間以上に物事をなしとげた生物はなく、科学技術は私たちに快適な生活を授けてきた。しかし、それらが自然界に（A.　　　　　）を与えることもある。自然と調和して（B.　　　　　）可能な生活を送るには、どうしたらよいか。科学作家のジャニン・ベニュスは、技術を（C.　　　　　）に適合させる「生物模倣」という方法を提案している。

① Science and technology have given us a comfortable life.

▶〈give＋人＋もの〉は「(人)に(もの)を与える[授ける]」。have givenは現在完了(結果)で「与えた」。

② Janine Benyus, a science writer, suggests a way to make our technology conform to nature: "biomimicry."

▶suggest a way to *do*は「～する方法を示唆[提案]する」、make ～ conform to ...は「～を…と一致[適合]させる」。

▶"biomimicry"「生物[生体]模倣」とは、生物の生態や機能をまねて新技術を開発すること。

③ No other living thing on earth has accomplished more than human beings.

▶No other ～で始まる比較級の文。「ほかのどんな～も…ない」の意味。

≒ Human beings have accomplished more than any other living thing on earth.

✍ 英文を完成させなさい。

どんな動物も、チーターほど速く走れない。

(　　　) (　　　) (　　　) can run faster than cheetahs.

④ We have created many useful things such as airplanes, trains, computers, cell phones, medicines and pesticides, as well as institutions such as schools, universities, hospitals and banks.

▶A as well as B は「Bだけでなく A も」の意味だが、ここではA and Bと同じ意味で使われている。A = many ～ pesticides、B = institutions ～ banksとなる。

▶～ such as ...は「…などの～」の意味で、many useful thingsとinstitutionsの具体例を挙げている。

⑤ Without them, the modern world would not exist.

▶〈Without ～, 主語＋would＋動詞の原形 ...〉は仮定法過去の文で、「もし～がなければ、…だろう(に)」という意味。Without ～は、If it were not for ～と書きかえられる。 ⇒p.132 G-❶

✍ 英文を完成させなさい。

水がなければ、どんな生物も存在できないだろう。

(　　　) (　　　), no living thing (　　　) exist.

▶themは、④の文で例示されたさまざまなものを指す。

⑥ These things let us travel far and wide, gather information quickly, educate ourselves, and treat diseases.

▶These thingsは④の文で述べられている人間が創り出したものを指す。

このセクションの内容 の答え→ A. (損)害 B. 持続 C. 自然

▶〈let＋人＋動詞の原形〉は「(人)に(許可して)～させる」→「(主語)のおかげで(人)は～することができる」の意味。動詞の原形には、travel、gather、educate、treatの4つが並列している。

▶far and wideは「広範囲に」(≒everywhere)、educate *oneself*は「自分自身を教育する」→「学ぶ、勉強する」。

⑦ However, things we have created can be harmful.

▶we have createdはthingsを後ろから修飾する節。

▶can be ～は「～であり得る」の意味で〈可能性〉を表す。

⑧ Pesticides kill insects but can poison the soil.

▶⑦の文で述べた「害になる」ことの1例。このcanも〈可能性〉を表す。「農薬は～するが、…するかもしれない」。poisonは「～を汚染する」。

⑨ We need cars, but CO_2 may be one of the main causes of global warming.

▶これも「害になる」ことの1例。車の排気ガス中に含まれるCO_2が、地球温暖化の主な原因の1つかもしれないということ。

▶may be ～も「～であるかもしれない」と〈可能性〉を表すが、can be ～より確信度がやや低い場合に用いる。

⑩ If we were to live in harmony with nature, could we maintain our comfortable way of living?

▶〈If＋主語＋were to＋動詞の原形〉は、未来について仮定や想像をする仮定法過去の表現。実現可能性の有無にかかわらず、仮定の話として前置きをするときに使われる。 ⇒p.133 G-❷

例 *If* I *were to* go abroad, I *would* go to Spain.
「仮に海外へ行くとしたら、私はスペインへ行くだろう」

▶in harmony with ～は「～と調和して」(≒in cooperation with ～)。

▶could we ～?も仮定法過去で、「私たちは～できるだろうか」の意味。maintainは「～を維持する」、way of livingは「生き方」。

⑪ In other words, how is it possible for us to live a sustainable life?

▶In other wordsは「言いかえれば、つまり」(≒To put it another way)。

▶how以下は〈it is ～ for ― to ...〉の疑問文で、⑩の文の問いを言いかえたもの。how is it possible for us to *do* ～?で「どうすれば私たちが～することが可能か」という意味。

▶live a ～ lifeは「～な生活を送る」、live a sustainable lifeで「持続可能な生活を送る」の意味。sustainable「持続可能な」は「地球環境と人間社会が未来にわたって調和・共存できるような」という意味で使われる。

教科書p.124　Section 2

- □ look to ～ for ...
- □ imitation [ìmɪtéɪʃən]
- □ imitate [ímɪtèɪt]
- □ sustain [səstéɪn]
- □ supporting [səpɔ́ːrtɪŋ]
- □ threaten [θrétn]
- □ ～ rather than ...
- □ her [hər]
- □ dream about ～
- □ hummingbird [hʌ́mɪŋbə̀ːrd]
- □ gram [grǽm]
- □ fuel [fjúːəl]
- □ many times ～
- □ weight [wéɪt]

2

①Janine Benyus suggests that the answer to this question may be found by looking to nature for inspiration. ②The word "biomimicry" comes from *bio*, meaning "life," and *mimicry*, meaning "imitation." ③She says that by imitating nature, we should be able to find a way to live in a nature-friendly way. ④After all, nature has been able to sustain a life-supporting environment for 3.8 billion years. ⑤But now that environment is threatened. ⑥We humans must learn how to sustain our environment by observing and trying to find inspiration from nature. ⑦Nature in Benyus's mind is our teacher and our model.

⑧Benyus reminds us that once we try to learn *from* nature, rather than *about* her, we may feel a sense of wonder. ⑨In fact, there are all sorts of plants and animals doing things we can only dream about. ⑩How about dragonflies, which move more quickly than our best helicopters? ⑪How about hummingbirds, which can fly hundreds of kilometers on less than three grams of fuel? ⑫How about ants, which can carry many times their body weight? They do these things without damaging nature.

このセクションの内容

自然は（A.　　　　　　）年の間、生命を支える環境を維持してきたが、いまやその環境はおびやかされている。私たちは、自然を（B.　　　　　　）として、自然に優しい方法で生きなければならない。実際、トンボ、ハチドリ、アリは、自然を（C.　　　　　　）ことなく、人間にはまったく不可能なことをやってのけている。

① Janine Benyus suggests that the answer to this question may be found by looking to nature for inspiration.

▶ suggest that ～は「～ということを示唆する」。

▶ that節の主語はthe answer to this question「この問いに対する答え」。this questionとは、Section 1の最後のhow is it possible for us to live a sustainable life?という問いを指す。

▶ may be foundは「見つけられるかもしれない」、by looking to nature for ～は「～を求めて自然に目を向けることによって」(look to ～ for ... ≒ depend on ～ for ...)。inspirationは「ひらめき、着想」のこと。

② The word "biomimicry" comes from *bio*, meaning "life," and *mimicry*, meaning "imitation."

▶ come from ～は「～に由来する」、... meaning ～は「～を意味する…」、imitationは「模倣」。動詞のimitateは「～を模倣する」(→③)。

③ She says that by imitating nature, we should be able to find a way to live in a nature-friendly way.

▶ that節内で、by imitating nature「自然を模倣することで」が主語の前に置かれていることに注意。

▶ shouldは「たぶん～だ、～のはずだ」と現在における可能性・推量を表す。

例 It *should* stop raining by noon.
「正午までに雨は止むだろう」

▶ in a nature-friendly wayは「自然に優しい方法で」。*cf.* earth-friendly「地球に優しい」、eco-friendly「環境[生態系]に優しい」

④ After all, nature has been able to sustain a life-supporting environment for 3.8 billion years.

▶「(ずっと)～することができている」という現在完了(継続)の文。

▶ After allは「結局」、sustainは「～を持続させる、～を維持する」、life-supporting environmentは「生命を支える(ための)環境」。

⑤ But now that environment is threatened.

▶「おびやかされている」という受け身の文。that environmentは、④の文のa life-supporting environmentを指す。

⑥ We humans must learn how to sustain our environment by observing and trying to find inspiration from nature.

▶ Weとhumansは同格。by V-ingは「～することによって」。observe and try to find ～は「観察し、～を見つけようと努力する」。

⑦ Nature in Benyus's mind is our teacher and our model.

▶ Nature in *one's* mindは「(人)の心の中の自然」→「(人)が考える自然」。

このセクションの内容 の答え→ A. 38億 B. 教師[モデル] C. 傷つける

⑧ Benyus reminds us that once we try to learn *from* nature, rather than *about* her, we may feel a sense of wonder.

▶〈remind + 人 + that節〉は「(人) に～ということを思い起こさせる[気づかせる]」、once ～は接続詞で「ひとたび～すると」の意味。

✍ 英文を完成させなさい。

彼女の電話で、数学の宿題があることに気づいた。

(　　　) call (　　　) (　　　) that I had math homework.

▶ A rather than B は「B よりもむしろ A、B ではなく A」(≒ A instead of B)。ここでは、*from* と *about* が対になっている。

✍ 次の英文を日本語に直しなさい。

You should take a bus rather than a taxi.

あなたは ＿＿＿＿＿＿＿＿＿＿＿＿＿＿＿＿ 利用すべきだ。

▶ her は nature を指す代名詞。sea「海」や ship「船」なども、she[her] で受けることがある。a sense of wonder は「不思議な感覚」。

⑨ In fact, there are all sorts of plants and animals doing things we can only dream about.

▶「実際、～をしているあらゆる種類の動植物が存在する」→「さまざまな動植物が～をしている」という文。we can only dream about は、前の things を後ろから修飾する節。

▶ dream about ～は「～のことを夢見る[空想する]」(≒ dream of ～)。

⑩ How about dragonflies, which move more quickly than our best helicopters?

▶ ⑩、⑪、⑫の文は、⑨の文で述べた「植物や動物がしていることで、人間には夢見るしかできないこと」の例。How about ～? は「(たとえば) ～はどうだろうか」。〈, which〉は非制限用法の関係代名詞で、which 以下が dragonflies について補足説明をしている。

⑪ How about hummingbirds, which can fly hundreds of kilometers on less than three grams of fuel?

▶ on ～は「～によって」と、手段や動力源を表す。hundreds of ～は「何百もの、数百の」、less than ～は「～未満」。

例 Many cars run *on* electricity today.
「今日、多くの自動車は電気で走る」

⑫ How about ants, which can carry many times their body weight?

▶ many times ～は「～の何倍も」(≒ much more than ～)。which 以下は、can carry things many times as heavy as their body weight ということ。

- □ in the right direction
- □ tunnel [tʌ́nl]
- □ turn to ～
- □ kingfisher [kíŋfìʃər]
- □ dive [dáɪv]
- □ splash [splǽʃ]
- □ Eastgate [í:stgèɪt]
- □ Harare [hərá:ri]
- □ Zimbabwe [zɪmbá:bwi]
- □ environmentally [ɪnvàɪərənméntəli]
- □ air conditioning [éər kəndíʃənɪŋ]
- □ termite [tə́:rmaɪt]
- □ mound [máund]
- □ repellent [rɪpélənt]
- □ rough [rʌ́f]
- □ surface [sə́:rfəs]
- □ dirt [də́:rt]
- □ roll off
- □ generation [dʒènəréɪʃən]
- □ sportswear [spɔ́:rtswèər]

3

①Benyus believes that we face environmental problems, not because there are no solutions, but because we have not been looking in the right direction. ②Actually, we can solve many problems, especially in the area of design, by looking to nature for inspiration.

Engineers in Japan had a problem: ③*Shinkansen* trains made a very loud sound when going into tunnels. ④To solve this problem, the engineers turned to the kingfisher, a bird that dives into water without a splash. ⑤They found the solution: they designed the nose of the train in the same shape as the kingfisher's beak.

⑥The Eastgate Center in Harare, Zimbabwe, is famous for its environmentally friendly air conditioning system. ⑦The architects who designed this building were inspired by termite mounds. ⑧Termites keep their living space at a comfortable temperature by opening and closing small holes in their mounds. The architects used a similar system for the Eastgate Center and saved electricity.

⑨Lotus leaves are one of the most water-repellent leaves in the world. ⑩Because of their rough surface, even a little wind causes water and dirt to roll cleanly off. ⑪Now, a rough surface has been introduced into a new generation of paint, glass, and cloth. ⑫It is especially useful for raincoats and sportswear.

このセクションの内容

デザインの分野では、多くの問題が解決された。カワセミの（A.　　　　　）の形をまねて、新幹線の「鼻」を設計した。シロアリの塚を参考にして、環境に優しい（B.　　　　　）システムを開発した。また、ハスの葉の特性を生かして、新世代の塗料や布などを開発し、そのでこぼこの表面は（C.　　　　　）やスポーツウェアに活用されている。

① Benyus believes that we face environmental problems, not because there are no solutions, but because we have not been looking in the right direction.

▶ we ～ directionまでがthat節の内容。faceは動詞で「～に直面する」。

▶ not A but Bの構文で、AとBにそれぞれbecauseの節が入っている。not because ～, but because ...で「～だからではなく、…だから」。

▶ have not been lookingは現在完了進行形で「ずっと見ていない」。in the right directionは「正しい方向に」（≒ in the right way）。

② Actually, we can solve many problems, especially in the area of design, by looking to nature for inspiration.

▶ Actuallyは「実際に、現に」、in the area of ～は「～の領域[分野]で」。

③ *Shinkansen* trains made a very loud sound when going into tunnels.

▶ make a soundは「音をたてる」。when going into tunnelsはwhen they (= *shinkansen* trains) were going into tunnelsのこと。

✍ 次の英文を日本語に直しなさい。

She looked happy when talking with you.

＿＿＿＿＿＿＿＿＿＿＿＿＿＿＿＿、彼女は幸せそうだった。

④ To solve this problem, the engineers turned to the kingfisher, a bird that dives into water without a splash.

▶ To solve ～は「～を解決するために」、turn to ～は「～に頼る、～を参照する」（≒ depend on ～ for help）。

▶ a bird ～ a splashは、kingfisherについて説明している（同格）。

▶ dive into ～は「～に飛び込む」、splashは「ザブン（など）という音」。

⑤ They found the solution: they designed the nose of the train in the same shape as the kingfisher's beak.

▶ Theyはthe engineersを指す。

▶ コロン (:) 以下は、solution「解決方法」の説明。nose「鼻」とは、電車の先端部分を指す語。the same ～ as ...は「…と同一の～、…と同じ種類の～」。

✍ 次の英文を日本語に直しなさい。

I went to the same college as yours.

私は＿＿＿＿＿＿＿＿＿＿＿＿＿＿＿＿＿＿＿＿＿＿＿に通った。

⑥ The Eastgate Center in Harare, Zimbabwe, is famous for its environmentally friendly air conditioning system.

▶ be famous for ～は「～で有名な」、itsは主語のThe Eastgate Centerを指す。environmentally friendlyは「環境に優しい」（≒ eco-friendly）。

⑦ The architects who designed this building were inspired by termite mounds.

▶ The ～ buildingが文の主語。whoは主格の関係代名詞。

▶ were inspired by ～は受け身で、「～によって触発された」。termite moundsは「シロアリの塚」で、その特徴は次の⑧の文に書かれている。

⑧ Termites keep their living space at a comfortable temperature by opening and closing small holes in their mounds.

▶ keep ～ at a comfortable temperatureは「～を快適な温度に保つ」。by V-ingは「～することによって」の意味でopeningとclosingが並列している。

⑨ Lotus leaves are one of the most water-repellent leaves in the world.

▶〈one of the＋形容詞の最上級＋複数名詞〉は「もっとも～な（名詞）の1つ」。water-repellentは形容詞で「水を通さない［はじく］」の意味。*cf.* repel（動詞）「～を追い払う、～を寄せつけない」

⑩ Because of their rough surface, even a little wind causes water and dirt to roll cleanly off.

▶ Because of ～は「～が原因で、～のために」（≒ Owing to ～）。theirはwater-repellent leavesを指す。

▶ cause ～ to *do*は「～に…させる、～が…する原因となる」、roll offは「転がり落ちる」（≒ move along a surface）。

⑪ Now, a rough surface has been introduced into a new generation of paint, glass, and cloth.

▶ has been introduced into ～は現在完了形の受け身で、「～に導入されている」。a new generation of ～は「～の新世代、新世代の～」。

✍ 英文を完成させなさい。

この祭りは2000年から毎年開催されている。

This festival (　　　) (　　　) (　　　) every year since 2000.

⑫ It is especially useful for raincoats and sportswear.

◆Itは⑪の文のa rough surfaceを指す。be useful for ～は「～に役立つ」。

このセクションの内容 の答え→　A. くちばし　B. 空調　C. レインコート

教科書p.128　Section 4

- ☐ aware [əwéər]
- ☐ forever [fərévər]
- ☐ judge [dʒʌ́dʒ]
- ☐ innovation [inəvéiʃən]
- ☐ powerful [páuərfəl]
- ☐ tool [tú:l]
- ☐ have an effect on ～
- ☐ survival [sərváivəl]

4

①Benyus believes that biomimicry may help us become more aware of nature, thus leading us to change our way of living. ②We cannot keep taking advantage of nature forever or keep dumping our waste into our environment.

③For too long, we have judged our innovations by whether they are good for us, or whether they make money. ④Benyus suggests that we put what is good for the whole earth first and trust that it will also be good for us humans. ⑤The new questions should be the following: Will it fit in? Is there a model for this in nature? What will it cost the earth and future generations?

⑥Biomimicry is a powerful tool that can play an important role in our future. In the early days, there were just a few of us humans in a very large world. ⑦Now, our population is growing rapidly, and we are beginning to have a bad effect on the environment. ⑧We are finally looking for an answer to the question: "How can we live on our home planet without destroying it?" ⑨Benyus believes that biomimicry is not only a new way of looking at nature but also a key to our survival on planet Earth. We have to learn to live on the earth. ⑩It is our home, but it is not ours alone.

このセクションの内容

人間が環境に（A.　　　　　）を及ぼし始めている今日、私たちは地球全体にとってよいことを第一に考えなければならない。ベニュスは「生物模倣」がその答えの１つだと信じている。それは（B.　　　　　）に対する新しい見方であるだけでなく、私たちの故郷である惑星を（C.　　　　　）せずに人間が生き残るための鍵だからだ。

① Benyus believes that biomimicry may help us become more aware of nature, thus leading us to change our way of living.

▶〈help + 人 + 動詞の原形〉は「(人)が〜するのを助ける」。become aware of 〜は「〜に気づく」→「〜への意識を高める」。

✍ 次の英文を日本語に直しなさい。

Most people are aware of the dangers of smoking.

ほとんどの人は、＿＿＿＿＿＿＿＿＿＿＿＿＿＿＿＿＿＿＿＿。

▶ thusは「したがって」。leadingは分詞構文で、it (=biomimicry) leadsの意味。〈lead + 人 + to *do*〉は「(人)に〜するように仕向ける[導く]」。

② We cannot keep taking advantage of nature forever or keep dumping our waste into our environment.

▶ 2つの〈keep V-ing〉「〜し続ける」が並列している。cannotは後ろの〈keep V-ing〉にもかかる。take advantage of 〜は「〜を利用する」、dump 〜 into ... は「〜(ごみなど)を…に捨てる」。

③ For too long, we have judged our innovations by whether they are good for us, or whether they make money.

▶ For too longは「あまりにも長い間」、have judgedは現在完了(継続)で、「(ずっと)判断してきた」。

▶ by whether 〜は「〜かどうかによって」。theyはour innovationsを指す。innovationは「発明、新しい手法」、make moneyは「お金をかせぐ」。

④ Benyus suggests that we put what is good for the whole earth first and trust that it will also be good for us humans.

▶ suggest that 〜は「〜ということを提案する」で、文末のhumansまでがthat節になる。提案、要求、命令を表す動詞にthat節が続くとき、that節内の動詞は原形、または〈should + 原形〉になる。これを仮定法現在といい、現在または未来の不確実な想像を表す。

⇒p.133 G-❸

✍ 英文を完成させなさい。

私は、誠が主将になってはどうかと提案した。

I suggested (　　　) Makoto (　　　) captain.

▶ put ～ firstは「～を第一に考える」、what is good for ～は「何が～にとってよいか」(whatは疑問詞)と考えても、「～にとってよいこと」(whatは関係代名詞)と考えてもよい。

▶ suggest that ～のthat節内に、and (we) trust that ... と別のthat節が含まれる。it willのitは直前のwhat is good for the whole earth「地球全体にとってよいこと」を指す。usとhumansは同格の関係。

⑤ **The new questions should be the following: Will it fit in? Is there a model for this in nature? What will it cost the earth and future generations?**

▶ コロン(:)のあとにThe new questions「新たな問い」が3つ続いている。should be ～は「たぶん～になるだろう」〈可能性・推量〉。

▶ 3つの問いのitとthisは④の文のwhat is good for the whole earthを指す。fit inは「うまくやる、調和する」。

▶ costは動詞で「(費用や労力など)がかかる」、What will it cost ～?で「～に何がかかるか」の意味。

⑥ **Biomimicry is a powerful tool that can play an important role in our future.**

▶ thatは主格の関係代名詞。play ～ roleは「～な役割を演じる[果たす]」。

⑦ **Now, our population is growing rapidly, and we are beginning to have a bad effect on the environment.**

▶ growは「増える、増大する」、have a bad effect on ～は「～に悪影響を及ぼす」(≒ have a bad influence on ～)。

⑧ **We are finally looking for an answer to the question: "How can we live on our home planet without destroying it?"**

▶ 「(現在)ようやく～を探しているところだ」という文。コロン(:)以下は、the questionの内容。

▶ home planet「故郷の惑星」とは地球のこと。without destroying it(=our home planet)は「それ(＝地球)を破壊することなく」。

⑨ **Benyus believes that biomimicry is not only a new way of looking at nature but also a key to our survival on planet Earth.**

▶ that節内は、not only ～ but also ...「～だけでなく…も」の構文。

▶ a new way of V-ingは「～する新しい方法」、a key to our survivalは「私たちの生存の鍵」→「私たちが生き残る手がかり」。

⑩ **It is our home, but it is not ours alone.**

▶ それぞれの主語Itとitは、⑨の文のplanet Earthを指す。ours aloneは「私たち(人間)のものだけ」。

このセクションの内容 の答え→ A. 悪影響 B. 自然 C. 破壊

Grammar for Communication

1　if節のない仮定法

if 〜の代わりに、副詞句、不定詞、主語の名詞句などを使って仮定の意味を表すことができる。

---

1. Without[But for] 〜：「もし〜がなければ」

◆ **Without[But for]** your help, I *couldn't finish* it.　＊仮定法過去
（あなたの助けがなければ、私はそれを終えられないだろう）

◆ **Without[But for]** your help, I *couldn't have finished* it. ＊仮定法過去完了
（あなたの助けがなかったら、私はそれを終えられなかっただろう）

≒ If it were not for your help, 〜 / Were it not for your help, 〜

★同様に、With 〜で「もし〜があれば」という仮定を表すこともできる。

With a little more effort, you *could have won* the game.
（もう少し努力していたら、あなたは試合に勝てただろう）

≒ If you had made a little more effort, you could have won the game.

2. 不定詞：「もし〜すれば」

◆ **To hear** him speak Japanese, you *would take* him for a Japanese.
（彼が日本語を話すのを聞けば、あなたは彼を日本人だと思うだろう）

≒ If you heard him speak Japanese, you would take him for a Japanese.

3. 主語の名詞句：「もし〜であれば、もし〜があったら」

◆ **A wise father** *would not do* such a thing to his son.　＊仮定法過去
（賢い父親であれば、息子にそんなことはしないだろう）

≒ If he were a wise father, he would not do such a thing to his son.

◆ **Your advice** *might have changed* her mind.　＊仮定法過去完了
（あなたが助言をしていれば、彼女の考えは変わったかもしれない）

≒ If you had given her advice, she might have changed her mind.

4. 副詞（句）など

◆ **One hundred years ago**, no one *could have believed* it.
（100年前だったら、だれもそれを信じなかっただろう）

◆ I got up earlier than usual; **otherwise**, I *would have missed* the plane.
（私はいつもより早く起きた。さもなければ飛行機に乗り遅れただろう）

≒ If I hadn't gotten up earlier than usual, I would have missed the plane.

2　未来に関する仮定法

〈if＋主語＋were to＋動詞の原形〉は、実現可能性の有無にかかわらず、未来について仮定[想像、空想]する表現。〈if＋主語＋should＋動詞の原形〉は、実現可能性が低いと思っていることを仮定する表現。

◆ **If** an accident **were to happen**, what *would* you *do*?
（仮に事故が起こるようなことがあれば、あなたはどうしますか）

◆ **If** the sun **were to** rise in the west, I *wouldn't agree* with you.
（たとえ太陽が西から昇ったとしても、私はあなたに同意しない）

◆ **If** I **should** make a mistake, she *would be disappointed.*
（万一私が間違うことがあれば、彼女はがっかりするだろう）

◆ **If** he **should** come to see me, *tell* him I've left for home.
（万一彼が私に会いに来たら、もう家に帰ったと伝えてください）

★〈If＋主語＋should＋動詞の原形〉のとき、帰結節[主節]には助動詞の過去形だけでなく、命令文や助動詞の現在形が使われることもある。

3　仮定法現在：提案・要求・命令を表す動詞＋that節

未来にすることを提案・要求・命令する文のthat節では、動詞の原形、または〈should＋動詞の原形〉を使う。このような表現を「仮定法現在」という。使われる動詞には、suggest、request、insist、require、advise、order、demandなどがある。アメリカ英語ではshouldを使わないことが多い。

◆ We **suggested that** he (should) **join** our team.
（私たちは、彼が私たちのチームに加わるように提案した）

◆ The officer **requested that** I (should) **show** my passport to him.
（係員は私にパスポートを見せるように求めた）

◆ The restaurant **insists that** people (should) **wear** a jacket.
（そのレストランは、人々は上着を着用すべきだと主張している）

◆ It is **required that** all the participants (should) **be** over 21 years old.
（参加者全員が21歳以上であることが求められている）　＊Itは形式主語

◆ My father **advised that** I (should) **be** more careful.
（父は私に、もっと注意するように忠告した）

◆ Our teacher **ordered that** we (should) **stay** in the classroom.
（先生は私たちに、教室にとどまっているように命じた）

確認問題

語彙・表現

1 次の語を（　）内の指示にしたがって書きかえなさい。

(1) harm（形容詞形に）　　(2) imitate（名詞形に）
(3) smooth（反意語に）　　(4) dirty（名詞形に）

2 第2音節にアクセント（強勢）のある語を2つ選び、記号で答えなさい。

ア　ex-ist　　イ　ed-u-cate　　ウ　main-tain
エ　hum-ming-bird　　オ　sur-face　　カ　sports-wear

3 日本語に合うように、（　）内に適切な語を入れなさい。ただし、最初の文字が指定されているときは、その文字で書き始めなさい。

(1) その知らせは四方八方に広まった。
The news spread (　　　) and (　　　).

(2) 言いかえれば、自然は私たちの教師なのだ。
(　　　) (　　　) words, nature is our teacher.

(3) 私たちは動物についてではなく、動物から学ぶべきだ。
We should learn from animals (r　　　) (　　　) about them.

(4) 姉は将来、科学者になることを夢見ている。
My sister (　　　) (a　　　) becoming a scientist in the future.

(5) 彼は寝ぼけていて、ベッドから転がり落ちた。
He was half asleep and (　　　) (　　　) the bed.

文のパターン・文法

1 各組の文がほぼ同じ意味になるように、（　）内に適切な語を入れなさい。

(1) Without your advice, we couldn't have built the robot.
(　　　) (　　　) your advice, we couldn't have built the robot.

(2) If you saw him dance, you would think he was a professional dancer.
(　　　) (　　　) him dance, you would think he was a professional dancer.

(3) If there were a good doctor, he or she could cure the illness.
(　　　) (　　　) (　　　) could cure the illness.

(4) Sally said to him, "Take a bus to the station."
Sally suggested that (　　　) (　　　) a bus to the station.

2 日本語に合うように、( )内に適切な語を入れなさい。

(1) 仮に宝くじに当たるようなことがあれば、あなたはどうしますか。
If you (　　　) (　　　) win the lottery, what (　　　) you do?

(2) 万一問題があれば、この機械は止まるだろう。
If there (　　　) (　　　) a problem, this machine would stop.

(3) 雪が降っていた。さもなければ私たちは買い物に行っただろう。
It was snowing; (　　　), we would (　　　) (　　　) shopping.

3 ( )内の語句を並べかえて、日本語に合う英文を作りなさい。

(1) この鍵がなかったら、私はこの箱を開けられなかっただろう。
(not / this key / were / it / for), I couldn't have opened this box.
____________________________, I couldn't have opened this box.

(2) 仮に留学するとしたら、私はカナダに行くだろう。
If (were / abroad / to / I / study), I would go to Canada.
If ____________________________, I would go to Canada.

(3) 彼女はそのイベントを土曜日に開くべきだと主張している。
She (that / held / the event / insists / be) on Saturday.
She ____________________________ on Saturday.

総合

次の文を読んで、あとの問いに答えなさい。

Biomimicry is a powerful tool that can (①) an important role in our future. In the early days, there were just a few of us humans in a very large world. Now, our population is growing rapidly, and ②we are beginning to have a bad effect on the environment. We are finally looking for an answer to the question: "How can we live on our home planet without destroying it?" Benyus believes that biomimicry is (③) only a new way of looking at nature but also a key to our ④(survive) on planet Earth. We have to learn to live on the earth. It is our home, but it is not ours alone.

問1　①、③の( )内に入る適語を書きなさい。

問2　下線部②を日本語に直しなさい。

問3　④の( )内の語を適切な形に直しなさい。

問4　私たちが最終的に求めているのは、どのような問いに対する答えだと書かれているか。日本語で説明しなさい。

Lesson 8 Invisible No Longer

教科書p.140 Section 1

- □ invisible [ɪnvízəbl]
- □ Côte d'Ivoire [kòutdiːvwáːr]
- □ related to ～
- □ nutritional [njuːtríʃənəl]
- □ take a moment to ～
- □ wage [wéɪdʒ]
- □ make a wage
- □ cacao [kəkáu]
- □ make money
- □ account [əkáunt]
- □ take ～ into account
- □ at the heart of ～
- □ industry [índəstri]

①A professor of women's studies is speaking to high school students about chocolate and the country where much of it is produced, Côte d'Ivoire.

1

②Good morning. Today, I would like to discuss with you something related to this *(showing chocolate)*.

Chocolate is one of our favorite foods, right? ③Japan has some of the biggest chocolate companies in the world, and you each eat around two kilos of chocolate a year.

When we talk about sweets, we think about taste, price, and nutritional value. ④But today I'd like you to take a moment to ask: "Where does chocolate actually come from? Do chocolate farmers make decent wages? Are their work conditions safe?"

⑤Chocolate is made from cacao beans. ⑥Almost 40 percent of the world's cacao beans are produced in Côte d'Ivoire, which is, in fact, the world's largest producer. Now, look at the map on the wall. Can you find Côte d'Ivoire?

The work on cacao farms is dangerous. ⑦Women do most of the work, yet they make very little money. One woman farmer says, "⑧Women do everything, right until the cacao dries. ⑨But the men take it, sell it, and never take us women into account."

Today, I'd like to talk to you about these women farmers. ⑩Some people call them the "invisible women" at the heart of the chocolate industry.

このセクションの内容

チョコレートの原料であるカカオ豆の（A.　　　　　）パーセント近くは、アフリカのコートジボワールで生産されている。そこの農園では、（B.　　　　　）な作業を含め、ほとんどの仕事を女性たちが行っていて、男性は女性の立場を（C.　　　　　）しようともしない。そのような女性農民たちを「目に見えない女性」と呼ぶ人々もいる。

① A professor of women's studies is speaking to high school students about chocolate and the country where much of it is produced, Côte d'Ivoire.

▶前置詞aboutの目的語がchocolateとthe countryで、where以下がthe countryを後ろから修飾している。much of itのitはchocolateを指す。

▶Côte d'Ivoire「コートジボワール」は、直前のthe country ～ producedと同格の関係で、「その（＝チョコレートの）多くの原産国であるコートジボワール」という意味。

② Good morning. Today, I would like to discuss with you something related to this (*showing chocolate*).

▶discussは「～を議論する」という他動詞で、目的語somethingの前にwith youが挿入されている。relatedはsomethingを修飾する過去分詞で、related to ～で「～に関連[関係]した」（≒ connected with ～）の意味。

✍ 次の英文を日本語に直しなさい。

She wants to get a job related to music.

彼女は ＿＿＿＿＿＿＿＿＿＿＿＿＿＿＿＿ つきたがっている。

▶(*showing chocolate*)は、教授が生徒にチョコレートを見せている様子を表す。

③ Japan has some of the biggest chocolate companies in the world, and you each eat around two kilos of chocolate a year.

▶some of the biggest ～は「最も大きな～のいくつか」。

▶you eachは「あなたたち１人１人」。kilosは、ここではkilogramsを短く表したもの。

④ But today I'd like you to take a moment to ask: "Where does chocolate actually come from? Do chocolate farmers make decent wages? Are their work conditions safe?"

▶I'd like you to *do*は「あなたたちに～してもらいたい」。take a moment to *do*は「～する時間をとる」（≒ take some time to *do*）の意味で、ここではコロン（:）のあとに続く問いについて考えてほしいということ。

▶ wageは「(主に肉体労働に対する)賃金」。make decent wagesで「適切な賃金をかせぐ」の意味。work conditionsは「労働条件」。

⑤ Chocolate is made from cacao beans.

▶ be made from ～は「～（の原料）から作られる」という受け身。*cf.* be made of ～「～（の材料）から作られる」

⑥ Almost 40 percent of the world's cacao beans are produced in Côte d'Ivoire, which is, in fact, the world's largest producer.

▶ Almost 40 percentは「ほぼ40パーセント」の意味で、厳密には40パーセントに達していないことを表す。

▶〈, which〉は非制限用法の関係代名詞で、which以下がCôte d'Ivoireについて補足説明をしている。「事実、コートジボワールが世界最大のカカオ豆の生産国である」ということ。

⑦ Women do most of the work, yet they make very little money.

▶ 接続詞yet「けれども」は、直前の内容と対照的な内容になる。

▶ make moneyは「お金をかせぐ」（≒ earn money）、littleは「少ししか[ほとんど]ない」という否定表現。

⑧ Women do everything, right until the cacao dries.

▶ right until ～は「実に～まで、～までずっと」、dryは「乾く、乾燥する」。

⑨ But the men take it, sell it, and never take us women into account.

▶ 2つのitはthe cacaoを指す。take itは「それを受け取る」。

▶ take ～ into accountは「～を考慮する」（≒ pay serious attention to ～）。usとwomenは同格の関係。

例 They didn't *take* my opinion *into account.*
「彼らは私の意見を考慮してくれなかった」

⑩ Some people call them the "invisible women" at the heart of the chocolate industry.

▶ Some people ～は「～する人たちもいる[いた]」。

▶〈call + O + C〉「OをCと呼ぶ」の文で、themは直前の文のthese women farmersを指す。the "invisible ～ industryがCにあたる。

▶ invisible womenは「見えざる[無視される]女性たち」。なお、表題のInvisible No Longerは「もう無視されていない」の意味。

▶ at the heart of ～は「～の中心にいる」（≒ at the most important part of ～）。

このセクションの内容 の答え→ A. 40 B. 危険 C. 考慮

教科書p.142　Section 2

- □ strap [strǽp]
- □ toddler [tádlər]
- □ tow [tóu]
- □ in tow
- □ pod [pád]
- □ the size of ～
- □ harvest [há:rvəst]
- □ attach [ətǽtʃ]
- □ attached to ～
- □ pole [póul]
- □ income [ínkʌ̀m]
- □ unfairness [ʌ̀nféərnəs]
- □ patriarchal [pèɪtriá:rkəl]
- □ have no say
- □ financial [faɪnǽnʃəl]
- □ aid [éɪd]
- □ gender [dʒéndər]
- □ gap [gǽp]

2

①One woman on a cacao farm in Côte d'Ivoire describes her typical day. ②She gets up at 4 a.m. and walks two kilometers to get water before making breakfast, cleaning the yard, and preparing the children for school. ③Then she walks several kilometers to the field to work, with her youngest baby strapped to her back and sometimes with a toddler in tow. ④Cacao beans grow in pods about the size of a football, which she harvests from trees using a knife attached to a long pole. ⑤In the evening, she returns home, carrying a heavy basket of cacao pods on her head, only to find more work waiting for her.

⑥Women do about 70 percent of the work on the farms but receive only about 20 percent of the income. They must also do all the housework. ⑦This unfairness is due to the country's patriarchal society, where men hold power and make most decisions. ⑧Women have no say about selling the cacao beans, and their husbands don't share the money. ⑨Women don't have access to training or financial aid which could help them lead a better life. ⑩There is a very large gender gap.

このセクションの内容

ある女性は、４時に起きて家事や育児をし、その後、カカオ農園に出かけて作業をする。帰宅後も次の仕事が待っているという。農園で働く女性たちは約（A.　　　　　）パーセントの仕事をするが、約20パーセントの賃金しか受け取れない。この（B.　　　　　）は、男性がほとんどの（C.　　　　　）を下すという家父長制社会によるもので、男女格差はきわめて大きい。

① One woman on a cacao farm in Côte d'Ivoire describes her typical day.

▶ One ～ Côte d'Ivoireが文の主語。One womanは「ある女性」の意味で、この段落はカカオ農園で働く女性の一日の例が述べられている。

② She gets up at 4 a.m. and walks two kilometers to get water before making breakfast, cleaning the yard, and preparing the children for school.

▶ walks two kilometersで「2キロの距離を歩く」、to get ～は「～を手に入れるために」。

▶ before V-ingは「～する前に」で、making、cleaning、preparingの3つが並列している。prepare ～ for ... は「…に備えて～に準備させる、～に…の用意をさせる」。水をくみに行って帰ってきたあと、朝食を作り、庭をそうじし、子どもに学校の準備をさせるということ。

③ Then she walks several kilometers to the field to work, with her youngest baby strapped to her back and sometimes with a toddler in tow.

▶ Then「それから」は、②の文の作業を終えてからということ。

▶ fieldは「(カカオ農園の)畑」、to workは「働くために」。

▶ 2つのwith ～は、「～しながら、そして時には…しながら」〈付帯状況〉の意味。

▶〈with＋名詞＋過去分詞(strapped)〉は「～がひもでしばられている状態で」→「～をひもでしばりつけて」。to her backは「彼女の背中に」。

▶ in towは「連れて、従えて」(≒ following closely)。with a toddler in towで「幼児を連れて」の意味。

✍ 英文を完成させなさい。

その少女は目に涙を浮かべて母親を待っていた。

The girl was waiting for her mother (　　　) (　　　) in her eyes.

④ Cacao beans grow in pods about the size of a football, which she harvests from trees using a knife attached to a long pole.

▶ podは「植物のさや」の意味。about the size of ～は「～ほどの大きさの」(≒ about the same size as ～)。

▶〈, which〉は非制限用法の関係代名詞で、先行詞はpods。

▶ using a knifeは「ナイフを使いながら」の意味で〈付帯状況〉を表す。attached to ～は「～に取りつけられた」(≒ using a knife tied to ～)。

⑤ In the evening, she returns home, carrying a heavy basket of cacao pods on her head, only to find more work waiting for her.

▶ carrying ～は「～を運びながら」、on her headは「頭の上に(のせて)」。

このセクションの内容 の答え→ A. 70 B. 不公平[不平等](さ) C. 決定

▶ only to *do* は結果を表す不定詞で、「(その結果は) ただ〜するだけだ」の意味。〈find + O + V-ing〉は「〜が…していることに気づく」。⇒p.149 G-❷

✍ 次の英文を日本語に直しなさい。

She tried it again, only to fail.

彼女はそれをもう一度試みたが、＿＿＿＿＿＿＿＿＿＿＿＿＿＿＿。

⑥ Women do about 70 percent of the work on the farms but receive only about 20 percent of the income.

▶ butをはさんで、女性たちの仕事量の割合と収入額の割合が対比されている。the income「その収入」は、カカオ農園の収入のこと。

⑦ This unfairness is due to the country's patriarchal society, where men hold power and make most decisions.

▶ This unfairness「この不公平[不平等]」は、⑥の文と直前の文の内容を指す。due to 〜は「〜が原因で、〜のためで」、patriarchalは「家父長制の」。

▶〈, where〉は非制限用法の関係副詞で、where以下はthe country's patriarchal societyについて補足説明をしている。

▶ make a decisionは「決定を下す」。〈most + 複数名詞〉で「たいていの〜、大多数の〜」の意味で、mostの前にtheはつけない。

⑧ Women have no say about selling the cacao beans, and their husbands don't share the money.

▶ sayは名詞で「発言権、決定権」の意味。have no sayで「発言権がない」(≒ have no opportunity to express *one's* opinion)。

✍ 次の英文を日本語に直しなさい。

The members of the group had no say about choosing their leader.

その団体のメンバーには＿＿＿＿＿＿＿＿＿＿＿＿＿＿＿＿＿＿。

⑨ Women don't have access to training or financial aid which could help them lead a better life.

▶ access to 〜は、ここでは「〜を利用する機会[権利]」のこと。trainingは「(職業) 訓練[教育]」、financial aidは「財政援助」。

▶ which以下はtraining or financial aidを後ろから修飾している。〈help + 人 + 動詞の原形〉は「(人) が〜するのを助ける[手伝う]」、lead a better lifeは「よりよい生活を送る」。

⑩ There is a very large gender gap.

▶ genderは「(社会的・文化的役割としての) 性」、gender gapは「性別の隔たり」→「男女(間の) 格差」。

- ☐ needless [ní:dləs]
- ☐ needless to say
- ☐ Fairtrade [fèərtréɪd]
- ☐ leadership [lí:dərʃip]
- ☐ management [mǽnɪdʒmənt]
- ☐ Edith [í:dɪθ]
- ☐ Rosine [roʊzí:n]
- ☐ transformation [træ̀nsfərméɪʃən]
- ☐ negotiate [nɪgóʊʃièɪt]
- ☐ task [tǽsk]
- ☐ budget [bʌ́dʒət]
- ☐ previously [prí:viəsli]
- ☐ in peace

3

①Needless to say, this gender gap must be closed. But how?

②In 2017, Fairtrade UK started a school called the Women's School of Leadership in Côte d'Ivoire. ③The school has transformed the students' lives by teaching confidence, money management, sustainable farming practices, and women's rights.

④Two of the graduates of the leadership school, Edith and Rosine, speak about their transformation.

Edith: "⑤Fairtrade training taught us how to talk to our husbands and make common decisions. In the past, our husbands sold the beans and didn't show us the money. ⑥Now we know how to negotiate with our husbands. We work together, exchange opinions, and share tasks. ⑦We support each other to share our problems and find a way through to a solution together. ⑧We feel empowered."

Rosine: "⑨Now my husband and I make a budget together and I'm afraid of nothing because I know how to manage my money. ⑩I am stronger."

⑪The school is open not only to women but also to men. ⑫A male graduate says, "Previously men denied women's rights, but after training we realized women needed to make decisions too." ⑬Now he helps his wife cook and clean. ⑭Some people make fun of him, but he doesn't care. ⑮He says, "My wife and I now live in peace."

このセクションの内容

男女格差を解消するためにコートジボワールに開設された学校では、自信、金銭管理、（A.　　　　　）な農業の実践、女性の（B.　　　　　）を教えることで、学生たちの生活を一変させた。学校の（C.　　　　　）は、夫婦で協力して仕事をし、家事も分担するようになった。

① Needless to say, this gender gap must be closed.

▶ Needless to say は「言うまでもなく」、close は動詞で「～(距離や差など)を詰める、縮める」。must be closed で「縮められなければならない」。

✍ 英文を完成させなさい。

言うまでもなく、スマートフォンは便利な道具だ。

(　　　) to (　　　), smartphones are convenient tools.

② In 2017, Fairtrade UK started a school called the Women's School of Leadership in Côte d'Ivoire.

▶ fairtrade（または fair trade）は「公正な取引[貿易]」の意味で、開発途上国の原料や製品を適正価格で継続的に購入し、途上国の生産者や労働者の生活改善と自立をめざす貿易システムのこと。

▶ called ～「～と呼ばれる」は school を後ろから修飾している。

③ The school has transformed the students' lives by teaching confidence, money management, sustainable farming practices, and women's rights.

▶ The school は②の文で述べられた学校を指す。transform ～は「～を一変させる」の意味。lives は life「生活」の複数形。

▶ by teaching ～のあとに、教える内容が4つ並んでいる。confidence は「自信」、management は「管理」、farming practice は「農業実践[実務]」。

④ Two of the graduates of the leadership school, Edith and Rosine, speak about their transformation.

▶ Edith and Rosine は2人の卒業生の名前。their transformation「彼女たちの変化」とは、教育によってもたらされた変化のこと。

⑤ Fairtrade training taught us how to talk to our husbands and make common decisions.

▶〈teach + 人 + how to *do*〉は「(人)に～する方法を教える」。

▶ make の前に how to が省略されている。make common decisions は「共通の決定を下す」→「同意した上で決定する」。

⑥ Now we know how to negotiate with our husbands.

▶ Now we know ～は「(学校で学んだ結果)今では私たちは～がわかっている」

ということ。negotiate with ～は「～と交渉する」。

⑦ **We support each other to share our problems and find a way through to a solution together.**

▶ support each otherは「お互いを支える、協力し合う」、a way through to a solutionは「解決に通じる道」→「解決策」。

⑧ **We feel empowered.**

▶ empoweredは過去分詞で、empowerは「～に力を与える、～の能力を高める」の意味。feel empoweredで「できると感じる」ということ。

⑨ **Now my husband and I make a budget together and I'm afraid of nothing because I know how to manage my money.**

▶ 2つの文が並列している。Now ～ togetherまでが1つ目の文。make a budgetは「予算を立てる」。

▶ I'm afraid of nothingは「私は何も恐れない」で、その理由がbecause以下に述べられている。

⑩ **I am stronger.**

▶学校で教育を受ける前とくらべている。than I used to be「かつての自分よりも」などの語句が省略されている。

⑪ **The school is open not only to women but also to men.**

▶ not only ～ but also ...「～だけでなく…も」の構文。open to ～は「～に門戸を開いている、～を受け入れている」の意味。

⑫ **A male graduate says, "Previously men denied women's rights, but after training we realized women needed to make decisions too."**

▶ Previouslyは「以前に(は)」、denyは「～を否定する[拒絶する]」。

▶ after training「訓練を受けたあと」は挿入句。realize (that) ～は「～ということをはっきり理解する」。

⑬ **Now he helps his wife cook and clean.**

▶ heは⑫の文のa male graduate「男性の卒業生」を指す。〈help + 人 + 動詞の原形〉は「(人)が～するのを助ける[手伝う]」。

⑭ **Some people make fun of him, but he doesn't care.**

▶ Some people *do*は「～する人たちもいる」、make fun of ～は「～をからかう」。doesn't careは、からかわれることを「気にしない」ということ。

✍ 次の英文を日本語に直しなさい。

He is always making fun of his younger brother.

彼はいつも ＿＿＿＿＿＿＿＿＿＿＿＿＿＿＿＿＿＿＿＿＿＿＿＿＿＿。

⑮ **He says, "My wife and I now live in peace."**

◆ in peaceは「平和に」(≒ peacefully)。

このセクションの内容 の答え→ A. 持続可能 B. 権利 C. 卒業生

教科書p.146 Section 4

- □ help *oneself*
- □ knowledge [nálidʒ]
- □ unstable [ʌnstéibl]
- □ Yaoua [jɑːúːə]
- □ worthy [wə́ːrði]
- □ go global
- □ Guatemala [gwɑ̀ːtəmɑ́ːlə]
- □ El Salvador [elsǽlvədɔ̀ːr]
- □ Indonesia [ìndəníːʒə]
- □ promote [prəmóut]
- □ empowerment [impáuərmənt]
- □ awareness [əwéərnəs]
- □ raise awareness

4

①If they are to achieve gender equality, women must work to help themselves. ②Graduates of the school are beginning to share their knowledge and training with other women in the community. ③Some women have started small businesses growing vegetables to protect their families from unstable cacao prices. ④Rosine and Yaoua, both graduates of the school, lead a women's society to help girls get an education. ⑤Yaoua says, "Women don't have to be behind men. We are worthy too."

⑥The project to help the invisible women farmers of Côte d'Ivoire has gone global. In Latin America, Fairtrade opened leadership schools in Guatemala and El Salvador. In Asia, Fairtrade also opened schools in Indonesia and India in 2019. ⑦The goal is to promote empowerment and raise awareness of human rights.

⑧I began by asking you to think about where chocolate comes from. ⑨Then we listened to the voices of the invisible women cacao farmers in Côte d'Ivoire. ⑩That led to the question of how to overcome the gender gap.

Now, let's think about our own lives and societies. ⑪How much have we accomplished and how much more do we have to do in order to close our own gender gap?

このセクションの内容

卒業生たちは男女（A.　　　　　）を達成するために、地域社会でさまざまな活動を始めている。コートジボワールでのプロジェクトは（B.　　　　　）に広がり、能力や人権意識の向上に役立っている。今度は私たちが、自分たちの生活や社会における男女（C.　　　　　）を知り、どのようにして克服するかを考える必要がある。

① If they are to achieve gender equality, women must work to help themselves.

▶主語のtheyはコートジボワールの人々のこと。are to achieveは「達成しようとする」〈意図〉の意味。

▶be to *do*は助動詞のような働きをし、予定・義務・可能・意図など、さまざまな意味を表す。「～する（ための）ことになっている」「～しなければならない」「～できる」「～するつもりだ」などの意味になる。 ⇒p.148 G-❶

▶help *oneself*は「自分で努力する、自立する」（≒ stand on *one's* own）。

② Graduates of the school are beginning to share their knowledge and training with other women in the community.

▶share ～ with ... は「～を…と共有する」で、ここではtheir knowledge and training「彼ら（＝卒業生）の知識と訓練」が目的語になる。

③ Some women have started small businesses growing vegetables to protect their families from unstable cacao prices.

▶growingはbusinessesを修飾する現在分詞。small businesses growing vegetablesで「野菜を栽培する小規模事業」。

④ Rosine and Yaoua, both graduates of the school, lead a women's society to help girls get an education.

▶挿入句のboth ～ schoolはRosine and Yaouaの補足説明。

▶leadは「～を率いる」、〈to help＋人＋動詞の原形〉は「（人）が～するのを助ける［手伝う］ために」。

⑤ Yaoua says, "Women don't have to be behind men. We are worthy too."

▶don't have to *do*は「～する必要はない、～しなくてよい」、be behind menは「男性の後ろ［裏側、陰］にいる」の意味。

✍ 英文を完成させなさい。

少数派が多数派の陰にいる必要はない。

Minorities (　　　) have to be (　　　) the majorities.

▶ We are worthy too.は直前の文を言いかえたもの。主語のWeは女性たちのこと。worthyは「価値がある」。

⑥ The project to help the invisible women farmers of Côte d'Ivoire has gone global.

▶ The project ～ Côte d'Ivoireが文の主語で、to以下がThe projectを後ろから修飾している。「～する(ための)プロジェクト[計画]」の意味。

▶ go globalは「世界規模になる」(≒ spread around the world)。has gone globalは現在完了で「世界規模になった[世界に広がった]」。あとに続く2文で具体例が挙げられている。

⑦ The goal is to promote empowerment and raise awareness of human rights.

▶〈S + V + C (= 不定詞)〉の文。promote empowermentは「(女性の)能力向上を促進する」、raise awarenessは「気づき[意識]を高める」(≒ increase interest and understanding)。

▶ empowerment「エンパワーメント」とは、教育や訓練などにより、困難な状況を打開したり、問題を解決したりする能力を身に付けること。

⑧ I began by asking you to think about where chocolate comes from.

▶ began by V-ingは「～することによって(私の話を)始めた」。

▶〈ask + 人 + to *do*〉は「(人)に～するように頼む」。where以下は間接疑問で、aboutの目的語になっている。

⑨ Then we listened to the voices of the invisible women cacao farmers in Côte d'Ivoire.

▶ listen to the voices of ～は「～の声に耳を傾ける」、invisible women cacao farmersは「見えざる[無視されている]女性カカオ農民」。

⑩ That led to the question of how to overcome the gender gap.

▶ That「そのこと」は、⑨の文の内容を指す。

▶ lead to ～は「～につながる、～を導く」、how to overcome the gender gapは「どのように男女格差を克服するか」。

⑪ How much have we accomplished and how much more do we have to do in order to close our own gender gap?

▶ 2つの問いが並んでいる文。1つ目の問いは、これまでの成果についてたずねる現在完了の疑問文。

▶ 2つ目の問いは、have to *do*の疑問文で、今後のことについてたずねている。how much more do we have to doは「私たちは、さらにどれだけのことをしなければならないか」という意味。in order to *do*は「～するために」。

このセクションの内容 の答え→ A. 平等 B. 世界 C. 格差

Grammar for Communication

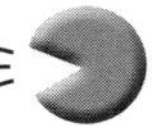

1 be to不定詞

be to不定詞のbe toは助動詞のような働きをし、予定・義務・命令・可能・運命・意図などの意味を表す。be to不定詞はかしこまった表現で、公式の場での発表や説明を行うときに使われることが多い。

---

1. 予定：「～すること[予定]になっている」

◆ Mr. Green **is to visit** London on business tomorrow.
（グリーンさんは明日に仕事でロンドンを訪れることになっている）
★「公式の予定になっている」という意味を表す。

◆ The welcome party **is to be** held next Monday.
（歓迎パーティーは今度の月曜日に開かれることになっている）

2. 義務・命令：「～しなければならない、～しなさい」

◆ You **are to return** the book to the library as soon as possible.
（あなたはできるだけすぐにその本を図書館に返さなければならない）
≒ You must[should] return the book to the library as soon as possible.

◆ You **are** not **to enter** this room with your shoes on.　＊禁止を表す
（あなたは靴をはいたままでこの部屋に入ってはいけない）
≒ You must not enter this room with your shoes on.

3. 可能：「～することができる」（主に受け身の否定文で）

◆ Not a sound **was to be** heard in the gym.
（体育館では物音ひとつ聞こえなかった）
≒ Not a sound could be heard in the gym.

◆ My smartphone **was** not **to be** found after all.
（結局、私のスマートフォンは見つからなかった）

4. 運命：「～する運命だ」（主に過去の文で）

◆ They **were** never **to see** each other again.
（彼らはお互いに二度と会うことはなかった[会うことのない運命だった]）

◆ Ten years later, the sailors **were to return** to Japan.
（10年後、その船員たちは日本に戻ることになった[戻る運命だった]）

5. 意図：「～するつもりだ、～したい」（主にif節で）

◆ If you **are to get** there by three, you had better take a taxi.
（3時までにそこに着くつもりなら、タクシーに乗るほうがいい）

◆ Practice harder if you **are to win** the marathon.
（マラソン大会で優勝するつもりなら、もっと懸命に練習しなさい）

2 結果を表す不定詞

不定詞の副詞的用法には、「…して（その結果）～する」と〈結果〉の意味を表すものがある。また、to *do*の前にonlyやneverの副詞が置かれることもある。

---

1. ... only to *do*：「…したが（その結果）～だった」

◆ I tried to persuade her, only **to fail**.
（私は彼女を説得しようとしたが、失敗した）

★only to *do*には「結局は～しただけの結果に終わった」という失望の気持ちが含まれる。

≒ I tried to persuade her, but unfortunately I failed.

◆ I went to see him only **to find** he had already left home.
（私は彼に会いに行ったが、彼はすでに家を出たことがわかった）

★次のonly to *do*は「～するためだけに」と〈目的〉を表す。
I went there *only to see* him. （私は彼に会うためだけにそこに行った）

2. ... never to *do*：「…したが（その結果）二度と～しなかった」

◆ He got angry, never **to speak** to me again.
（彼は腹を立て、二度と私に話しかけなかった）

≒ He got angry and never spoke to me again.

◆ We said goodbye at the station, never **to meet** again.
（私たちは駅で別れを告げ、二度と会うことはなかった）

≒ We said goodbye at the station and never met again.

3. ... to *do*：「…して（その結果）～」

◆ She grew up **to be** a great guitarist.
（彼女は成長して偉大なギタリストになった）

◆ I woke up **to find** that the town was covered with snow.
（目覚めると、町が雪でおおわれているのがわかった[おおわれていた]）

◆ My grandmother lived **to be** 100 years old.
（祖母は100歳まで生きた）

確認問題

語彙・表現

1 次の語をそれぞれ名詞形に書きかえなさい。

(1) aware　(2) transform
(3) know　(4) empower

2 第2音節にアクセント (強勢) のある語を3つ選び、記号で答えなさい。

ア ca-ca-o　イ in-dus-try　ウ pre-vi-ous-ly
エ fi-nan-cial　オ man-age-ment　カ ne-go-ti-ate

3 日本語に合うように、( ) 内に適切な語を入れなさい。ただし、最初の文字が指定されているときは、その文字で書き始めなさい。

(1) 私は宇宙に関することを何か勉強したい。
I want to study something (r　　) (　　) space.
(2) ちょっと時間をとって昼食を食べよう。
Let's (　　) a (m　　) to eat lunch.
(3) 私たちは彼の年齢を考慮に入れるべきだ。
We should (　　) his age (　　) (a　　).
(4) 私たちは将来、どうすれば平和に暮らせるだろうか。
How can we live (　　) (　　) in the future?
(5) 言うまでもなく、彼は最優秀サッカー選手の1人だ。
(　　) to (　　), he is one of the best soccer players.

文のパターン・文法

1 各組の文がほぼ同じ意味になるように、( ) 内に適切な語を入れなさい。

(1) The concert will start at seven in the evening.
The concert (　　) (　　) start at seven in the evening.
(2) You must finish the work without any help.
You are (　　) (　　) the work without any help.
(3) Not a star can be seen tonight.
Not a star (　　) (　　) (　　) seen tonight.
(4) If you want to be healthy, you must eat breakfast.
If you (　　) (　　) (　　) healthy, you must eat breakfast.

2 次の文を〈結果〉を表す不定詞を使って書きかえなさい。

(1) I woke up, and I found myself lying in a dark room.
_______________ lying in a dark room.

(2) Beth opened the box, but she found it empty.
Beth opened the box, _______________.

(3) He left his hometown, and he never came back.
He left his hometown, _______________.

3 (　) 内の語句を並べかえて、日本語に合う英文を作りなさい。

(1) スミス夫妻は明日、東京に到着する予定だ。
Mr. and Mrs. Smith (arrive / Tokyo / are / tomorrow / in / to).
Mr. and Mrs. Smith _______________.

(2) その日は、彼らにとって忘れられない日となった。
The day (was / forgotten / them / be / never / to / by).
The day _______________.

(3) 私は急いで家を出たが、会合には遅れてしまった。
I left home in a hurry, (late / only / be / the meeting / to / for).
I left home in a hurry, _______________.

総合

次の文を読んで、あとの問いに答えなさい。

Women do about 70 percent of the work on the farms but receive only about 20 percent of the income. They must also do all the housework. ①This unfairness is due to the country's patriarchal society, where men hold power and make most decisions. ②Women have no say about selling the cacao beans, and their husbands don't share the money. Women don't have (③) to training or financial aid which could help them lead a better life. ④There is a very large (　　) (　　).

問1　下線部①の具体的な内容を２つ日本語で説明しなさい。

問2　下線部②を日本語に直しなさい。

問3　③の (　) 内に入る最も適切な語を選びなさい。

ア meaning　イ access　ウ time　エ nature

問4　下線部④が「とても大きな男女格差がある」という意味になるように、(　) 内に入る最も適切な２語を書きなさい。

Lesson 9 Nudges

教科書p.160　Section 1

- □ nudge [nʌ́dʒ]
- □ get *one's* attention
- □ stranger [stréɪndʒər]
- □ what's more
- □ Stockholm [stɑ́khòʊm]
- □ Sweden [swí:dn]
- □ step on ～
- □ at the same time
- □ experimental [ɪkspèrɪméntl]
- □ result in ～
- □ come to popular attention
- □ Richard H. Thaler [rítʃərd éɪtʃ θéɪlər]
- □ Cass R. Sunstein [kǽs ɑ́:r sʌ́nsti:n]
- □ basic [béɪsɪk]
- □ at least
- □ effective [ɪféktɪv]

①A "nudge" is a gentle push a friend gives you to get your attention. ②However, you can also be nudged by strangers for other purposes. ③What's more, you may not even know what's happening.

1

You are at a subway station in Stockholm, Sweden. You get off the subway and look for a way to get to the street. ④You find stairs of black and white keys—like huge piano keys—leading up to the exit. When you step on the keys, they make piano-like sounds. ⑤You can take the escalator if you want, but you'll probably choose the musical stairs because they are so much fun. ⑥At the same time, you will be exercising. ⑦The experimental piano stairs resulted in a 66% increase in the use of steps.

⑧A "nudge" is a little change that leads you to do something you may not have planned to do. ⑨Nudges came to popular attention in 2008 when Richard H. Thaler and Cass R. Sunstein published *Nudge: Improving Decisions about Health, Wealth, and Happiness.* ⑩The basic idea is to design an environment which makes it easy for people to do the right thing, or at least to do what you want them to do. ⑪In many countries, nudges have proved to be effective.

このセクションの内容

踏むとピアノのような音を出す階段は楽しく、人々は（A.　　　　　）に乗らずに階段を利用する。それはまた、よい（B.　　　　　）になる。このように、好ましいことへ人々を仕向ける穏やかなひと押しを「ナッジ」といい、多くの国でナッジに（C.　　　　　）があると証明されている。

① A "nudge" is a gentle push a friend gives you to get your attention.

▶ nudge「ナッジ」は「(ひじで)軽く押す、(ある方向に)穏やかに説得する」の意味を表す動詞で、その行為自体を表す名詞としても使われる。

▶ a friend ～ attentionはa gentle push「穏やかなひと押し」を後ろから修飾する節。to get your attentionは「あなたの注意[関心]を引くために」(≒ to attract your interest)。

② However, you can also be nudged by strangers for other purposes.

▶ can be nudgedは受け身で「軽く押されることもあり得る」。ここでは、nudgeが動詞として使われている。strangerは「見知らぬ人」。

③ What's more, you may not even know what's happening.

▶ What's moreは「さらに」(≒ In addition)の意味で、情報を付け加えるときに使われる。may not even know ～は「～さえわからないかもしれない」、what's happeningは「何が起こっているか[起こっていること]」。つまり、知らないうちに「ナッジされて」いる可能性があるということ。

④ You find stairs of black and white keys—like huge piano keys—leading up to the exit.

▶ stairs of black and white keysは「白黒の鍵盤のような階段」の意味で、ofの前後は〈同格〉の関係になる。さらにダッシュ(—)ではさまれた語句で、black and white keysについて補足説明を加えている。

▶ find ～ V-ingは「～が…しているのを見つける」、lead up to ～は「～につながる[続く]」。

⑤ You can take the escalator if you want, but you'll probably choose the musical stairs because they are so much fun.

▶ if you wantはif you want to take the escalatorを簡潔に表したもの。

▶ becauseのあとのtheyはthe musical stairsを指す。

⑥ At the same time, you will be exercising.

▶ At the same timeは「同時に、その上」の意味で、ここでは「楽しいだけでなく」ということ。will be exercisingは「運動をしているだろう」と未

来における進行中の動作を表す。 ⇒p.164 G-❶

⑦ **The experimental piano stairs resulted in a 66% increase in the use of steps.**

▶主語はThe experimental piano stairs「その実験的なピアノ階段」。result in ～は「～という結果になる」、increase in ～は「～における増加」。つまり、ピアノ階段によって、階段利用者が66パーセント増えたということ。

⑧ **A "nudge" is a little change that leads you to do something you may not have planned to do.**

▶thatは主格の関係代名詞で、先行詞はa little change「小さな変化」。〈lead＋人＋to *do*〉は「(人)に～するように仕向ける」。

▶you may not have planned to do「(以前には)しようと計画していなかったかもしれない」は、somethingを後ろから修飾する節。

⑨ **Nudges came to popular attention in 2008 when Richard H. Thaler and Cass R. Sunstein published *Nudge: Improving Decisions about Health, Wealth, and Happiness.***

▶come to popular attentionは「世間[大衆]の注目を集める、広く知られるようになる」(≒ be noticed by many people)。

▶when以下は関係副詞の節で2008年についての説明。イタリック体[斜体]が本のタイトルになる。improving decisions about ～は「～についての意思決定を改良する[よりよくする]こと」という意味。

⑩ **The basic idea is to design an environment which makes it easy for people to do the right thing, or at least to do what you want them to do.**

▶〈S＋V＋C(＝不定詞)〉の文。to design ～は「～を設計すること」。

▶関係代名詞which以下(文の最後まで)がan environmentを後ろから修飾している。

▶make it easy for people to do ～, or at least to do ... は「人々が～することや、少なくとも…することを容易にする[しやすくする]」の意味で、itは後ろの2つのto doを指す形式目的語。what you want them to doは「彼ら[人々]にしてもらいたいこと」。

✍ 次の英文を日本語に直しなさい。

Do for others what you want them to do for you.

________________________________ 他人にしなさい。

⑪ **In many countries, nudges have proved to be effective.**

▶prove to be ～は「～だと証明する[わかる]」の意味。

 このセクションの内容 の答え→ A. エスカレーター B. 運動 C. 効果

教科書p.162　Section 2

- □ experiment [ɪkspérɪmənt]
- □ properly [prápərli]
- □ loudspeaker [láudspìːkər]
- □ sensor [sénsər]
- □ underground [ʌ̀ndərgráund]
- □ Mumbai [mʊ̀mbáɪ]
- □ honk [háŋk]
- □ capital [kǽpətl]
- □ manner [mǽnər]
- □ come up with ～
- □ reset [rìːsét]
- □ signal [sígnl]
- □ horn [hɔ́ːrn]
- □ decibel [désɪbèl]

2

①Also in Sweden, there was an experiment to encourage people to throw their trash away properly. ②A loudspeaker and a sensor were placed inside an ordinary trash can. ③When you dropped something into the can, it made a long falling sound as if the bottom was deep underground. ④People loved it and because of the little nudge, the streets became much cleaner.

⑤The Indian city of Mumbai is known as "the honking capital of the world." Mumbai drivers are always honking. They even honk at traffic lights. ⑥To encourage better manners, police have come up with the "Honk More, Wait More" system. ⑦The system resets the red signal every time the sound of horns goes above 85 decibels: a little nudge to be patient.

We can also find examples of nudges in schools. ⑧Many schools in the U.S. use a nudge in their cafeterias to encourage healthy choices. ⑨Research shows that if you put fruit in an attractive bowl at the start of the line, more students make the healthy choice: they choose fruit.

このセクションの内容

スウェーデンでは、ゴミ箱の中にゴミを落とすと長い（A.　　　　　）が聞こえるようにすると、人々はそれを気に入り、通りはきれいになった。ムンバイでは、運転手によりよいマナーを身につけてもらうために（B.　　　　　）のある場所でクラクションの音量が一定量を超えると待ち時間をリセットするようにした。アメリカの学校の食堂でも、魅力的なボウルや陳列の場所を工夫することで、より多くの生徒が（C.　　　　　）を選ぶようになった。

① **Also in Sweden, there was an experiment to encourage people to throw their trash away properly.**

▶ an experiment to ～は「～するという実験」の意味。to以下はexperimentと〈同格〉の関係になる。

例 She made *the decision to buy* the expensive sweater.
「彼女はその高価なセーターを買う決心をした」

▶〈encourage + 人 + to *do*〉は「(人)が～するように促す[勧める]」、throw ～ away（またはthrow away ～）は「～を捨てる」、properlyは「適切に」。

② **A loudspeaker and a sensor were placed inside an ordinary trash can.**

▶ loudspeakerは、ここでは「スピーカー」(= speaker)のこと。

▶ were placedは受け身で、「置かれた、設置された」、ordinaryは「普通の」。

▶ trash canは、アメリカ英語で「ゴミ[くず]箱」のこと。なお、イギリス英語ではdustbinと言う。

③ **When you dropped something into the can, it made a long falling sound as if the bottom was deep underground.**

▶ the canは、②の文の「スピーカーとセンサーが付いたゴミ箱」のこと。

▶ itはthe canを指す。a long falling soundは「長い落下音」。

▶〈as if + 仮定法過去〉は「まるで～かのように」の意味で、実際と異なることを表す。as if the bottom was deep undergroundで「まるで(ゴミ箱の)底が地下深くにあるかのように」となる。be動詞はwereを使うのが正式であるが、会話などくだけた場面ではwasを使うことがある。

✍ 次の英文を日本語に直しなさい。

Mike talked to me as if he were my brother.

マイクは、＿＿＿＿＿＿＿＿＿＿＿＿＿＿＿＿＿＿＿＿＿＿＿＿＿＿＿。

④ **People loved it and because of the little nudge, the streets became much cleaner.**

▶ itは②と③の文で述べられているゴミ箱を指す。

▶ because of the little nudge「その小さなナッジのために」とは、③の文のゴミ箱の仕掛けのこと。

▶ muchは「ずっと～」と比較級を強調する副詞。ほかにa lot、even、stillなども使われる。cleanerのあとにthan beforeが省略されている。

⑤ **The Indian city of Mumbai is known as "the honking capital of the world."**

▶ The Indian city of Mumbaiは「ムンバイというインドの都市」で、ofの前後は〈同格〉の関係。be known as ～は「～として知られている」。

このセクションの内容 の答え→ A. 落下音 B. 信号(機) C. 果物

▶ honking は honk「(車の) クラクションを鳴らす」の現在分詞。honking capital「クラクション (による騒音) の首都」とは比喩表現で、「(世界で) 最も車のクラクションがうるさい都市」ということ。

⑥ To encourage better manners, police have come up with the "Honk More, Wait More" system.

▶ To encourage better manners とは、To encourage drivers to have better manners「運転手によりよいマナーを身につけてもらうために」ということ。

▶ come up with ～は「～を思いつく、～を考え出す」(≒ think of ～)。

✍ 英文を完成させなさい。

あなたはおもしろい計画を何か思いつきましたか。

Have you (　　　) (　　　) with any interesting plans?

▶ "Honk More, Wait More"は「もっとクラクションを鳴らして、もっと待て」の意味。この制度[システム]の内容は⑦の文で述べられる。

⑦ The system resets the red signal every time the sound of horns goes above 85 decibels: a little nudge to be patient.

▶ reset the red signal「赤信号をリセットする」とは、赤信号の待ち時間をもとに戻す[信号が変わった直後の状態に戻す]ということ。

▶ every time ～は「～するたびに」、go above ～は「～を超える」。

▶ コロン (:)「つまり～」のあとは、「がまん[忍耐]強くなるためのちょっとしたナッジだ」という意味。

⑧ Many schools in the U.S. use a nudge in their cafeterias to encourage healthy choices.

▶ to encourage ～は「～を促すために」。healthy choice「健康的な選択」とは、健康によい食べもののこと。アメリカの学校では、自分で好きなものを大皿から取って食べるビュッフェ形式が多い。

⑨ Research shows that if you put fruit in an attractive bowl at the start of the line, more students make the healthy choice: they choose fruit.

▶ Research shows that ～は「調査は～ということを示している」→「調査によると～だ」。

▶ if you put ～の you は一般の人を指す代名詞。attractive は「魅力的な」。

▶ at the start of the line「列の最初に」とは、生徒が列をつくって並ぶ大皿の陳列のいちばん前のこと。make a choice は「選ぶ」。

▶ コロン (:) 以下は、直前の内容を言いかえている。choose fruit「果物を選ぶ」は make the healthy choice「健康的な選択をする」の言いかえ。

- □ socially [sóuʃəli]
- □ beneficial [bènɪfíʃl]
- □ neither [ní:ðər]
- □ nor [nɔ́:r]
- □ neither ～ nor ...
- □ online [ɑ̀nláɪn]
- □ trial [tráɪəl]
- □ subscription [səbskrípʃən]
- □ automatically [ɔ̀:təmǽtɪkəli]
- □ involuntary [ɪnvɑ́ləntèri]
- □ purchase [pə́:rtʃəs]
- □ make a purchase
- □ target [tɑ́:rgət]
- □ careless [kéərləs]
- □ cancel [kǽnsl]
- □ trick [trík]
- □ in *one's* best interest
- □ stay on the job
- □ close to ～
- □ salary [sǽləri]
- □ on *one's* own

3

①Not all nudges promote healthy or socially beneficial behavior. ②Some nudges are neither healthy nor beneficial.

③Some online services offer free trial subscriptions, and then automatically charge you when the trial period ends. ④The nudge of a free trial leads you to make involuntary purchases. It targets careless people. ⑤Canceling the subscription can be a lot of trouble. ⑥You might have to contact a call center at strange hours or argue with the sales staff. ⑦You will have been tricked by a nudge.

⑧Sometimes nudges lead us to do things that are not in our best interests or those that are even dangerous. An example is a part-time taxi driver who has finished work for the day. ⑨She is too tired to drive safely, but the taxi company wants her to stay on the job. ⑩They could simply order her to stay on. ⑪However, one American company uses nudges rather than orders. ⑫They send the driver a notice that she is close to meeting a target which will raise her salary. They also send the location of a nearby customer. ⑬The driver decides on her own to stay on the job. ⑭She has been "nudged" to do something which is neither healthy nor socially beneficial.

このセクションの内容

すべてのナッジが健全で有益とは限らない。（A.　　　　　）のお試し期間終了後に（B.　　　　　）的に課金するオンラインサービスや、昇給をほのめかして（C.　　　　　）の運転手に追加勤務をさせる会社もある。

① Not all nudges promote healthy or socially beneficial behavior.

▶ Not all ～は「すべての～が…とは限らない」の意味で、部分否定を表す。Not all nudges promote ～は、Not every nudge promotes ～としても同じ。

✍ 次の英文を日本語に直しなさい。

Not all elderly people who live alone feel lonely.

一人暮らしの高齢者がみな、＿＿＿＿＿＿＿＿＿＿＿＿＿＿。

▶ healthyは「健全な」、socially beneficialは「社会的に有益な」。

② Some nudges are neither healthy nor beneficial.

▶ neither A nor Bは「AもBも（～し）ない」「AでもBでもない」。

例 Most of the students *neither* know *nor* care about it.
「ほとんどの生徒は、それについて知りもせず関心も持たない」

③ Some online services offer free trial subscriptions, and then automatically charge you when the trial period ends.

▶ 健全でも有益でもないナッジの例を挙げている。online services「オンラインサービス」はインターネットを介したサービスのことで、映画や音楽の配信サービスやオンラインゲームなどがある。

▶ offerは「～を提供する」、free trial subscriptionsは「無料のお試し購読[購入]」。subscriptionとは、サービスの利用者が毎月決まったお金を支払うシステムのこと。

▶ automatically charge youは「自動的に支払いを請求する」、when the trial period endsは「お試し期間が終わったときに」。

④ The nudge of a free trial leads you to make involuntary purchases.

▶ The nudge of a free trialは「無料のお試しというナッジ」の意味。ofの前後は〈同格〉の関係。

▶ 〈lead + 人 + to *do*〉は「（人）を～するように仕向ける[導く]」。make a purchaseは「購入する、買う」（≒ buy）の意味で、make involuntary purchasesで「非自主的な購入をする」→「思わず知らず買う」ということ。

⑤ Canceling the subscription can be a lot of trouble.

▶ canは〈可能性・推量〉を表す。a lot of troubleは「多くの困難[面倒]」。つまり、キャンセルする手続きが非常に面倒かもしれないということ。

⑥ You might have to contact a call center at strange hours or argue with the sales staff.

▶ might have to *do*は「～しなければならないかもしれない」（推量）で、*do*にあたる動詞はcontactとargueの２つ。

▶ at strange hours「変な時間帯」とは、例えば、夜中など通常の営業時間

このセクションの内容 の答え→ A. 無料 B. 自動 C. タクシー

外の時間のこと。argue with ～は「～と口論する」、sales staff「販売員」。

⑦ You will have been tricked by a nudge.

▶ will have been trickedは未来完了形（受け身）で、未来の時点までに予想される完了・結果、経験、継続を表す。ここでは「だまされてしまっているだろう」（完了）の意味。 ⇒p.164 G-❷

⑧ Sometimes nudges lead us to do things that are not in our best interests or those that are even dangerous.

▶ things that ～と those that ～がorをはさんで並列している。thoseはthingsを言いかえたもの。

⑨ She is too tired to drive safely, but the taxi company wants her to stay on the job.

▶ too ～ to *do*「とても～なので…できない」の文。主語のSheは直前の文のa part-time taxi driverを指す。

▶〈want＋人＋to *do*〉は「（人）に～してもらいたい」、stay on the jobは「仕事にとどまる」→「仕事を続ける」（≒keep working）。

⑩ They could simply order her to stay on.

▶ Theyは、⑨の文のthe taxi companyで働いている人たち（＝タクシー運転手の上司）のこと。couldは「（しようと思えば）～することもできる」の意味で、潜在的な能力を表す。

▶〈order＋人＋to *do*〉は「（人）に～するように命じる」。

⑪ However, one American company uses nudges rather than orders.

▶ rather than ordersは「命令よりはむしろ」→「命令する代わりに」。

⑫ They send the driver a notice that she is close to meeting a target which will raise her salary.

▶〈send＋人＋もの〉は「（人）に（もの）を送る」。a notice ～ salaryが〈もの〉にあたる。noticeは「通知」で、that以下がその内容になる。

▶ close to ～は「～に近い」（≒nearly ～）、close to meeting a targetは「目標の達成に近づいている」となる。whichは主格の関係代名詞。つまり、もう少しで目標を達成して給料が上がるということ。

⑬ The driver decides on her own to stay on the job.

▶ decide to *do*は「～することに決める」、toの前にon *one's* own「自分一人で」（≒by *oneself*）が挿入されている。

⑭ She has been "nudged" to do something which is neither healthy nor socially beneficial.

▶ be "nudged" to do ～は「～をするように『ナッジされ』てしまう」。

教科書p.166　Section 4

□ reminder [rɪmáɪndər]
□ cautious [kɔ́:ʃəs]
□ propose [prəpóʊz]
□ misleading [mìslí:dɪŋ]
□ reject [rɪdʒékt]
□ welfare [wélfèər]
□ proper [prápər]
□ improper [ɪmprápər]
□ evaluate [ɪvǽljuèɪt]
□ basis [béɪsɪs]
□ on the basis of ～
□ fool [fú:l]

4

①Nudges are supposed to give people a gentle reminder to do something they are already interested in doing or which will be socially beneficial. ②But as we have seen, nudges are powerful tools that can lead us to do things that may not be in our best interests. ③It is best to be cautious.

④Richard H. Thaler, the author of *Nudge*, proposes three principles:

1. ⑤All nudging should be clear and never misleading.
2. ⑥It should be as easy as possible to reject a nudge.
3. ⑦There should be good reasons to believe that the encouraged behavior will improve the welfare of those who are being nudged.

⑧These are the keys to deciding whether a nudge is proper or improper. ⑨Now, think about the nudges you have just read about and evaluate them on the basis of Thaler's principles.

⑩You are being nudged all day. ⑪Pay attention. Welcome the good nudges. ⑫Don't let yourself be fooled by the bad ones.

このセクションの内容

ナッジは本来、興味があることや社会の（A.　　　　　）になることへの行動を促すものだが、私たちが望まないことをさせる強力な（B.　　　　　）にもなる。私たちは、セイラーが提案する３つの原則をもとに、ナッジが適切かどうかを判断し、悪いナッジに（C.　　　　　）ように注意しなければならない。

① Nudges are supposed to give people a gentle reminder to do something they are already interested in doing or which will be socially beneficial.

▶ be supposed to *do*は「〜することになっている、〜しなければならない」。

例 Everyone *is supposed to follow* this rule.
「だれもがこの規則に従うことになっている」

▶〈give＋人＋もの〉「(人)に(もの)を与える」の文。a gentle reminder to do somethingは「何かをする親切な催促」。reminderは「思い出させる[気づかせる]もの」。*cf.* remind「(人)に(〜を)思い出させる」

▶ somethingの後ろに２つの節が続いている。something they are already interested in doingは「彼らがすでにすることに興味を持っている何か」、or (something) which will be socially beneficialは「または社会的に有益な何か」。orの後ろにsomethingが省略されている。

② But as we have seen, nudges are powerful tools that can lead us to do things that may not be in our best interests.

▶ as we have seenは「私たちがこれまで見てきたように」。

▶ powerful tools that 〜のthatは関係代名詞で、thatから文末までがpowerful toolsの説明。このthat節内に、thingsを説明するthat節を含む構造になる。全体で、「私たちの最善の利益にならないかもしれないことをするように、私たちに仕向ける可能性がある強力な道具」という意味。

③ It is best to be cautious.

▶ Itはto beを指す形式主語。cautiousは「注意[用心]深い」。

④ Richard H. Thaler, the author of *Nudge*, proposes three principles:

▶ proposeは「〜を提案する」、principleは「原則」。

⑤ All nudging should be clear and never misleading.

▶ ３つの原則の１つ。nudgingは「ナッジすること」。

▶ should be 〜は「〜であるべきだ」、never misleadingは「決して誤解を与えない[まぎらわしくない]」。*cf.* mislead「(人)を誤解させる」

⑥ It should be as easy as possible to reject a nudge.

▶ ２つ目の原則。Itはto reject a nudge「ナッジを拒否すること」を指す形式主語。as 〜 as possibleは「できる限り〜な[に]」。

⑦ There should be good reasons to believe that the encouraged behavior will improve the welfare of those who are being nudged.

▶ ３つ目の原則。reasons to believe that 〜は「〜ということを信じる理由」。

▶ the encouraged behavior「促された行動」とは、ナッジによって促され

このセクションの内容 の答え→ A. 利益 B. 道具 C. だまされない

る行動のこと。

▶ the welfare of those who are being nudgedは「ナッジされている人々の幸福[福利]」の意味。those who ～は「～する[している]人々」(≒ people who ～)、〈be being＋過去分詞〉は受け身の進行形。 ⇒p.165 G-❸

✍ 英文を完成させなさい。

駅前に新しいホテルが建てられている。

A new hotel (　　　) (　　　) (　　　) in front of the station.

⑧ These are the keys to deciding whether a nudge is proper or improper.

▶ Theseは、⑤～⑦の文の3つの原則を指す。keysは、ここでは「手がかり、秘訣」の意味。

▶ whether A or Bは「AかBかどうか」の意味。decide whether a nudge is proper or improperで「ナッジが適切か不適切かを決める」となる。

✍ 次の英文を日本語に直しなさい。

We need to decide whether we will order a pizza delivery or eat out.

____

⑨ Now, think about the nudges you have just read about and evaluate them on the basis of Thaler's principles.

▶ 文頭のNowは「さあ」と相手に強く促している。thinkとevaluateで始まる2つの命令文が続いている。

▶ think about ～ and evaluate ... は「～について考え、…を評価しなさい」。evaluateは「価値や重要性などを見極めて判断する」という意味。

▶ you have just read about「あなたが先ほど読んだ」は、the nudgesを修飾する節。このnudgesは、Lesson 9で紹介されたすべてのナッジのこと。

▶ on the basis of ～は「～に基づいて、～を根拠にして」(≒ based on ～)。

⑩ You are being nudged all day.

▶ are being nudged「ナッジされている」は、受け身の進行形〈be being＋過去分詞〉。つまり、「私たちはさまざまなナッジにさらされている」ということ。all dayは「1日中」。

⑪ Pay attention. Welcome the good nudges.

▶ 2つの命令文。pay attentionは「注意を払う、細かい点に気を配る」、welcomeは「～を喜んで受け入れる」。

⑫ Don't let yourself be fooled by the bad ones.

▶〈let＋人＋*do*〉「(人)に～させる」の否定の命令文。let *oneself do*は「自分自身に～させる」、be fooled by ～は「～にだまされる」。全体で「あなたは悪いもの(＝ナッジ)にだまされないようにしなさい」となる。

Grammar for Communication

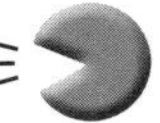

1　未来進行形：will be V-ing

〈will be V-ing〉の形を未来進行形といい、未来のある時に動作や出来事が進行していることを表す。進行の含意がなく、単に予定を表したり、丁寧表現として使われる場合もある。

---

1. 未来に進行中の動作：「～しているだろう」

◆ I **will be jogging** around the park tomorrow morning.
（明日の朝、私は公園のまわりをジョギングしているだろう）

◆ We **will be thinking** about the school festival when we finish the exam.
（試験が終わったら、私たちは学園祭のことを考えているだろう）

2. 予定：「～することになるだろう[なっている]」

◆ We **will be arriving** at Nagoya Station at 3:20.
（私たちは３時20分に名古屋駅に着くことになっている）

◆ I **will be seeing** Ms. Ito after school today.
（私は今日の放課後に、伊藤先生に会うことになっている）

★〈will be V-ing〉は、成り行きや事情で決まっていることを表す。

《比較》　I *am seeing* Ms. Ito after school today.
＊予定に向けて心づもりや準備を進めていることを表す

I *will see* Ms. Ito after school today.　＊意志を表す

3. 丁寧表現

◆ **Will** you **be staying** in Japan long?　（日本には長くご滞在の予定ですか）

★相手の予定や都合を丁寧にたずねるときに使われる。

◆ How **will** you **be paying** for the ticket? Cash or card?
（チケットのお支払いはどうなさいますか。現金ですか、カードですか）

2　未来完了形：will have＋過去分詞

〈will have＋過去分詞〉の形を未来完了形といい、未来のある時までに予想される動作や状態の完了・結果、経験、継続を表す。

---

1. 完了[結果]:「〜して(しまって)いるだろう」

◆ The sun **will have set** before we reach the coast.
(私たちが海岸に着く前に日が沈んでしまうだろう)

◆ Ten years from now, most of them **will have forgotten** the accident.
(今から10年後には、彼らのほとんどがその事故を忘れているだろう)

2. 経験:「〜したことになる(だろう)」

◆ If I visit Okinawa next month, I **will have been** there three times.
(来月沖縄を訪れたら、私はそこに3回行ったことになる)

◆ I **will have read** this book five times if I read it again.
(もう一度読んだら、私はこの本を5回読んだことになる)

3. 継続:「ずっと〜していることになる(だろう)」

◆ We **will have lived** in this city for seven years in October.
(10月になると、私たちはこの都市に7年間住んだことになる)

◆ They **will have been** married for five years next month.
(来月で、彼らは結婚して5年になる)

3 受け身の進行形:be being+過去分詞

〈be being+過去分詞〉の形は受け身の進行形で、「〜されているところだ」という意味を表す。過去のことはbe動詞を過去形にする。

◆ Cookies **are being baked** in the kitchen now.
(今、台所でクッキーが焼かれているところだ)

◆ A big fireworks display **is** now **being held** in Nagaoka City.
(今、大花火大会が長岡市で開かれているところだ)

◆ Christmas songs **were being played** during the party.
(パーティーの間中ずっと、クリスマスソングが流れていた)

◆ The students **were being taught** how to cook at that time.
(そのとき生徒たちは料理の仕方を教わっていた)

未来のことについて「〜されているだろう」と言うときは、〈will be being+過去分詞〉で表す。

◆ This old wall **will be being painted** white around this time tomorrow.
(この古い壁は、明日の今頃には白く塗られているだろう)

確認問題

語彙・表現

1 次の語を（　）内の指示にしたがって書きかえなさい。

(1) basis（形容詞形に）　　(2) remind（名詞形に）
(3) careful（反意語に）　　(4) proper（反意語に）

2 第２音節にアクセント（強勢）のある語を２つ選び、記号で答えなさい。

ア　ex-per-i-ment　　イ　loud-speak-er　　ウ　un-der-ground
エ　ben-e-fi-cial　　オ　pur-chase　　カ　e-val-u-ate

3 日本語に合うように、（　）内に適切な語を入れなさい。ただし、最初の文字が指定されているときは、その文字で書き始めなさい。

(1) 今日は暑く、その上、じめじめしている。
It's hot today, at the (　　　) (　　　), humid.
(2) このテーブルは少なくとも20キロはある。
This table weighs (　　　) (　　　) 20 kilograms.
(3) 彼らの努力は成功に終わるだろう。
Their efforts will (r　　　) (　　　) success.
(4) 私はついに最善の解決策を思いついた。
I finally (c　　　) (　　　) (　　　) the best solution.
(5) 彼女の助言に基づいて私たちの決定は下された。
Our decisions were made (　　　) (　　　) (　　　) of her advice.

文のパターン・文法

1 各文を、（　）内の指示にしたがって書きかえなさい。

(1) It is snowing heavily now.　（下線部を tomorrow morning に変えて）
It ______________________________ tomorrow morning.
(2) They were discussing global warming during the meeting.
（下線部を主語にして受け身の文に）
Global warming ______________________________ during the meeting.
(3) Beth has been sick in bed for a week.
（tomorrow を加えて未来完了形の文に）
______________________________ tomorrow.

2 日本語に合うように、(　) 内に適切な語を入れなさい。

(1) 明日の今頃、彼は太平洋上を飛んでいるだろう。
He (　　　) (　　　) (　　　) over the Pacific Ocean around this time tomorrow.

(2) 私が家に着くまでには、彼らは夕食を終えているだろう。
They (　　　) (　　　) (　　　) dinner by the time I get home.

3 (　) 内の語句を並べかえて、日本語に合う英文を作りなさい。

(1) 私は明後日、その行事に参加することになっている。
I (attending / will / the event / be) the day after tomorrow.
I ________________________________ the day after tomorrow.

(2) 招待状は7月末までに送られるだろう。
The invitations (by / been / will / the end / sent / have) of July.
The invitations ________________________________ of July.

(3) あそこに建てられているのは何ですか。
What (built / there / is / being / over)?
What ________________________________?

総合

次の文を読んで、あとの問いに答えなさい。

①Sometimes nudges lead us to do things that are not in our best interests or those that are even dangerous. An example is a part-time taxi driver who has finished work for the day. She is too tired to drive safely, but the taxi company wants her to stay on the job. They could simply order her to stay on. However, one American company uses nudges rather than orders. They send the driver a notice that she is close to meeting a target which will raise her salary. They also send the location of a nearby customer. ②The driver decides on (　　　) (　　　) to stay on the job. She has been "nudged" to do something which is (③) healthy nor socially beneficial.

問1　下線部①を日本語に直しなさい。

問2　下線部②が「運転手は自分で、働き続けると決める」という意味になるように、(　) 内に適切な語を入れなさい。

問3　③の (　) 内に入る適切な語を書きなさい。

問4　タクシー会社が運転手に送る通知の内容を2つ、日本語で書きなさい。

Lesson 10 Are We Alone?

教科書p.176　Section 1

- □ Richard Dawkins [rítʃərd dɔ́ːkɪnz]
- □ for sure
- □ uncertainty [ʌnsə́ːrtənti]
- □ orbit [ɔ́ːrbət]
- □ galaxy [gǽləksi]
- □ universe [júːnɪvə̀ːrs]
- □ in total
- □ astronomer [əstránəmər]
- □ unlikely [ʌnláɪkli]
- □ be unlikely to ～
- □ explode [ɪksplóud]
- □ deal in ～

①From ancient times, people have wondered if there are other planets like Earth. ②That is still an open question today. ③Richard Dawkins tells us that we are getting closer to an answer.

1

Is there life on other planets? ④Nobody knows for sure, but I'd say yes. ⑤One day we may have clear evidence of life on other planets, but for now, the best we can do is to reduce the uncertainty.

⑥The first thing we might ask is how many planets there are. ⑦People used to believe that the ones orbiting our sun were the only ones. But now we know that in our galaxy most stars have planets. ⑧So, we can probably conclude that most of the stars in the universe have planets.

⑨The number of stars in our galaxy is about 100 billion, and the number of galaxies in the universe is about the same. ⑩That means 10,000 billion billion stars in total.

According to astronomers, only about 10 percent of stars are like the sun. ⑪Stars that are very different from the sun are unlikely to support life on their planets for various reasons: for example, stars that are much bigger than the sun will not last long enough before exploding. ⑫But even if we are talking only about the planets orbiting sun-like stars, we are dealing in billions of billions.

このセクションの内容

宇宙のほかの惑星に、（A.　　　　　）は存在するのか。宇宙には膨大な数の恒星と、それらを周回する惑星がある。（B.　　　　　）に似た恒星は約10パーセントだが、それらの惑星の数は数十億の数十億倍に達する。いつの日か、それらの惑星に生命の明確な（C.　　　　　）が見つかるかもしれない。

① From ancient times, people have wondered if there are other planets like Earth.

▶ have wondered if ～は現在完了（継続）で、「～ではないかと（ずっと）思って[考えて]きた」。

▶ planets like Earth「地球のような惑星」とは、「地球のように生命の存在する惑星」ということ。惑星の「地球」という意味では、Mars「火星」やJupiter「木星」と同様にEarthと表記することが多い。

② That is still an open question today.

▶ That「そのこと」とは、①の文のif以下に示された問いを指す。openは、ここでは「閉じていない」→「未解決の」。

③ Richard Dawkins tells us that we are getting closer to an answer.

▶ we are getting closer to ～は「～に近づいてきている」。an answerは、①の文のif以下に示された問いに対する「１つの答え」。

④ Nobody knows for sure, but I'd say yes.

▶ for sureは「確かに」（≒ for certain）。直前の疑問文を受けているので、sureのあとにthat there is life on other planets「ほかの惑星に生命がいること」が省略されている。I'd（= I would）say yesは、直前の疑問文に「はい」と答えるだろうということ。

⑤ One day we may have clear evidence of life on other planets, but for now, the best we can do is to reduce the uncertainty.

▶ One dayは「いつか（きっと）」（≒ Someday）。clear evidence of lifeは「生命の明確な証拠」。

▶ for nowは「今のところ」。the best we can doは後半の文の主語で、「私たちができる最善のこと」の意味。we can doはthe bestを修飾する節。to reduce the uncertaintyは「不確かなことを減らすこと」。

⑥ The first thing we might ask is how many planets there are.

▶〈S + V + C（= 間接疑問）〉の文。主語はThe first thing we might ask「私たちが問うかもしれない最初のこと」→「私たちがまず知りたいこと」。

▶ how many ～は間接疑問なので、there areの語順になっている。

⑦ People used to believe that the ones orbiting our sun were the only ones.

▶ used to ～は「(以前は) ～した(ものだった)」。

▶ the ones (= the planets) V-ingは「～している惑星群」。that以下は「太陽を周回している惑星群が(宇宙で)唯一の惑星群だ」という意味。

⑧ So, we can probably conclude that most of the stars in the universe have planets.

▶ can probably conclude that ～は「たぶん[高い確率で] ～と結論することができる」。most of ～は「～の多く[大部分]」。

⑨ The number of stars in our galaxy is about 100 billion, and the number of galaxies in the universe is about the same.

▶ The number of ～は「～の数」、billionは「十億」。ひとつの銀河に約一千億の恒星があり、全宇宙に銀河も同じ数(約一千億)ある。

⑩ That means 10,000 billion billion stars in total.

▶ That「そのこと」とは、⑨の文の内容を指す。10,000 billion billionは、銀河の中の恒星の数と銀河の数をかけた数(＝100 billion ×100 billion)。

▶ in totalは「合計で、全部で」(≒ all together)。

⑪ Stars that are very different from the sun are unlikely to support life on their planets for various reasons: for example, stars that are much bigger than the sun will not last long enough before exploding.

▶ 文の前半の主語はStars ～ sunで、thatは主格の関係代名詞。

▶ be unlikely to *do*は「～しそうもない」(≒ probably will not *do*)、support lifeは「生命を維持する」、for various reasonsは「さまざまな理由で」。

✍ 次の英文を日本語に直しなさい。

The situation is unlikely to improve.

____

▶ コロン(:)以下は、直前のvarious reasons「さまざまな理由」の例。will not last long enoughは「十分長くは続かない」→「寿命が長くない」。

⑫ But even if we are talking only about the planets orbiting sun-like stars, we are dealing in billions of billions.

▶ even if ～は「たとえ～だとしても」、the planets orbiting sun-like starsは「太陽に似た恒星を周回している惑星」。

▶ deal in ～は「～を扱う」、billions of billionsは、billions (of planets) of billions (of sun-like stars)のことで、数十億ある太陽に似た恒星を周回する数十億の惑星の数を表す。

 このセクションの内容 の答え→ A. 生命(体) B. 太陽 C. 証拠

教科書p.178　Section 2

- □ out there
- □ extra-solar [èkstrəsóulər]
- □ unsuitable [ʌ̀nsú:təbl]
- □ as we know it
- □ proportion [prəpɔ́:rʃən]
- □ rocky [ráki]
- □ extraterrestrial [èkstrətəréstriəl]
- □ regard [rɪgá:rd]
- □ regard ～ as ...
- □ essential [ɪsénʃl]
- □ liquid [líkwɪd]
- □ will[won't] do
- □ steam [stí:m]
- □ Mars [má:rz]
- □ if not ～
- □ Europa [juəróupə]
- □ Jupiter [dʒú:pətər]
- □ be covered with ～
- □ a sea of ～
- □ take the place of ～
- □ rare [réər]

2

①There being so many planets in the universe, the chances are great that there is life somewhere out there. ②But not all planets support life. ③Most extra-solar planets are "gas giants," which are unsuitable for life as we know it. ④Of course, that doesn't mean that life as we know it is the only possible kind of life. ⑤There might be life on gas giants, although I doubt it. ⑥We don't know what proportion of planets are rocky like Earth. ⑦But even if the proportion is quite low, the number will still be high because the total is so huge.

⑧Scientists searching for extraterrestrial life regard water as essential. If there is no water in liquid form, life can probably not exist. ⑨Ice won't do, nor will steam. ⑩Mars shows evidence of liquid water, in the past if not today. ⑪Europa, one of the moons of Jupiter, is covered with ice and under the ice there could be a sea of liquid water.

⑫People once thought Mars was the most likely planet to have extraterrestrial life within our solar system. ⑬Now Europa has taken the place of Mars, but most scientists think we must keep looking. ⑭Evidence suggests that water is not particularly rare on extra-solar planets.

このセクションの内容

地球のような岩石型惑星には、生命が存在する可能性がある。また、生命が存在するためには、(A.　　　　　　)の水が不可欠だ。太陽系内では、(B.　　　　　　)には過去に水が存在した証拠があり、(C.　　　　　　)の衛星エウロパの氷の下には、大量の水があるかもしれない。

① There being so many planets in the universe, the chances are great that there is life somewhere out there.

▶ There being ～は〈理由〉を表す分詞構文。主節の主語（the chances）と主語が異なるときは、分詞の前にも主語を置く。there is構文の場合はThere being ～とする。 ⇒p.180 G-❶

▶ the chances are great that ～は「～という機会が大きい」→「～である可能性が非常に高い」。that以下はchancesと同格の関係（同格のthat）。本来はthe chances that ～ are greatとなるが、主語が長くなるのを避けるために、that節を後ろに置いている。

▶ somewhere out thereは「どこか外に[その辺に]」（≒ somewhere in space）。

② But not all planets support life.

▶ not all ～ ... は「すべての～が…というわけではない」で、部分否定を表す。

✍ 次の英文を日本語に直しなさい。

Not all the members supported the plan.

____

③ Most extra-solar planets are "gas giants," which are unsuitable for life as we know it.

▶ extra-solar planetsは「太陽系外惑星（太陽系の外にある惑星）」、gas giantsは「巨大ガス惑星」で、太陽系内では木星と土星がそれにあたる。

▶〈, which〉は非制限用法の関係代名詞で、"gas giants"の補足説明。

▶ unsuitable for ～は「～に適していない」、life as we know itは「私たちが知っている生命」→「今地球に存在するような生命」（≒ life as it is here and now）。

④ Of course, that doesn't mean that life as we know it is the only possible kind of life.

▶ 主語のthat「そのこと」は、③の文の内容を指す。the only possible kind of lifeは「唯一可能な種類の生命」。つまり、私たちが知っている生命だけが、唯一の生命というわけではないということ。

⑤ There might be life on gas giants, although I doubt it.

▶ There might be ～は「～が存在するかもしれない」、although I doubt itは「私はそれを疑っているが」。

⑥ We don't know what proportion of planets are rocky like Earth.

▶ what proportion of planetsは「惑星の何割」、rockyは「岩石の多い」。なお、水星、金星、地球、火星は岩石惑星になる。

⑦ But even if the proportion is quite low, the number will still be high because the total is so huge.

▶ even if ～は「たとえ～でも」、the number「その数」とは「岩石惑星の数」

このセクションの内容 の答え→ A. 液体 B. 火星 C. 木星

のこと。the totalは「(惑星の)合計(数)」。

⑧ **Scientists searching for extraterrestrial life regard water as essential.**

▶ Scientists ～ lifeが文の主語。regard ～ as ...は「～を…とみなす」(≒ consider ～ as ...)。extraterrestrial「地球外の」(形容詞)は、「地球外生物」を意味する名詞としても使われ、E.T.と略される。

⑨ **Ice won't do, nor will steam.**

▶ 直前の文「液体の水がなければ生命は存在できないだろう」を受けて、ice「氷」とsteam「水蒸気」について述べている。

▶ won't (= will not) doは「(生命が存在するのに)適さないだろう」ということ。nor ～は接続詞で、「そしてまた～も…しない」。norのあとは〈(助)動詞＋主語〉の倒置構文になる。 ⇒p.181 G-❷

⑩ **Mars shows evidence of liquid water, in the past if not today.**

▶ evidence of ～は「～の証拠」、in the past if not todayは「今日ではないにしても過去に」の意味。つまり、火星には過去に液体の水が存在した証拠があるということ。

✍ 次の英文を日本語に直しなさい。

Most, if not all, of the students could not answer the question.

________________________ その問題に答えられなかった。

⑪ **Europa, one of the moons of Jupiter, is covered with ice and under the ice there could be a sea of liquid water.**

▶ moonは「衛星」の意味。be covered with ～は「～でおおわれている」。

▶ couldは〈可能性〉を表し、there could be ～で「～がある可能性がある」。

▶ a sea of ～は「大量の～」(≒ a large amount of ～)。

⑫ **People once thought Mars was the most likely planet to have extraterrestrial life within our solar system.**

▶ the most likely planet to *do*は「最も～しそうな惑星」、within our solar systemは「私たちの太陽系内で」。

⑬ **Now Europa has taken the place of Mars, but most scientists think we must keep looking.**

▶ take the place of ～は「～に取って代わる」(≒ replace ～)、keep lookingは「探索し続ける」。

⑭ **Evidence suggests that water is not particularly rare on extra-solar planets.**

▶ Evidence suggests that ～は「証拠は～ということを示唆する」→「～ということを示す証拠がある」。not particularly ～は「特に～というわけではない」。

- □ boil [bɔ́ɪl]
- □ freeze [fríːz]
- □ Gliese 581 [glíːzə fáɪv éɪt wʌ́n]
- □ assume [əsjúːm]
- □ strictly [stríktli]
- □ mass [mǽs]
- □ have an impact upon ～
- □ gravity [grǽvəti]
- □ three times as great as ～
- □ rhinoceros [raɪnásərəs]
- □ nickel [níkl]
- □ coal [kóul]

3

①What other conditions are necessary to support life? Temperature is important. ②It must not be too hot or too cold. ③The orbit of Earth is "just right": not too close to the sun, where water would boil, and not too far from the sun, where water would freeze.

④In 2011, a planet was found orbiting a star called Gliese 581. ⑤This planet is rocky and appears to have the right temperature. ⑥Nobody is suggesting that it has life. ⑦But since it was discovered soon after we started looking, we assume that there are lots of life-supporting planets out there.

Size is also important. ⑧A planet's size—more strictly its mass—has an impact upon life because of gravity. ⑨If Earth were made of gold, the gravity would be over three times as great as it is now. ⑩The gravity would be so strong that a mouse would need thick bones and walk like a tiny rhinoceros, which is unlikely to happen.

⑪Just as gold is heavier than iron, nickel and the other things that Earth is made of, coal is much lighter. ⑫If Earth were made of coal, the gravity would be about one-fifth as strong as it is now. ⑬A rhinoceros could jump around on thin legs like a spider, which is, again, unlikely to happen.

このセクションの内容

生命を維持するためには、（A.　　　　　）からのちょうどよい距離、つまり水が液体で存在できる惑星の（B.　　　　　）が重要である。また、惑星の質量も重要である。質量の大きさは惑星の（C.　　　　　）の大きさに比例する。生命を維持するためには適切な質量でなければならない。

① What other conditions are necessary to support life?

▶ What other conditions「ほかのどんな条件」が文の主語。to support ～は「～を支える[維持する]ために」。

② It must not be too hot or too cold.

▶ Itは天気・気候を表すit。「暑すぎても寒すぎてもならない」の意味。

③ The orbit of Earth is "just right": not too close to the sun, where water would boil, and not too far from the sun, where water would freeze.

▶ orbitは「(恒星を周回する)軌道」。コロン(:)以下は、"just right"「ちょうどよい」とはどういうことかを説明している。

▶ 2つのnot too ～は「～すぎない」で、直前にthe orbit of Earth isが省略されている。2つの〈, where〉は非制限用法の関係副詞で、直前の内容がどのような場所か説明している。wouldは「～するだろう」〈推量〉の意味。

④ In 2011, a planet was found orbiting a star called Gliese 581.

▶ orbiting ～は「～を周回している」。we found a planet orbiting ～〈S + V + O + C (= V-ing)〉の文の受け身。a star called ～は「～と呼ばれる恒星」。

⑤ This planet is rocky and appears to have the right temperature.

▶ appear to ～は「～するように見える[思える]」、the right temperatureは「(生命を維持できる)適切な温度」。

⑥ Nobody is suggesting that it has life.

▶ Nobody ～は「だれも～ない」。そこ(＝発見された惑星)に生命がいるかどうかはだれにもわからないということ。

⑦ But since it was discovered soon after we started looking, we assume that there are lots of life-supporting planets out there.

▶ since ～は「～なので」、soon after ～は「～してすぐに」。

▶ assume that ～は「～と想定する、～を本当だと思う」、life-supporting planetは「生命を支える[維持する]惑星」。

⑧ A planet's size—more strictly its mass—has an impact upon life because of gravity.

▶ more strictly its massは「より厳密にはそれ(＝惑星)の質量」、have an

impact upon ～は「～に影響を及ぼす」(≒ influence ～)。

▶ because of gravityは「重力のために」。質量が大きければ重力も大きくなり、生命に影響があるということ。

⑨ If Earth were made of gold, the gravity would be over three times as great as it is now.

▶「(実際はそうではないが) もし～ならば…だろう」という仮定法過去の文。

▶ be made of ～は「～でできている」、three times as great as ～は「～の3倍大きい」(≒ three times greater than ～)。

✍ ほぼ同じ意味を表すように、英文を完成させなさい。

Tokyo Tower is over ten times taller than this building.

Tokyo Tower is over ten times (　　　) (　　　) (　　　) this building.

▶ it is nowはthe gravity is nowのことで、「現在の重力(の状態)」を表す。

例 John used to be much more sociable than *he is now.*
「ジョンは今よりずっと社交的だった」

⑩ The gravity would be so strong that a mouse would need thick bones and walk like a tiny rhinoceros, which is unlikely to happen.

▶仮定法過去の文。If Earth were made of gold, が省略されている。

▶ so ～ that ... は「とても～なので…」。

▶〈, which〉は非制限用法の関係代名詞で、「そしてそのことは」と直前の内容を指す。be unlikely to *do*は「～しそうにない」。

⑪ Just as gold is heavier than iron, nickel and the other things that Earth is made of, coal is much lighter.

▶ Just as ～は「～とまったく同じように」、iron, nickel and the other things that Earth is made ofは「地球が作られている[地球を構成している]鉄、ニッケル、その他のもの」。

⑫ If Earth were made of coal, the gravity would be about one-fifth as strong as it is now.

▶仮定法過去の文。one-fifth as ～ as ... は「…の5分の1～」。

✍ 英文を完成させなさい。

日本はフランスの約3分の2の大きさだ。

Japan is about (　　　) (　　　) large as France.

⑬ A rhinoceros could jump around on thin legs like a spider, which is, again, unlikely to happen.

▶仮定法過去の文。jump around on thin legsは「細い脚で跳ね回る」。

▶〈, which〉は非制限用法の関係代名詞で、直前の内容を指す。

このセクションの内容 の答え→　A. 恒星　B. 温度[気温]　C. 重力

教科書p.182　Section 4

- □ sum [sʌ́m]
- □ to sum up
- □ in order for ~ to ...
- □ habitable [hǽbɪtəbl]
- □ so-called [sóʊkɔ́:ld]
- □ Goldilocks [góʊldilɑ̀ks]
- □ zone [zóʊn]
- □ extreme [ɪkstrí:m]
- □ random [rǽndəm]
- □ scientific [sàɪəntífɪk]
- □ equip [ɪkwíp]
- □ seek [sí:k]
- □ seek out ~
- □ meaningful [mí:nɪŋfl]
- □ identify [aɪdéntəfàɪ]
- □ 比較級 than S+V
- □ sensible [sénsəbl]
- □ implausible [ɪmplɔ́:zəbl]
- □ investigation [ɪnvèstɪgéɪʃən]
- □ discovery [dɪskʌ́vəri]
- □ fiction [fíkʃən]

4

①To sum up, in order for a planet to support life, it has to satisfy certain conditions. ②First, it must have water in liquid form. ③Second, the temperature must be just right—not too hot or not too cold—so that water may remain liquid. ④Third, the mass, which determines the gravity of the planet, must be just right—not too big or not too small. ⑤In short, a habitable planet must be in a so-called “Goldilocks Zone”: “just right” between two extremes. ⑥Even though the conditions which sustain life are very special, it is likely that life exists elsewhere because there are so many planets.

⑦Although we have not discovered life on other planets, I hope to have shown how much science can tell us. ⑧Our search for life is not random; our scientific knowledge equips us to seek out meaningful information and to identify habitable planets. ⑨We need much more information than we have now, but we can at least ask sensible questions and get sensible answers. ⑩We don’t have to invent implausible stories; we have the joy of real scientific investigation and discovery. ⑪In the end, that is more exciting than science fiction.

このセクションの内容

惑星に生命が存在するためには、液体の（A.　　　　　）と適切な温度と適切な（B.　　　　　）が必要で、そのような生存可能領域は「ゴルディロックス・ゾーン」と呼ばれている。地球外生命はまだ未発見だが、（C.　　　　　）的知識によって、生命が存在する惑星を特定することができるだろう。

① To sum up, in order for a planet to support life, it has to satisfy certain conditions.

▶ To sum upは「要約すると」。*cf.* to conclude「結論を言うと」

▶ in order to *do*「〜するために」のtoの前に不定詞の意味上の主語が置かれている。in order for 〜 to *do*で「〜が…するために」となる。

▶ satisfyは「〜を満たす」(*cf.* satisfied「満足した」)、certain conditionsは「特定の諸条件」。

② First, it must have water in liquid form.

▶ ①のcertain conditionsの1つ目。itはa planet to support life「生命を維持することができる惑星」のこと。in liquid formは「液体の状態で、液状で」。

③ Second, the temperature must be just right—not too hot or not too cold—so that water may remain liquid.

▶ ①のcertain conditionsの2つ目。ダッシュ(—)ではさまれた語句はjust right「ちょうどよい」の補足説明。

▶ so that 〜は、「〜するために、〜するように」(≒ in order that 〜)。

✍ 次の英文を日本語に直しなさい。

You should hurry up so that you can catch the last train.

____________________________________、急いだほうがいいですよ。

④ Third, the mass, which determines the gravity of the planet, must be just right—not too big or not too small.

▶ ①のcertain conditionsの3つ目。which 〜 planetはthe mass「質量」の補足説明。determine 〜は「〜を決定する」。

⑤ In short, a habitable planet must be in a so-called "Goldilocks Zone": "just right" between two extremes.

▶ In shortは「一言で言えば、要するに」。

▶ habitableは「居住可能な」→「生命が生存できる」、must be in 〜は「〜に存在しなければならない」、so-called 〜は「いわゆる〜」。

▶ Goldilocks Zoneという呼称は、「ちょうどよい」ものを常に選ぶ童話の主人公の名前に由来する。一般的には「ハビタブル・ゾーン」と呼ばれる。

▶ コロン(:)以下はGoldilocks Zoneの説明。between two extremesは「2つの極端(な状態)の間に」で、「温度が熱すぎず冷たすぎず、重力が大きすぎず小さすぎない」→「ちょうどよい」ということ。

⑥ Even though the conditions which sustain life are very special, it is likely that life exists elsewhere because there are so many planets.

▶ Even though 〜は「(現実に)〜だけれども」、the conditions which

このセクションの内容の答え→ A. 水 B. 質量[重力] C. 科学

sustain lifeは「生命を維持する条件」でwhichは関係代名詞。

▶主節はit is ~ that ...「…ということは~だ」の文。likelyは「ありそうな、~しそうな」(*cf.* unlikely)、elsewhereは「ほかのどこか[場所]に」。

⑦ Although we have not discovered life on other planets, I hope to have shown how much science can tell us.

▶Although ~は「~だけれども」、have not discovered ~は「まだ~を発見していない」。

▶hope to have *done*〈hope + 完了不定詞〉は「(未来に) ~することを願う[~したい]」、how much science can tell usは間接疑問で、「科学が(どれほど)多くのことを私たちに教えてくれるか」。

✍ 次の英文を日本語に直しなさい。

I hope to have read this book by next Sunday.

私は、＿＿＿＿＿＿＿＿＿＿＿＿＿＿＿＿と願っている。

⑧ Our search for life is not random; our scientific knowledge equips us to seek out meaningful information and to identify habitable planets.

▶search for ~は「~の探求」、randomは「でたらめの、思いつきの」で、ここでは「非科学的な」の意味で使われている。

▶セミコロン(;)以下は無生物主語構文で、〈equip + 人 + to *do*〉は「(人)に~する力をつけさせる」→「(人)が(主語)によって~する力をつける」。

▶seek out ~は「~を探し出す」(≒ search hard for and find ~)、identifyは「~を確認[特定]する」。

⑨ We need much more information than we have now, but we can at least ask sensible questions and get sensible answers.

▶much moreは「ずっと多くの」の意味で、muchは比較級を強める。than we have nowは「私たちが現在持っている(情報)よりも」

▶sensibleは「(科学的に)賢明な」の意味で、but以下は「私たちは少なくとも賢明な問いをたてて、賢明な答えを得ることができる」という意味。

⑩ We don't have to invent implausible stories; we have the joy of real scientific investigation and discovery.

▶invent implausible stories「信じがたい話を発明する」とは、「非科学的な空想をする」ということ。

▶have the joy of ~は「~の喜びを持って[知って]いる」、real scientific investigation and discoveryは「本当の科学的調査と発見」。

⑪ In the end, that is more exciting than science fiction.

▶In the endは「最後に、結局」、thatは⑩の文のthe joy以下の内容を指す。

Grammar for Communication

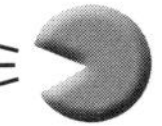

1 独立分詞構文

分詞の主語が主節の主語と異なるときには、分詞の前にその主語を置く必要がある。この形を独立分詞構文といい、主に文章体（書き言葉）で使われる。

1. 基本形

◆ **It being** a holiday, almost all the shops were closed.
（祝日だったので、ほとんどすべての店は閉まっていた）
≒ Since[Because, As] *it was* a holiday, ...

◆ **There being** nothing to do, they went home early.
（することが何もなかったので、彼らは早く帰宅した）
★There is 構文の場合は、There being 〜になる。
≒ Since[Because, As] *there was* nothing to do, ...

◆ **Their work done**, they went out to have dinner.
（仕事が終わって、彼らは夕食を食べに出かけた）
≒ After *their work was done*, ...

◆ **The event being** over, the audience began to leave the hall.
（イベントが終わって、観客はホールを出始めた）
≒ When *the event was* over, ...

◆ **All things considered**, you have done quite well.
（いろいろ考えてみると、あなたはとても[かなり]よくやった）

2. 慣用的な分詞構文

分詞構文には慣用化したものがあり、主節の主語にかかわらず、分詞の意味上の主語は示さなくてよい。これらは会話でよく使われる。

◆ **Frankly speaking**, he isn't very kind.　＊分詞の意味上の主語はI
（率直に言って、彼はそれほど親切ではない）
≒ If I speak frankly, ...

◆ **Weather permitting**, I'll go swimming in the river.
（天候が許せば[よければ]、私は川へ泳ぎに行くつもりだ）

◆ **Generally speaking**, a woman lives longer than a man.
（一般的に言って[概して]、女性は男性より長生きだ）

◆ **Strictly speaking**, the earth is not a perfect sphere.
（厳密に言うと、地球は完全な球体ではない）

◆ **Talking about** fruit, I like peaches the best.
（果物について言うと、私は桃がいちばん好きだ）

◆ **Judging from** her way of speaking, she must be from Osaka.
（話し方から判断すると、彼女は大阪出身に違いない）

2　倒置

強調などのために〈S + V〉の語順が〈V + S〉に入れ替わることがある。これを〈倒置〉という。

---

1. 慣用的な倒置

◆ Nick likes making plastic models. — **So do I**.　＊肯定文への同意
（ニックはプラモデルを作るのが好きだ。—私も好きだ）
≒ I do, too. / Me, too.

◆ I have never been to Hawaii. — **Neither[Nor] have I**.　＊否定文への同意
（私はハワイに行ったことがない。—私もない）
≒ I haven't, either. / Me, neither.

◆ It wasn't my bag, **nor was it** my sister's.
（それは私のバッグでも、姉[妹]のものでもなかった）
≒ 〜, and it was not my sister's, either.

◆ On the left **is the house** where the writer was born.
（左手にあるのは、その作家が生まれた家だ）
★副詞句が前に置かれると、そのあとが〈動詞＋主語〉になることがある。

2. 否定の強調のための倒置

◆ **Never** before have I been asked to do such a thing.
（私は今まで、こんなことをするように言われたことはない）
≒ I have never been asked to do such a thing before.

◆ **Little** did I understand what the little girl was saying.
（私にはその少女が言っていることがほとんど理解できなかった）
≒ I little understood what the little girl was saying.

◆ **Hardly** had he left home when it began to rain hard.
（彼が家を出るとすぐに、雨が激しく降ってきた）
≒ He had hardly left home when it began to rain hard.

確認問題

語彙・表現

1 次の語を（　）内の指示にしたがって書きかえなさい。

(1) essence（形容詞形に）　　(2) science（形容詞形に）
(3) investigate（名詞形に）　　(4) discover（名詞形に）

2 第2音節にアクセント（強勢）のある語を3つ選び、記号で答えなさい。

ア　as-tron-o-mer　　イ　u-ni-verse　　ウ　hab-it-a-ble
エ　e-quip　　オ　or-bit　　カ　re-gard

3 日本語に合うように、（　）内に適切な語を入れなさい。ただし、最初の文字が指定されているときは、その文字で書き始めなさい。

(1) 確かなことはだれにもわからないが、彼らは生存しているに違いない。
Nobody knows (　　　) (s　　　), but they must be alive.
(2) 私たちのチームは次の試合に勝てそうもない。
Our team is (　　　) (　　　) win the next game.
(3) 彼は私の10倍くらいCDを持っている。
He has about ten (　　　) (　　　) many CDs (　　　) I do.
(4) 新しい科学技術が人間の労働に取って代わった。
New technology has (　　　) (　　　) (　　　) of human labor.

文のパターン・文法

1 各組の文がほぼ同じ意味になるように、（　）内に適切な語を入れなさい。

(1) After lunch was over, we went to the gym to play basketball.
(　　　) (　　　) over, we went to the gym to play basketball.
(2) Since Jane caught a cold, her parents were worried about her.
(　　　) (　　　) a cold, her parents were worried about her.
(3) I have never been to the museum. — I haven't, either.
I have never been to the museum. — (　　　) (　　　) I.

2 日本語に合うように、（　）内に適切な語を入れなさい。

(1) 外はとても暑かったので、私は1日中家にいた。
(　　　) (　　　) so hot outside, I stayed home all day.

(2) 率直に言って、彼らの計画は失敗するよ。
( ) ( ), their plan will fail.
(3) 彼女のEメールから判断すると、サリーは誠実な人だと思う。
( ) ( ) her emails, I think Sally is a decent person.

3 ( ) 内の語句を並べかえて、日本語に合う英文を作りなさい。
(1) 私はこんなにおもしろいSF小説を読んだことがない。
Never (read / such / I / interesting / an / have) science fiction book.
Never ______________________ science fiction book.
(2) ここであなたに会おうとは夢にも思わなかった。
(I / I / did / dream / would / little / that) see you here.
______________________ see you here.
(3) 雨がやむとすぐに、私たちはジョギングを始めた。
Hardly (when / the rain / had / started / we / stopped) jogging.
Hardly ______________________ jogging.

総合

次の文を読んで、あとの問いに答えなさい。

①To ( ) ( ), in order for a planet to support life, it has to satisfy certain conditions. First, it must have water in liquid form. Second, the temperature must be just right—not too hot or not too cold—so that water may remain liquid. Third, the mass, which determines the gravity of the planet, must be just right—not too big or not too small. In short, a habitable planet must be in a so-called "Goldilocks Zone": ②"just right" between two extremes. Even though the conditions which sustain life are very special, it is likely that life exists elsewhere because there are so many planets.

問1 下線部①が「要約すると」という意味になるように、( ) 内に適切な語を書きなさい。

問2 下線部②を次のように説明するとき、( ) 内に適切な語を書きなさい。
The ( ) must be neither too hot nor ( ) ( ), and the ( ) must be neither too big nor ( ) ( ).

問3 筆者はなぜ、宇宙のどこかに生命が存在する可能性があると考えているのか。日本語で説明しなさい。

Reading 2 Miracle on the Hudson

教科書p.190〜p.191 *l*.2 I

- □ Hudson [hʌ́dsən]
- □ start out
- □ (be) no different from 〜
- □ passenger [pǽsɪndʒər]
- □ aboard [əbɔ́:rd]
- □ airways [éərwèɪz]
- □ Chesley Sully Sullenberger [tʃézli sʌ́li sʌ́lənbə̀:rgər]
- □ Jeff Skiles [dʒéf skáɪlz]
- □ LaGuardia [ləgwá:rdɪə]
- □ Charlotte [ʃá:rlət]
- □ North Carolina [nɔ́:rθ kæ̀rəláɪnə]
- □ clear 〜 for ...
- □ takeoff [téɪkɔ̀:f]
- □ controller [kəntróʊlər]
- □ routine [rù:tí:n]
- □ checklist [tʃéklìst]
- □ All hell broke loose.

①It started out as a day no different from any other day for the crew and passengers aboard US Airways Flight 1549. ②One hundred seconds later, it became a day they would never forget.

③On Thursday, January 15, 2009, Captain Chesley "Sully" Sullenberger and his first officer, Jeff Skiles, arrived at LaGuardia Airport in New York City to prepare for a flight from New York City to Charlotte, North Carolina.

④At 3:25 p.m., Sully and Skiles were ready, and the LaGuardia tower cleared their flight for takeoff. ⑤The flight was identified as radio call sign Cactus 1549 by the air traffic controllers.

⑥For Sully, it was like nearly every other flight he'd made for 42 years. ⑦Cactus 1549 was completely routine ... for the first 100 seconds.

⑧During those seconds, Cactus 1549 continued climbing and Skiles, who was at the controls, asked for the after-takeoff checklist, a task pilots must perform at that stage of a flight.

⑨And then, all hell broke loose.

このセクションの内容

2009年1月15日、機長のサリーと（A.　　　　　）のスカイルズは、ニューヨーク市からノースカロライナ州のシャーロットへのフライトの準備を整えた。彼らはいつもの手順どおり（B.　　　　　）とやりとりし、飛行機は上昇し始めたが、離陸して（C.　　　　　）秒後、大混乱が発生した。

① It started out as a day no different from any other day for the crew and passengers aboard US Airways Flight 1549.

▶ It started out as ～は「最初は～として始まった、事の始まりは～」の意味。主語のItは「その日」の意味で、その日に起こったことはこれから述べられる。start outはstartとほぼ同じ意味。

▶ a day no different from ～は、a day that[which] was no different from ～と同じで、「～と何も変わらない日」(≒ a day the same as ～)の意味。

▶ any other dayは「ほかのどの日」、for the crew and passengersは「乗務員[クルー]と乗客にとって」。

▶ aboardは前置詞で、「(乗り物に)乗っている」。

✍ 次の英文を日本語に直しなさい。

There were few passengers aboard the pleasure boat.

その遊覧船には ＿＿＿＿＿＿＿＿＿＿＿＿＿＿＿＿＿＿＿＿＿＿。

② One hundred seconds later, it became a day they would never forget.

▶ they ～ forgetはa dayを後ろから修飾する節。

③ On Thursday, January 15, 2009, Captain Chesley "Sully" Sullenberger and his first officer, Jeff Skiles, arrived at LaGuardia Airport in New York City to prepare for a flight from New York City to Charlotte, North Carolina.

▶ 西暦2009年は、two thousand (and) nineと読むのが一般的。なお、2020年は、two thousand (and) twentyまたはtwenty twentyと読む。

▶ Captain ～ Skilesまでが文の主語。"Sully"と引用符が付いているのは、彼がそのように呼ばれているから。この文章でも以後はSullyと書かれている。first officerは「副操縦士」のこと。

▶ to prepare for ～は「～の準備をするために」、flightは「フライト、(航空)便」で、a flight from ～ to ...は「～から…までのフライト」。

④ At 3:25 p.m., Sully and Skiles were ready, and the LaGuardia tower cleared their flight for takeoff.

▶ were readyは「(離陸の)準備ができた」、the LaGuardia towerは管制塔の名称。

▶ clear ～ for ...は「～に…の許可を与える」(≒ give ～ permission for ...)。takeoffは「離陸」。*cf.* take off「離陸する」

✍ 次の英文を日本語に直しなさい。

This plane hasn't been cleared for takeoff yet.

この飛行機はまだ ＿＿＿＿＿＿＿＿＿＿＿＿＿＿＿＿＿＿＿＿＿＿。

このセクションの内容 の答え→ A. 副操縦士 B. (航空)管制官 C. 100

⑤ The flight was identified as radio call sign Cactus 1549 by the air traffic controllers.

▶「…によって〜された」という受け身の文。be identified as 〜は「〜として識別[認定、確認]される」。

✍ 英文を完成させなさい。

その遺体は、行方不明の女性のものと確認された。

The body (　　　) (　　　) (　　　) that of the missing woman.

▶ radio call sign 〜は「〜という無線コールサイン[呼出符号]」、air traffic controllerは「航空管制官」。

⑥ For Sully, it was like nearly every other flight he'd made for 42 years.

▶ itは⑤の文のthe flightを指す。like nearly 〜は「〜とほぼ同じの」。

▶ he'd (= he had) made for 42 yearsは、every other flight「ほかのあらゆるフライト」を修飾する節。make a flightは「フライトを行う、飛行する」。

⑦ Cactus 1549 was completely routine ... for the first 100 seconds.

▶ completelyは「完全に」、routineは「平常どおり、いつもの手順」。

例 It is his *routine* to drink coffee after each meal.
「毎食後にコーヒーを飲むのが彼の習慣だ」

▶途中の"..."は、読み手に時間の空白やひと呼吸を与え、文に臨場感を生む効果がある。

⑧ During those seconds, Cactus 1549 continued climbing and Skiles, who was at the controls, asked for the after-takeoff checklist, a task pilots must perform at that stage of a flight.

▶ continued climbingは「上昇し続けた」、who was at the controls「操縦席にいた」はSkilesの補足説明。controlsは「運転[操縦]装置」。

▶ ask for 〜は「〜を要求する」、the after-takeoff checklistは「離陸後のチェックリスト」。ここでは、スカイルズがサリーにチェックリストの項目を確認することを求めたということ。

▶ a task 〜は、チェックリストの確認作業の補足説明で、「フライトのその段階でパイロットが実行しなければならない職務」という意味。pilots以下はa taskを修飾する節。

⑨ And then, all hell broke loose.

▶ And thenは「そしてそれから」、all hell breaks looseは慣用表現で、「地獄が一気に解き放たれる」→「大混乱が生じる、大騒ぎになる」(≒ everything goes wrong all at once)という意味。

教科書p.191 *ll*.3〜23　Ⅱ

- □ 316 feet a second
- □ avoid [əvɔ́ɪd]
- □ recall [rɪkɔ́:l]
- □ thump [θʌ́mp]
- □ thud [θʌ́d]
- □ strike [stráɪk]
- □ shudder [ʃʌ́dər]
- □ rumble [rʌ́mbl]
- □ engine [éndʒɪn]
- □ runway [rʌ́nwèɪ]
- □ take action
- □ ignition [ɪgníʃən]
- □ recover [rɪkʌ́vər]
- □ aircraft [éərkræ̀ft]
- □ auxiliary [ɔ:gzíliəri]
- □ unit [jú:nɪt]
- □ APU [éɪ pí: jú:]
- □ backup [bǽkʌ̀p]
- □ electrical [ɪléktrɪkl]
- □ take control of 〜

①"I saw the birds three seconds before we hit them; we were traveling 316 feet a second and could not avoid them," Sully later recalled.

②They could feel and hear the thumps and thuds as they struck the birds, followed by a shuddering, and then a rumbling sound coming from the engines. ③They felt the engines "rolling back," meaning failing.

④"We got one roll ... both of them rolling back!" Sully said as his engines made a strange noise that he had never heard before.

⑤"This can't be happening," he thought. ⑥And the next moment, "This doesn't happen to me."

⑦Sully finally saw that his flight would probably not end safely on a runway. ⑧And so, within two-and-a-half-seconds of Flight 1549 hitting the birds, he began to take action.

⑨He turned on the engine ignition so that, if the engines could recover, they would. ⑩He also started the aircraft's auxiliary power unit (APU) to provide backup electrical power. ⑪After turning on the APU, Sully took control of the aircraft.

このセクションの内容

「ぶつかる３秒前に（A.　　　　　）を見たが、避けられなかった」とサリーはのちに回想した。エンジンは２基とも故障したらしく、今まで聞いたこともない（B.　　　　　）を立てた。サリーは飛行機が無事に（C.　　　　　）に着陸しそうにないだろうと悟った。サリーはエンジンの回復をはかり、さらに、補助電源装置をオンにして、バックアップ電力を供給した。

Reading 2

① "I saw the birds three seconds before we hit them; we were traveling 316 feet a second and could not avoid them," Sully later recalled.

▶ three seconds before ～は「～の３秒前に」、travel 316 feet a secondは「秒速316フィート（時速約347km）で移動する」。

▶ セミコロン（;）は接続詞の働きをし、前後の文が関連していることを示す。

② They could feel and hear the thumps and thuds as they struck the birds, followed by a shuddering, and then a rumbling sound coming from the engines.

▶ Theyは機長と副操縦士を指す。

▶ thumpは強くなぐったときの鈍い音、thudは重いものが落ちた音。the thumps and thudsで「ゴツン、ドスンという音」。as ～は「～したとき」。

▶ (being) followed by ～は分詞構文で、その後に続いて起こったことを表す。be followed by ～は「～が（あとに）続く」。

例 The meal *was followed by* ice cream.
「食事のあとにアイスクリームが出た」

▶ a shuddering (sound), and then a rumbling soundは「激しく振動する音と、それからゴロゴロ鳴る音」、comingは現在分詞で、soundを修飾する。

③ They felt the engines "rolling back," meaning failing.

▶〈feel + O + V-ing〉は「Oが～するのを感じる」。

✍ 英文を完成させなさい。

私は背中で何かが動いているのを感じた。

I (　　　) (　　　) (　　　) on my back.

▶ roll backは本来「後退する、巻き戻る」の意味だが、ここでは「（エンジンが）回転しなくなる」ということ。航空用語なので引用符（“ ”）が使われている。さらに、meaning failing「（つまり）故障［停止］を意味する」を続けて、“rolling back”を説明している。

④ "We got one roll ... both of them rolling back!" Sully said as his engines made a strange noise that he had never heard before.

▶ 引用符（“ ”）内はサリーの言葉。We got one rollは「１つ（のエンジン）は動いているぞ」。直後の“...”は、サリーの言葉の少しの間を表す。

▶ both of themのthemは２基のエンジンのこと。themのあとにareが省略されている。

▶ as ～は「～したとき」、that以下はa strange noiseを説明する関係代名詞の節。had never heard beforeは「以前に一度も聞いたことがない」。

このセクションの内容 の答え→　A. 鳥　B.（奇妙な）音　C. 滑走路

✍ 次の英文を日本語に直しなさい。

I found an insect that I had never seen before.

____

⑤ "This can't be happening," he thought.

▶ This can't be happeningとは「こんなこと(＝両方のエンジンが停止すること)は起こるはずがない[ありえない]」。heは機長のサリーのこと。

⑥ And the next moment, "This doesn't happen to me."

▶ the next moment「次の瞬間」のあとにhe thoughtが省略されている。

⑦ Sully finally saw that his flight would probably not end safely on a runway.

▶ see that ～は「～ということがわかる」。

✍ 次の英文を日本語に直しなさい。

At first, I didn't see that he had a rich imagination.

最初、私は彼が____________________________。

▶ would not ～ end safely on a runwayは「滑走路上で安全に終わらないだろう」→「無事に滑走路に着陸しないだろう」。

⑧ And so, within two-and-a-half-seconds of Flight 1549 hitting the birds, he began to take action.

▶ within two-and-a-half-secondsは「2.5秒以内に」、of Flight 1549 hitting the birdsは「1549便が鳥に衝突してから」。

例 I live *within* 100 meters *of* my school.
「私は学校から100メートル以内に住んでいる」

▶ take actionは「行動を起こす」(≒ act)。

⑨ He turned on the engine ignition so that, if the engines could recover, they would.

▶ turn on ～は「～をつける[オンにする]、～の電源を入れる」、engine ignitionは「エンジンの点火装置」。so that ～は「～するために」。

▶ 挿入されているif ～は「もしエンジンが回復できるなら」、so that they would「それら(＝エンジン)が回復するように」ということ。

⑩ He also started the aircraft's auxiliary power unit (APU) to provide backup electrical power.

▶ aircraft's auxiliary power unitは「航空機の補助電源装置」。to provide backup electrical powerは「バックアップ電力を供給するために」。

⑪ After turning on the APU, Sully took control of the aircraft.

▶ take control of ～は「～を管理[制御]する」(≒ take charge of ～)→「～を操縦する」。

教科書p.191 *l*.24～p.192 *l*.22　Ⅲ

- □ desperately [déspərətli]
- □ the best course of action
- □ smoothly [smú:ðli]
- □ make a choice
- □ stick with ～
- □ send out a call
- □ Mayday [méɪdèɪ]
- □ Cactus fifteen thirty-nine.
- □ Hit birds.
- □ thrust [θrʌ́st]
- □ fate [féɪt]
- □ end up

①In the next few seconds, Sully and his first officer desperately tried to figure out the best course of action. Sully later recalled, "②Even though Jeff and I had just met for the first time three days before, if you had watched us work together, you would have thought we had been working together for years. ③We were able to work smoothly in an emergency when there was not enough time to talk about what had just happened."

④Sully was aware that every decision he made would be examined carefully later. ⑤But that did not stop him from making hard choices and sticking with them.

Around 20 seconds after losing power in both engines, Sully sent out a call for help: "⑥Mayday! Mayday! Mayday! This is Cactus fifteen thirty-nine. ⑦Hit birds. We've lost thrust on both engines. ⑧We're turning back toward LaGuardia."

⑨The air traffic controller immediately began to try to get them back to a runway at LaGuardia.

⑩However, by then, Sully had realized what his ultimate fate was going to be. ⑪"We may end up in the Hudson," he told the controller.

⑫At 3:29 p.m.—two minutes and 18 seconds after the bird strike—Sully repeated what he had said earlier. ⑬"We're going to be in the Hudson." ⑭Only this time, he was sure.

このセクションの内容

エンジンが止まった約20秒後、サリーは救助要請を出して、ラガーディア空港に（A.　　　　　）ことを伝えた。管制官もそれを試みたが、サリーは最終的にどうなる（B.　　　　　）かを理解し、（C.　　　　　）に着水するつもりだと管制官に伝えた。

① In the next few seconds, Sully and his first officer desperately tried to figure out the best course of action.

▶ desperatelyは「必死に」、figure out ～は「～を探し出す[考え出す]」、the best course of actionは「最善の行動方針」(≒ the best thing to do)。

② Even though Jeff and I had just met for the first time three days before, if you had watched us work together, you would have thought we had been working together for years.

▶ Even though ～は「(実際は)～とはいえ、～だったのだが」。had just met(過去完了)は、事故が起こった時より以前のことを表す。

▶ if以下は仮定法過去完了の文で、過去の事実に反する仮定を表す。if you had watched us work togetherは「もし私たちがいっしょに働くのを(人が)見たら」、would have thought (that) ～は「～と思っただろう」。

▶ had been working togetherは「(それまで)ずっといっしょに働いていた」(過去完了進行形)、for yearsは「何年間も」。

✍ 英文を完成させなさい。

Sally told me that she had been waiting here for two hours.

サリーは私に、＿＿＿＿＿＿＿＿＿＿＿＿＿＿＿＿と言った。

③ We were able to work smoothly in an emergency when there was not enough time to talk about what had just happened.

▶ whenは関係副詞で、when以下がan emergency「緊急時」を説明している。there was not enough time to *do*は「～する時間が十分になかった」。

▶ what had just happenedは「何が起こったのか[起こったばかりのこと]」、つまりエンジンが故障したことを指す。

④ Sully was aware that every decision he made would be examined carefully later.

▶ be aware that ～は「～ということがわかっている」、every decision he madeは「彼が下すすべての決定」。

▶ 過去における未来はwouldを使う。be examinedは「調査される」。

⑤ But that did not stop him from making hard choices and sticking with them.

▶主語のthat「そのこと」は④の文のthat以下の内容を指す。〈stop + O + from V-ing〉は「Oが～するのを妨げる」。

✍ 英文を完成させなさい。

彼が嵐の中を外出するのをだれも止められなかった。

No one could stop (　　　) (　　　) (　　　) out in the storm.

▶make a choiceは「選択をする」(≒ choose)、stick with ～は「(方針など)を守る」(≒ not change *one's* mind about ～)、themはhard choicesを指す。

⑥ Mayday! Mayday! Mayday!

▶船や飛行機が無線で緊急事態を知らせるときに使う語で、3回繰り返す。

⑦ Hit birds. We've lost thrust on both engines.

▶= We hit birds.「鳥にぶつかった」。緊急連絡なので主語を省いている。

▶thrust on both enginesは「両エンジンの推進力」。

⑧ We're turning back toward LaGuardia.

▶「～しかけている」と、動作の途中を表す現在進行形。turn back toward ～は「～に引き返す」。

⑨ The air traffic controller immediately began to try to get them back to a runway at LaGuardia.

▶try to get them back to ～は「彼らを～に戻そうとする」。

⑩ However, by then, Sully had realized what his ultimate fate was going to be.

▶had realizedは「すでに理解していた」、what his ultimate fate was going to beは「彼の最終的な運命がどうなるか」→「最終的にどうしなければならないのか」。その内容は次の文に書かれている。

⑪ "We may end up in the Hudson," he told the controller.

▶end up ～は「最後は[結局]～に終わる」(≒ finish)。つまり、最終的にはハドソン川に着水することになるということ。

⑫ At 3:29 p.m.—two minutes and 18 seconds after the bird strike—Sully repeated what he had said earlier.

▶ダッシュ(—)ではさまれた語句は3:29 p.m.の補足説明。what he had said earlier「彼がすでに前に言ったこと」とは、⑪の文でサリーが言ったこと。

⑬ "We're going to be in the Hudson."

▶サリーがくり返した言葉だが、⑪の文では可能性を表すmayが使われているのに対し、この文では予定を表すbe going to *do*が使われている。

⑭ Only this time, he was sure.

▶Only this time「今回だけは」とは、⑬の文をサリーが言ったときのこと。飛行機をハドソン川に着水させることを、サリーは確信していたということ。

このセクションの内容 の答え→ A. 引き返す[戻る] B. 運命 C. ハドソン川

教科書p.192 *l*.23〜p.193 *l*.14 Ⅳ

□ smooth [smúːð]
□ attempt [ətémpt]
□ neighborhood [néɪbərhùd]
□ novel [návl]
□ set priorities
□ sacrifice [sǽkrɪfàɪs]
□ in control
□ brace [bréɪs]
□ in unison
□ unison [júːnɪsn]
□ Heads down!

①He realized the only place in the entire city of New York that was long enough, wide enough, and smooth enough to even attempt landing a jet was the Hudson River. ②Before landing in the river, he would have to first avoid tall buildings and crowded neighborhoods.

③Sully was attempting something he had never done or even practiced before. "④This was a completely novel event that I had never trained for. ⑤Yet I was able to set clear priorities. ⑥I took what I did know and applied it in a new way to solve a problem I'd never seen before," he recalled.

⑦Sully made his decision: he would have to sacrifice the airplane to save lives.

⑧He made his one and only announcement to the passengers and crew. ⑨He just had a few seconds, but he wanted to sound in control. ⑩He knew that one person's confidence can give other people courage.

"This is the Captain. ⑪Brace for impact," Sully told the crew and passengers. ⑫Immediately, the three flight attendants started shouting their commands to the passengers in unison: "Brace, brace, brace! Heads down! Stay down!"

このセクションの内容

サリーは、ハドソン川がニューヨーク市全体でジェット機を着陸させることができる（A.　　　　　）の場所だと気づいた。彼は、以前にやったことも練習したこともないことに（B.　　　　　）していたが、自分の知識を費やして、それを解決する新たな方法に適用した。彼は乗客と乗務員に向けて、（C.　　　　　）に備えるようにとアナウンスした。

① He realized the only place in the entire city of New York that was long enough, wide enough, and smooth enough to even attempt landing a jet was the Hudson River.

▶ the only place ～ a jetは長い主語で、関係代名詞の節that ～ a jetがthe only place in the entire city of New York「ニューヨークの市全体の中の唯一の場所」を後ろから修飾している。

▶ long enough, wide enough, and smooth enough to even attempt landing a jetは「ジェット機の着陸を試みることさえできる十分な長さと幅と滑らかさを備えた」。evenは強調を表す副詞で、attemptを修飾することを明確にする目的で、toのあとに置かれている(分離不定詞)。

✍ 次の英文を日本語に直しなさい。

Mr. Suzuki asked his students to quietly leave the classroom.

鈴木先生は生徒に、＿＿＿＿＿＿＿＿＿＿＿＿＿＿＿＿＿＿＿＿。

② Before landing in the river, he would have to first avoid tall buildings and crowded neighborhoods.

▶ would have to first *do*は「まず～しなければならなかった」の意味で、過去における未来のことなので、wouldが使われている。crowded neighborhoodsは「混雑している地域、住宅密集地」。

③ Sully was attempting something he had never done or even practiced before.

▶ was attemptingは「試みていた、挑戦していた」。

▶ he had ～ beforeはsomethingを修飾する節で、「以前にやったことも練習したこともない(こと)」の意味。

④ This was a completely novel event that I had never trained for.

▶ サリーの発言の内容。This「このこと」とは、飛行機を川へ着水させること。

▶ that以下がnovel event「今までにない[まったく新しい]出来事」を修飾している。I had never trained forは「(それに対して)訓練したことがない」。*cf.* train for a marathon「マラソンの練習をする」

⑤ Yet I was able to set clear priorities.

▶ Yetは「しかし、それでも」、set prioritiesは「優先順位を設定する」(≒ decide what is most important)。

⑥ I took what I did know and applied it in a new way to solve a problem I'd never seen before

▶ took what I did knowは「私が確かに知っていることを取り出した」→「私の持てる確かな知識を費やした」。did knowはknewの強調。

▶ applied it「それを適用した」のitはwhat I did knowを指す。to solve ～

 このセクションの内容 の答え→ A. 唯一[ただ1つ] B. 挑戦 C. 衝撃

は「〜を解決するために」。I'd never seen before「それまで見たこともない」はa problemを修飾する節。

⑦ Sully made his decision: he would have to sacrifice the airplane to save lives.

▶ make *one's* decisionは「決断する」。コロン(:)以下は「決断」の内容。

▶ would have to 〜は「〜しなければならなかった」、to save livesは「命を救うために」。

⑧ He made his one and only announcement to the passengers and crew.

▶ make his one and only announcementは「彼のただ一度の[一度だけの]アナウンス[告知]をする」。crewは集合名詞で「乗組員」の総称。

✍ 英文を完成させなさい。

ベスは私の唯一無二のカナダ人の友人だ。

Beth is (　　　) (　　　) (　　　) (　　　) Canadian friend.

⑨ He just had a few seconds, but he wanted to sound in control.

▶ just had 〜は「〜しか(時間が)なかった」。

▶ wanted to sound in controlは「(自分の声が乗客に)落ち着いて聞こえてほしいと思った」。soundは「〜に聞こえる[響く、思われる]」、in controlは「自分を制御して、自制して」(≒ calm)。

⑩ He knew that one person's confidence can give other people courage.

▶ サリーが⑨の文のように思った理由。one person's confidenceは「ある人の自信」、give other people courageは「ほかの人々に勇気を与える」。

⑪ Brace for impact

▶ braceは「(困難・不快なことに対して)準備をする、覚悟をする」の意味で、この文のBrace for 〜は「〜に備えてください」、impactは「(着水するときの)衝撃」。

例 Bob *braced for* the worst when he heard the fire alarm.
「火災報知機の音を聞いたとき、ボブは最悪の事態を覚悟した」

⑫ Immediately, the three flight attendants started shouting their commands to the passengers in unison: "Brace, brace, brace! Heads down! Stay down!"

▶ flight attendantは「旅客機の客室乗務員」、commandは「命令、要求」、in unisonは「声をそろえて、一致して」(≒ together)。

▶ Heads down!は「頭を下げて! [伏せて!]」(≒ Put your heads down!)、Stay down!は「しゃがんだままでいて!」。

教科書p.193 *l*.15～p.194　V

□ 3,020 feet
□ bank left
□ high-rise [háɪràɪz]
□ steady [stédi]
□ altitude [ǽltɪtjùːd]
□ touch down
□ send up ～
□ spray [spréɪ]
□ intact [ɪntǽkt]
□ at the same moment
□ drift [dríft]
□ current [kə́ːrənt]
□ take on ～
□ up and down
□ aisle [áɪl]
□ rescue [réskjuː]
□ ferry [féri]
□ shore [ʃɔ́ːr]
□ tale [téɪl]
□ get in touch with ～
□ cut ～ off

①Sully began to carefully guide his plane for a landing on the river. ②When they were at 3,020 feet, he banked left and pointed the plane down toward the river. Soon, it was lower than many of the high-rise buildings. ③As people watched from windows on both sides of the river, Sully steadied the airplane and prepared for a water landing. ④Skiles began calling out the plane's speed and altitude to help Sully judge the height at which to begin the landing.

⑤Shortly after 3:30 p.m.—just five and a half minutes after takeoff, less than three and a half minutes since the thrust loss—Cactus 1549 touched down on the Hudson, sending up a huge spray of water.

⑥Sully could tell the plane was intact. ⑦He and Skiles looked at one another and said, almost at the same moment, "That wasn't as bad as I thought!"

The plane did not sink immediately. Instead, it drifted in strong currents. ⑧Frightened passengers began climbing out the exits into freezing cold air and onto the wings of the plane, which began taking on water. ⑨When everyone was safely out, Sully walked up and down the aisle twice to make sure that no one was left behind. ⑩He was the last to leave the plane.

Within four minutes, the first rescue boats arrived. ⑪Both pilots, the three flight attendants, and all the passengers, including a baby, were picked up by ferries and other rescue boats as

Cactus 1549 continued to drift south. Everyone reached shore safely.

⑫Sully had lived to tell a tale that was almost a miracle. But his job wasn't over.

⑬On the ferry, once he realized that his phone was still dry enough, he called US Airways to tell them what had happened.

⑭He got in touch with the airline operations manager. ⑮That person, however, cut him off, saying he could not talk since they had a plane down in the Hudson.

"I know," Sully said. "⑯I'm the guy."

このセクションの内容

川の（A.　　　　　）で人々が見守るなか、飛行機はハドソン川に着水した。機体は無傷で、すぐには沈まなかった。（B.　　　　　）たちは出口から出て翼に乗り、その後、全員無事に救出された。最後に飛行機を出たサリーは航空会社に（C.　　　　　）をして、自分が事故の当人だと伝えた。

① Sully began to carefully guide his plane for a landing on the river.

▶ guide ～ for ... は「～を…に導く」、landing on the river は「川への着水」。

② When they were at 3,020 feet, he banked left and pointed the plane down toward the river.

▶ at 3,020 feet（≒920 meters）は飛行機の高度のこと。bank left は「左に傾ける[旋回させる]」（≒ turn to the left）で、飛行機の方向を変えるときの操作。point ～ down toward ... は「…に向かって～を下降させる」。

③ As people watched from windows on both sides of the river, Sully steadied the airplane and prepared for a water landing.

▶ As ～は「～するとき、～する間」、windows on both sides of the river「川の両側の窓」とは、川沿いに立っているビルの窓のこと。steady は「～を安定させる」。

④ Skiles began calling out the plane's speed and altitude to help Sully judge the height at which to begin the landing.

▶ call out ～は「～を大声で叫ぶ」、altitude は「高度」。

▶〈to help + 人 + 動詞の原形〉は「(人)が～するのを助けるために」、the height at which to begin ～は「(その地点で)～を始める高度」（≒ the height at which he should begin the landing)。

⑤ **Shortly after 3:30 p.m.—just five and a half minutes after takeoff, less than three and a half minutes since the thrust loss—Cactus 1549 touched down on the Hudson, sending up a huge spray of water.**

▶ Shortly after ～は「～の少しあと」。ダッシュ(—)ではさまれた語句は3:30 p.m.の補足説明。less than ～は「～未満」、thrust lossは「推力喪失」。

▶ touch downは「(飛行機などが)着陸する」(≒ land)。

▶ sending up ～は分詞構文で、続いて起こる動作や様子を表す(≒ and sent up)。send up a huge spray of waterは「大量の水しぶきを上げる」(≒ send a huge spray of water into the air)。

✍ 次の英文を日本語に直しなさい。

A woman approached me, asking me to help her carry her bags.

---

⑥ **Sully could tell the plane was intact.**

▶ could tell (that) ～は「～だとわかった」、intactは「損傷を受けていない」。

⑦ **He and Skiles looked at one another and said, almost at the same moment, "That wasn't as bad as I thought!"**

▶ one anotherは「お互い」、挿入句のalmost at the same momentは「ほとんど同時に」(≒ almost at the same time)。

▶ not as ～ as ... は「…ほど～ない」、as I thoughtは「思ったほど」。

⑧ **Frightened passengers began climbing out the exits into freezing cold air and onto the wings of the plane, which began taking on water.**

▶ Frightened passengersは「おびえた乗客」。climbはここでは「(苦労して)移動する」の意味で、climb out (of) ～ into ... and onto — は「～から出て…の中を進み、—の上に乗る」となる。

▶〈, which〉は非制限用法の関係代名詞で、そのときのthe planeの様子を補足している。take on ～は「～を取り込む」(≒ absorb ～)。

⑨ **When everyone was safely out, Sully walked up and down the aisle twice to make sure that no one was left behind.**

▶ up and downは「行ったり来たり」(≒ back and forth)。

▶ to make sure that ～は「～ということを確かめるために」、no one was left behindは「だれもあとに残されて[残って]いない」。

⑩ **He was the last to leave the plane.**

▶ the last to *do*は「～する最後の人」(≒ the last person to *do*)。

このセクションの内容 の答え→ A. 両側(の窓) B. 乗客 C. 連絡[電話]

⑪ **Both pilots, the three flight attendants, and all the passengers, including a baby, were picked up by ferries and other rescue boats as Cactus 1549 continued to drift south.**

▶ Both ～a babyが文の主語。including ～は「～を含む」。

✍ 英文を完成させなさい。

女性３人を含むその一行は、６時に頂上に到達した。

The group, (　　　) (　　　) (　　　), reached the summit at six.

▶ be picked up by ～は「～によって拾われる」→「～に救助される」。as ～は「～する間」、drift southは「南に（向かって）漂流する」。

⑫ **Sully had lived to tell a tale that was almost a miracle.**

▶ live to tell a taleは「生きて[生き延びて]ある話をする」、a tale that was almost a miracleは「ほとんど奇跡とも言える話」。つまり、危険な状況下を奇跡的に生き残ったということ。live[survive] to tell the taleは慣用表現で、「困難[危険]な状況を乗り切る」の意味。

⑬ **On the ferry, once he realized that his phone was still dry enough, he called US Airways to tell them what had happened.**

▶ once ～は「～するとすぐに」、still dry enoughは「まだ（使えるだけ）十分乾いている」。his phoneは、ここではサリーの携帯電話のこと。

▶ to tell them what had happenedは「何が起こったのかを伝えるために」で、themは「USエアウェイズの社員」を指す。

⑭ **He got in touch with the airline operations manager.**

▶ get in touch with ～は「～と連絡を取る」（≒ make contact with ～）。

例 Could you *get in touch with* her?　「彼女と連絡が取れましたか」

▶ airline operations managerは「航空会社の運航管理責任者」。

⑮ **That person, however, cut him off, saying he could not talk since they had a plane down in the Hudson.**

▶ That personは⑭の文のthe airline operations managerを指す。cut ～ offは「～（の話）をさえぎる」の意味。つまり、サリーの電話に出た責任者は、サリーが話しているのをさえぎったということ。

▶ saying ～は分詞構文で、続いて起こる動作を表す（≒ and said ～）。saying以下は、責任者がサリーの話をさえぎって言った内容になる。

▶ since ～は「～なので」、they had a plane down in the Hudsonは「彼ら（＝USエアウェイズ）の飛行機がハドソン川に着水した」。

⑯ **I'm the guy.**

▶ guyは「男、やつ」で、manよりくだけた語。「私はその男だ」とは「私がその（飛行機をハドソン川に着水させた）当人だよ」ということ。

確認問題

語彙・表現

1 第２音節にアクセント（強勢）のある語を４つ選び、記号で答えなさい。

ア	pas-sen-ger	イ	rou-tine	ウ	check-list
エ	run-way	オ	air-craft	カ	aux-il-ia-ry
キ	e-lec-tri-cal	ク	des-per-ate-ly	ケ	sac-ri-fice
コ	al-ti-tude	サ	in-tact	シ	cur-rent

2 日本語に合うように、（　）内に適切な語を入れなさい。ただし、最初の文字が指定されているときは、その文字で書き始めなさい。

(1) 私たちはコンテストで３位に終わった。
We (e　　　) (　　　) in third place in the contest.

(2) 飛行機は無事に滑走路に着陸した。
The plane (　　　) (d　　　) safely on the runway.

(3) 日本に着いたらすぐに、私に連絡してください。
Please (　　　) (　　　) (　　　) with me as soon as you arrive in Japan.

(4) 私が話しているときはさえぎらないでもらいたい。
I don't want you to (c　　　) me (　　　) when I'm talking.

(5) 私たちは最初の計画を守るべきだ。
We should (　　　) (w　　　) what we planned in the beginning.

(6) NGO のメンバーは環境を守るために行動を起こした。
The members of the NGO (　　　) (　　　) to protect the environment.

文のパターン・文法

1 各組の文がほぼ同じ意味になるように、（　）内に適切な語を入れなさい。

(1) I was late for the meeting because of a car accident.
A car accident stopped (　　　) (　　　) arriving in time for the meeting.

(2) The problem was less difficult than I thought.
The problem (　　　) as difficult (　　　) I thought.

2 日本語に合うように、（　）内に適切な語を入れなさい。

(1) もしそのとき彼女と話していたら、あなたは彼女に同意しただろう。
If you (　　　) (　　　) to her then, you (　　　) (　　　) agreed with her.

(2) その責任者はイベントが始まる時間を変更した。
The manager changed the time (　　) (　　) the event would start.

3 (　)内の語句を並べかえて、日本語に合う英文を作りなさい。

(1) それはほかのメロンと変わらないメロンに見える。
It looks like (from / a melon / any / melon / different / no / other).
It looks like ______________________________.

(2) 最も広い国はロシアで、次にカナダが続く。
The largest country (Canada / followed / is / Russia / by / ,).
The largest country ______________________________.

(3) 私は部屋にだれも残っていないことを確かめた。
I (in / nobody / made / left / sure / was) the room.
I ______________________________ the room.

総合

次の文を読んで、あとの問いに答えなさい。

He realized the only place in the entire city of New York that was long enough, wide enough, and smooth enough to even attempt landing a jet (①) the Hudson River. Before landing in the river, he would have to first avoid tall buildings and crowded neighborhoods.

②Sully was attempting something he had never done or even practiced before. "This was a completely novel event that I had never trained for. Yet I was able to set clear priorities. I took what I did know and applied ③it in a new way to solve a problem I'd never seen before," he recalled.

Sully made his decision: he would have to sacrifice the airplane to save lives.

He made his one and only announcement to the passengers and crew. He just had a few seconds, but he wanted to sound in control.

問1　①の(　)内に入る適切な1語を書きなさい。
問2　下線部②を日本語に直しなさい。
問3　下線部③のitは何を指すか、日本語で答えなさい。
問4　Sullyはどのような声でアナウンスしたいと思ったか。日本語で説明しなさい。

Optional Lesson

The Sustainability of Happiness

教科書p.196～p.197 *l*.12 I

- □ conference [kάnfərəns]
- □ Rio+20 [ríːou plʌ́s twénti]
- □ Rio de Janeiro [rìːoudeɪʒənérou]
- □ poverty [pάvərti]
- □ participant [pərtísɪpənt]
- □ José "Pepe" Mujica [xosé pépe muxíkɑ]
- □ Uruguay [júərəgwàɪ]
- □ lifestyle [láɪfstàɪl]
- □ consumption [kənsʌ́mpʃən]
- □ resource [ríːsɔːrs]

The United Nations Conference on Sustainable Development (Rio+20) was held in Rio de Janeiro in 2012. Leaders from 192 states met to plan the future. ①The focus was on creating a sustainable environment and leading the world out of poverty.

One of the participants was José "Pepe" Mujica, President of Uruguay. ②Mujica, known as "the world's poorest president" because of his simple lifestyle, had a message that surprised many of the participants: Don't forget human happiness.

③We've been talking all afternoon about sustainable development, about how to get the masses out of poverty. But what are we thinking? Do we want to follow the model of development and consumption of the rich countries? I ask you now: ④What would happen to this planet if Indians had the same proportion of cars per household as Germans? ⑤How much oxygen would we have left to breathe?

⑥Does our planet have enough resources so that seven or eight billion people can have the same level of consumption and waste that we have today in rich countries? This level of consumption is harming our planet.

⑦Will that ever be possible?

このセクションの内容

2012年に開催された「リオ＋20」で、（A.　　　　　）のムヒカ大統領のスピーチが参加者たちの心を動かした。彼は、すべての人間が（B.　　　　　）国と同じレベルの開発と消費をすれば、地球はどうなるだろうか、地球にはそれほど十分な（C.　　　　　）があるだろうかと訴えた。

① **The focus was on creating a sustainable environment and leading the world out of poverty.**

▶ be on V-ingは「～することについてだ」、creating以下は「持続可能な環境を創出し、世界を貧困から連れ出す[抜け出させる]こと」。

② **Mujica, known as "the world's poorest president" because of his simple lifestyle, had a message that surprised many of the participants: Don't forget human happiness.**

▶挿入句のknown as ～「～として知られている」は、who is known as ～と同じ。because of ～は「～のために、～が理由で」。

▶ had a message that surprised ～は「～を驚かせたメッセージを伝えた」。コロン(:)以下はメッセージの内容。

③ **We've been talking all afternoon about sustainable development, about how to get the masses out of poverty.**

▶「ずっと～してきた」という現在完了進行形の文。how to get ～ out of ... は「～を…から抜け出させる方法」、the massesは「大衆」。

④ **What would happen to this planet if Indians had the same proportion of cars per household as Germans?**

▶仮定法過去の疑問文。What would happen ～?で「何が起こるだろうか。」という意味。the same ～ as ... は「…と同じ～」、proportion of cars per householdは「1世帯当たりの車の割合」。

⑤ **How much oxygen would we have left to breathe?**

▶④の文から続く仮定法過去の疑問文。left to breathe「(私たちが)息をするために残されている」は過去分詞句で、修飾される名詞はoxygen「酸素」。ガソリン車は燃料と空気中の酸素を反応させて動力を得るため、車が増えれば空気中の二酸化炭素が増える。

⑥ **Does our planet have enough resources so that seven or eight billion people can have the same level of consumption and waste that we have today in rich countries?**

▶〈enough ～ so that + S + V〉は「SがVするほど十分な～、SがVするだけの～」。この文では、Sはseven or eight billion people「70億から80億の人々」、Vはcan have「～を持つことができる」。

▶ the same ～ that ... は「…と同じ～」。the same以下は、「今日の裕福な国々と同じ量[レベル]の消費と廃棄物」となる。

⑦ **Will that ever be possible?**

▶ thatは⑥の文で述べた十分な資源を持つことを指す。

▶ everは強調語で、疑問文中では「いったい、そもそも」の意味。

このセクションの内容 の答え→ A. ウルグアイ B. 裕福な[豊かな] C. 資源

教科書p.197 *l*.13～p.198 *l*.10 Ⅱ

☐ discussion [dɪskʌ́ʃən]
☐ competition [kɑ̀mpətíʃən]
☐ globalization [glòubələzéɪʃən]
☐ be aware of ～
☐ be in control of ～
☐ ruthless [rú:θləs]
☐ importance [ɪmpɔ́:rtəns]
☐ summit [sʌ́mɪt]
☐ on the contrary
☐ slip away
☐ worth [wə́:rθ]
☐ slip through *one's* fingers
☐ consume [kənsjú:m]

We must start a different type of discussion. ①We are the ones who have created this civilization in which the market economy and competition have produced great material progress. ②The market economy has given us globalization, which means being aware of the whole planet.

③But are we in control of globalization or is globalization in control of us? We talk about "being all together." ④How is that possible in an economy based on ruthless competition? How far does our "being all together" go?

I am not questioning the importance of this summit meeting. ⑤On the contrary, we are facing a huge challenge. But it is not environmental. It is a political challenge.

⑥Today, we are no longer in control of the forces we created. Rather, these forces are controlling us. We did not come onto this planet simply to develop it. We came onto this planet to be happy. ⑦Life is short and it slips away from us. ⑧Nothing we own is worth as much as life. ⑨But our lives are slipping through our fingers as we work harder and longer just to be able to consume more.

このセクションの内容

市場経済と競争は大きな（A.　　　　）的進歩をもたらしたが、私たちは今やグローバリゼーションに支配されている。私たちは単に開発するためではなく、（B.　　　　）になるために生まれてきたのであって、人生以上に価値のあるものはない。しかし（C.　　　　）のために懸命に働いている間に、私たちの人生はあっという間に過ぎてしまう。

① **We are the ones who have created this civilization in which the market economy and competition have produced great material progress.**

▶ the ones who 〜は「〜する人々」。in whichは〈前置詞＋関係代名詞〉で先行詞はthis civilization。the market economy and competitionは「市場経済と（市場）競争」、material progressは「物質的進歩」。

② **The market economy has given us globalization, which means being aware of the whole planet.**

▶〈, which〉以下はglobalization「グローバル化」の補足説明。be aware of 〜は「〜を意識［認識］する」（≒ recognize 〜）。

③ **But are we in control of globalization or is globalization in control of us?**

▶ be in control of 〜「〜を管理している」（≒ control 〜）。

④ **How is that possible in an economy based on ruthless competition?**

▶「どうすればそれは可能か」→「そんなことは不可能だ」と反語の意味を含む。thatは直前の文にある"being all together"を指す。economy based on 〜は「〜に基づく経済」、ruthlessは「冷酷な」。

⑤ **On the contrary, we are facing a huge challenge.**

▶ On the contraryは「それどころか、むしろ」の意味で、直前の内容を否定しながら、反対の事実を示すときに使われる。

⑥ **Today, we are no longer in control of the forces we created.**

▶ no longer 〜は「もはや〜ない」、the forces we created「私たちが創り出した力」とは、市場経済がもたらしたグローバル化の力のこと。

⑦ **Life is short and it slips away from us.**

▶ slip awayは「（こっそりと）立ち去る、消え去る」（≒ disappear）。

⑧ **Nothing we own is worth as much as life.**

▶ Nothing is 〜 as much as ...は「…ほど〜なものは何もない、どんなものも…ほど〜ではない」、we ownはNothingを修飾する節。

⑨ **But our lives are slipping through our fingers as we work harder and longer just to be able to consume more.**

▶ slip through *one's* fingersは「（人）の指をすべり落ちる」（≒ pass quickly）、as 〜は「〜につれて」、just to be able to *do*は「〜できるようになるためだけに」。消費の欲望のためだけにあくせく働いていると、あっという間に人生が終わってしまうということ。

このセクションの内容 の答え→ A. 物質 B. 幸福［幸せ］ C. 消費

教科書p.198 *l*.11～p.199 *l*.7 Ⅲ

- □ consumer [kənsjúːmər]
- □ fall into ～
- □ stagnation [stægnéɪʃən]
- □ nevertheless [nèvərðəlés]
- □ bulb [bʌ́lb]
- □ long-lasting [lɔ̀ːŋlǽstɪŋ]
- □ manufacture [mæ̀njəfǽktʃər]
- □ trap [trǽp]
- □ vicious [víʃəs]
- □ cave dweller [kéɪv dwèlər]
- □ monument [mánjəmənt]
- □ backwardness [bǽkwərdnəs]
- □ indefinitely [ɪndéfənətli]

We live in a consumer society. Consumption drives everything. ①If consumption slows, the economy slows, and if the economy slows, we fall into stagnation. We know that too much consumption is harming our planet. Nevertheless, we need to keep consuming. ②We make things that have a short life in order to sell more. ③So we make light bulbs that do not last longer than 1,000 hours, even though we can make light bulbs that last 100,000 hours! ④The long-lasting bulbs are not manufactured because everyone has to work to sustain this "use-and-throw-away" society.

⑤We are trapped in a vicious cycle. These are political problems. ⑥It is time to start fighting for a different culture.

⑦I'm not talking about returning to the days of the cave dweller, or building a "monument to backwardness." ⑧But we cannot continue like this, indefinitely, being ruled by the market. ⑨On the contrary, we have to rule over the market.

このセクションの内容

私たちは（A.　　　　　）に生きており、過剰な消費が地球を害しているとわかっていても消費を続け、「（B.　　　　　）」社会を維持しなければならない。この悪循環は政治的な問題であり、今こそ現状とは異なる文化を築き始める時期に来ている。大昔に戻ろうと言っているのではない。いつまでも（C.　　　　　）に支配されているのではなく、それを支配しなければならないのだ。

① If consumption slows, the economy slows, and if the economy slows, we fall into stagnation.

▶ slowは「遅くなる、鈍る」、fall into ～は「～に陥る」（≒ be caught in ～）、stagnationは「（経済の）停滞、低迷」。今日の経済の悪循環を示す文。

② We make things that have a short life in order to sell more.

▶ things that have a short lifeは「（製品の）寿命が短いもの」、in order to *do*は「～するために」。

③ So we make light bulbs that do not last longer than 1,000 hours, even though we can make light bulbs that last 100,000 hours!

▶ light bulbs that do not last longer than ～は「～を超えて長持ちしない電球」、even though ～は「（実際は）～だが」。

④ The long-lasting bulbs are not manufactured because everyone has to work to sustain this "use-and-throw-away" society.

▶ The long-lasting bulbs「長い寿命の電球」は③の文で述べたような10万時間を超える寿命の電球のこと。to sustain this "use-and-throw-away" societyは「『使い捨ての』社会を維持するために」。

⑤ We are trapped in a vicious cycle.

▶ be trapped in ～は「～に陥る」、vicious cycleは「悪循環」。

⑥ It is time to start fighting for a different culture.

▶ It is time to *do*は「～する時だ」、fight for ～は「～を求めて戦う」。a different culture「異なる文化」とは、過剰消費とは異なる文化のこと。

⑦ I'm not talking about returning to the days of the cave dweller, or building a "monument to backwardness."

▶ the days of the cave dwellerは「洞窟の住人の時代、石器時代」、monument to backwardnessは「後退[後進性]の記念碑」。つまり、時代を逆行させるべきだと主張しているのではないということ。

⑧ But we cannot continue like this, indefinitely, being ruled by the market.

▶ like this「このように」とは、今日の過剰消費の文化を指す。indefinitelyは「無期限に、いつまでも」。being ruled by the marketは〈付帯状況〉を表す分詞構文で、「市場（経済）に支配されたまま」の意味。

⑨ On the contrary, we have to rule over the market.

▶ On the contraryは「それどころか、むしろ」、rule over ～は「～を支配する」。つまり、市場に私たちが支配されるのではなく、私たちが市場を支配しなければならないということ。

このセクションの内容 の答え→ A. 消費社会　B. 使い捨て(の)　C. 市場(経済)

教科書p.199 *l*.8〜p.200 *l*.16 Ⅳ

- ☐ in *one's* way of thinking
- ☐ humble [hʌ́mbl]
- ☐ thinker [θíŋkər]
- ☐ Epicurus [èpɪkjúərəs]
- ☐ Seneca [sénɪkə]
- ☐ Aymara [àɪmərɑ́ː]
- ☐ characteristic [kæ̀rəktərístɪk]
- ☐ salute [səlúːt]
- ☐ agreement [əgríːmənt]
- ☐ crisis [kráɪsɪs]
- ☐ revise [rɪváɪz]
- ☐ fertile [fə́ːrtl]
- ☐ a few more than ～
- ☐ export [ekspɔ́ːrt]
- ☐ dairy [déəri]

①This is why, in my humble way of thinking, the problem we are facing is political. ②The old thinkers ... Epicurus, Seneca, and even the Aymara put it this way, "A poor person is not someone who doesn't have much but someone who always needs more, and more and more." This is a cultural characteristic.

③So I salute the efforts and agreements being made at this conference. And as a president I will follow them. ④I know some things I'm saying are not easy to digest. ⑤But we must change our way of thinking that the water crisis and the destruction of the environment are the main issues. ⑥In fact, the main issue is the model of civilization that we have created.

⑦We must completely revise our way of life.

I live in a small country with lots of natural resources. Almost 90 percent of the land is fertile. ⑧There are only a few more than three million people, but there are 13 million cows—some of the best in the world—and eight to ten million excellent sheep. We export food, dairy products, and meat.

このセクションの内容

私たちが直面している問題は政治的な問題だ。「(A.　　　　　) 人というのは、多くを持たない人ではなくより多くのものを求める人だ」と昔の思想家たちが言ったように、主要な問題は水問題と (B.　　　　　) ではなく、私たちが創り出してきた (C.　　　　　) のモデルである。私たちは、私たちの生活スタイルを全面的に見直さなければならない。

① This is why, in my humble way of thinking, the problem we are facing is political.

▶ This is (the reason) why ～は「これが～の理由だ、だから～だ」、the problem we are facingは「私たちが直面している問題」。

▶ in my (humble) way of thinkingは「私の（謙虚な）考え方では」→「私見によれば」（≒ in my view）。

② The old thinkers ... Epicurus, Seneca, and even the Aymara put it this way, "A poor person is not someone who doesn't have much but someone who always needs more, and more and more."

▶ put it this wayは「このように[次のように]述べている」。itは話題に挙がっている問題のこと。

▶ A poor person is not A but B「貧しい人というのは、AではなくBである」という文。AとBがそれぞれsomeone who ～になる。

③ So I salute the efforts and agreements being made at this conference.

▶ saluteは「～に敬意を表する」、the efforts and agreements being made at～は「～でなされている努力と合意」。*cf.* make an effort「努力する」

④ I know some things I'm saying are not easy to digest.

▶ some things I'm sayingは「私が言っているいくつかのこと」、not easy to digestは「消化しにくい」→「理解しにくい」。

⑤ But we must change our way of thinking that the water crisis and the destruction of the environment are the main issues.

▶ our way of thinking that ～は「～という私たちの考え方」。the main issuesは「主要な問題」。

⑥ In fact, the main issue is the model of civilization that we have created.

▶ In factは「（いや）実際は」で、⑤の文のthat以下の内容を否定している。

▶ the model of civilization that we have created「私たちが創り出した文明のモデル」とはつまり、過剰に消費し続けることで成り立つ社会のこと。

⑦ We must completely revise our way of life.

▶ completely reviseは「全面的に改める、一から見直す」。

⑧ There are only a few more than three million people, but there are 13 million cows—some of the best in the world—and eight to ten million excellent sheep.

▶ a few more than ～は「～より少し多い数、～強」（≒ a little more than ～）。

このセクションの内容 の答え→ A. 貧しい B. 環境破壊 C. 文明

教科書p.200 *l*.17〜p.201 V

☐ fellow [félou]
☐ workday [wə́ːrkdèɪ]
☐ payment [péɪmənt]
☐ rheumatic [rumǽtɪk]
☐ precious [préʃəs]
☐ element [élɪmənt]

My fellow workers fought hard for the eight-hour workday. ①Now they are working to make that six hours. That's progress. ②However, the person who works six hours, now gets two jobs and works longer than before. Why? ③Because he needs to make more money to pay for the motorcycle, the car, for more and more and more. ④The payments pile up, and before you know it, he is a rheumatic old man, like me, and his life is already over.

⑤Is this our fate as human beings?

⑥What I am saying now is very basic: development cannot be the enemy of happiness. ⑦It has to work to increase human happiness, to promote love of our Earth, human relationships, caring for children, having friends, meeting our basic needs.

Happiness is the most precious treasure we have. Happiness! ⑧When we fight for the environment, we must remember that the essential element of the environment is human happiness.

このセクションの内容

ウルグアイでは現在、１日６時間労働の実現に取り組んでいる。それは進歩だが、実際には（A.　　　　　）をし、以前より長時間働く人がいる。車などの（B.　　　　　）が山積みで、もっとかせぐ必要があるからだ。そしていつの間にか年を取り、人生が終わる。これが人間の運命なのだろうか。開発は幸福を妨げるものではなく、幸福を増進するためのものでなければならない。（C.　　　　　）のために戦うのであれば、その基本要素は人間の幸福であることを忘れてはならない。

① Now they are working to make that six hours.

▶ theyは直前の文のMy fellow workers「私の同士である労働者」を指す。またthatは、eight-hour workday「1日8時間労働」のこと。

② However, the person who works six hours, now gets two jobs and works longer than before.

▶ the person who works six hours「6時間労働の職員」が文の主語。せっかく1日6時間労働になったのに、副業をして以前より長時間働いている、ということ。その理由は、③の文に述べられている。

③ Because he needs to make more money to pay for the motorcycle, the car, for more and more and more.

▶ heは、②の文のthe person who works six hoursを指す。to pay for ～は「～の代金を支払うために」。for more and more and moreは、支払いがまだまだある（＝多くの支払いに追われている）ことを表している。

④ The payments pile up, and before you know it, he is a rheumatic old man, like me, and his life is already over.

▶ pile upは「山積みになる」、before you know itは「それ（＝山積みの支払いがあること）に気づく前に」、his life is already overは「彼の人生はもう終わっている」。

⑤ Is this our fate as human beings?

▶ thisは③と④の文の内容、つまり消費への限りない欲望によって支払いに追われ、人生を棒に振ることを指す。fate as human beingsは「人間としての運命[宿命]、人間として避けられないこと」。

⑥ What I am saying now is very basic: development cannot be the enemy of happiness.

▶ What I am saying now「今私が言っていること」が文の主語。コロン(:)は「つまり」の意味。cannot be ～は「～であるはずがない」。

⑦ It has to work to increase human happiness, to promote love of our Earth, human relationships, caring for children, having friends, meeting our basic needs.

▶ Itはdevelopmentを指す。workは「機能する、役立つ」。to increase human happiness「人間の幸福を増進するために」は、直後のto promote ～「～を促進するために」で言いかえられている。

⑧ When we fight for the environment, we must remember that the essential element of the environment is human happiness.

▶ When we fight for the environment「私たちが環境のために戦うとき」とは、つまり「この会議で環境問題を扱うのであれば」ということ。

このセクションの内容の答え→ A. 副業[2つの仕事]　B. 支払い　C. 環境

確認問題

語彙・表現

1 次の語を（　）内の指示にしたがって書きかえなさい。

(1) poor（名詞形に）　(2) important（名詞形に）
(3) character（形容詞形に）　(4) agree（名詞形に）

2 第2音節にアクセント（強勢）のある語を2つ選び、記号で答えなさい。

ア　con-fer-ence　イ　fer-tile　ウ　sum-mit
エ　nev-er-the-less　オ　in-def-i-nite-ly　カ　sa-lute

3 日本語に合うように、（　）内に適切な語を入れなさい。ただし、最初の文字が指定されているときは、その文字で書き始めなさい。

(1) 彼は冬山登山の危険性に気づいていましたか。
Was he (a　　　) (　　　) the dangers of winter mountain climbing?

(2) メアリーは昨夜、パーティーをこっそり抜け出した。
Mary (s　　　) (　　　) from the party last night.

(3) 市の職員は、彼らが予算を管理できていると話した。
The city officials said that they were in (　　　) (　　　) the budget.

(4) 私の考えでは、お金で幸せを買うことはできない。
In (　　　) (w　　　) of (　　　), money cannot buy happiness.

(5) 彼は裕福ではない。それどころか、多額の借金がある。
He is not rich. (　　　) (　　　) (　　　), he has a huge debt.

(6) オスカー・ワイルドは次のように述べている、「人生は芸術を模倣する」。
Oscar Wilde (　　　) it (　　　) (　　　), "Life imitates art."

文のパターン・文法

1 各組の文がほぼ同じ意味になるように、（　）内に適切な語を入れなさい。

(1) I believe health is the most precious thing.
I believe (　　　) is worth as (　　　) (　　　) health.

(2) We need more time to finish this assignment.
We need more time (　　　) (　　　) we can finish this assignment.

(3) They want to build a society where people can live in peace.
They want to build a society (　　　) (　　　) people can live in peace.

2 (　)内の語句を並べかえて、日本語に合う英文を作りなさい。

(1) 現在のような地球にしてしまったのは私たちだ。
We are (made / who / Earth / the ones / have) what it is today.
We are ______________________________ what it is today.

(2) これが、私たちが過剰な消費をやめられない理由だ。
(stop / this / cannot / why / we / is) excessive consumption.
______________________________ excessive consumption.

(3) 私たちはお金がいちばん大事だという考え方を変えなければならない。
We must (that / way / of / change / thinking / our) money is the most important thing.
We must ________________ money is the most important thing.

(4) もし大気中に酸素がなければ、私たちに何が起こるだろうか。
(happen / us / would / what / if / to) there were no oxygen in the atmosphere?
____________________ there were no oxygen in the atmosphere?

総合

次の文を読んで、あとの問いに答えなさい。

We live in a consumer society. Consumption drives everything. If consumption slows, the economy slows, and if the economy slows, we fall (①) stagnation. We know that too much consumption is harming our planet. Nevertheless, we need to keep consuming. ②<u>We make things that have a short life in order to sell more.</u> So we make light bulbs that do not last longer than 1,000 hours, even though we can make light bulbs that last 100,000 hours! The long-lasting bulbs are not manufactured because everyone has to work to sustain this "use-and-throw-away" society.

③<u>We are trapped in a vicious cycle.</u> These are political problems. ④<u>(start / is / for / it / to / fighting / time) a different culture.</u>

問1　①の(　)内に入る適切な語を書きなさい。

問2　下線部②を日本語に直しなさい。

問3　下線部③について、私たちが陥っている悪循環とは何か、日本語で説明しなさい。ただし、「経済」「消費」「地球」という言葉を使うこと。

問4　下線部④の(　)内の語を並べかえて、英文を完成させなさい。

解答

Lesson 1

▶ Section 1

⑤ 招待されてうれしかった

⑥ How, say

▶ Section 2

③ being called

⑨ too, to

▶ Section 3

② 彼が理解できない

⑧ be seen

▶ Section 4

④ 私のスマートフォンがこわれている

⑫ 私に質問させてください

確認問題

《語彙・表現》

1 (1) loss
(2) attractive
(3) simplicity
(4) breathe

2 ア、エ、オ

3 (1) into, mind
(2) defined as
(3) translate, into
(4) if not
(5) in, way

《文のパターン・文法》

1 (1) for, to
(2) of, to
(3) not, but
(4) it, that[when]

2 (1) what this Japanese word means
(2) to be taken to the hospital
(3) was nice of you to
(4) being loved very much by

《総合》

問1 not read

問2 without

問3 英語を学ぶことは私たちが異なる[さまざまな]方法で世界を見ることを可能にする。

問4 翻訳によって(何か)失われるものがあるかもしれないということ。

Lesson 2

▶ Section 1

④ よく近くの川で釣りをした(ものだ)

⑧ wonder if

▶ Section 2

⑤ 公園を掃除するのを手伝って

⑩ keep yourself

▶ Section 3

① whose mother

⑪ ここで昼食を食べてもいいですか[かまいませんか]

▶ Section 4

④ made, cry

⑨ It, us

確認問題

《語彙・表現》

1 ウ、エ、キ

2 (1) Thanks, attend
(2) if, with
(3) part in
(4) took, out
(5) wish, could
(6) absorbed in

《文のパターン・文法》

1 (1) whose roof
(2) my[me] using
(3) which
(4) have been
(5) was built

2 (1) about my mother reading my diary
(2) at that store being closed
(3) seems to have already gone
(4) is said to have influenced

《総合》

問1 translated
問2 It takes, to
問3 enjoying picture books I help to make
問4 人生に小さな変化をもたらすため[人生を少し変えるため]（の簡単な第一歩だった）

Lesson 3

▶Section 1

④ 音楽を聞きながら
⑥ all, way, despite
⑨ 十分なお金を持っていなかったので

▶Section 2

③ difficulty sleeping
⑧ Having lost
⑪ 小学校の先生として働くことを誇りに思っている

▶Section 3

④ Less than
⑦ not to

▶Section 4

④ it, to
⑩ 多くの観光客に日本を訪れて

確認問題

《語彙・表現》

1 (1) unfortunately
(2) disability
(3) accessibility
(4) objective

2 ア、イ、カ

3 (1) all, way
(2) more, more, tend
(3) difficulty finding[getting]
(4) makes it, to
(5) proud to

《文のパターン・文法》

1 (1) Walking in the park
(2) Born in the countryside
(3) Not being busy
(4) Having read the book

2 (1) is my mother's curry that I
(2) was ten years ago that
(3) was when he was five that

《総合》

問1 ① 例えば、レストランの入り口には、しばしば外の区域から建物を分ける段差がある。
⑤ 私は、もし私たちがこれらの課題に対処すれば、より大きなビジネスの機会を得られるだろうと提案する。

問2 ② like
③ In
④ in

問3 10 to 15 percent of the world population is disabled

問4 彼ら[障がいを持つ人々]がしばしばグループで、または家族といっしょに旅行すること

Lesson 4

▶Section 1

⑤ regardless of
⑥ had been waiting
⑧ もうすぐ日本に着くと書いてあるEメールを

▶Section 2

③ times when
⑪ not to eat[have]

▶ Section 3

② led, to
⑤ 私には理解することが
⑪ it, to

▶ Section 4

② こわれたドアを修理するのに役立つ
④ much as

確認問題

《語彙・表現》

1 (1) organization
(2) decision
(3) agree
(4) belief

2 イ、オ

3 (1) as, result
(2) Put[Clear], away
(3) regardless of
(4) put, action
(5) confidence in
(6) beyond help

《文のパターン・文法》

1 (1) when
(2) where
(3) when

2 (1) how she could be of help
(2) were ordered not to speak
(3) me which chair I can sit on
(4) friends to play soccer with

《総合》

問1 twenty-eight thousand

問2 小さな病院が1つあるだけで、そこには看護師が2人、タミル人の医師が2人、通訳、そして医療従事者がいるだけだった

問3 with

問4 them simple questions and decided what to do

Lesson 5

▶ Section 1

④ in which

▶ Section 2

④ problem(s) waiting
⑧ どんなに時間がかかっても

▶ Section 3

④ 私がいつおばを訪ねても
⑧ 彼らが何を言っても

▶ Section 4

⑤ spent hours reading

確認問題

《語彙・表現》

1 (1) toughness
(2) encourage
(3) shoot
(4) positive

2 ア、イ

3 (1) long run
(2) were plagued
(3) all time
(4) Are, for
(5) the moment

《文のパターン・文法》

1 (1) in which
(2) in which
(3) to whom

2 (1) Whenever
(2) Whatever
(3) No matter how

3 (1) that my sister takes care of
(2) stopped us from going out
(3) sudden return made us surprised

《総合》

問1 spent hours imaging what she wanted to do

問2 エ

問3 down, to

問4 練習中にプレッシャー［重圧］を感じることは、彼女が試合当日に緊張を和らげることに役立つ。

Reading 1

▶ Section I

① had, left

⑩ had known

⑫ 近くに雷が落ちたときだった

▶ Section II

③ as possible

⑭ ドアをノックするのを聞いた

▶ Section III

⑬ it would take

▶ Section IV

⑤ most, had ever

確認問題

《語彙・表現》

1 (1) acceptance
  (2) muddy
  (3) refusal
  (4) asleep

2 ウ、エ

3 (1) a flash
  (2) was, about
  (3) take off
  (4) filled, with

《文のパターン・文法》

1 (1) too, for, to
  (2) told, had been
  (3) woke me
  (4) Having nothing
  (5) with, back

2 (1) happiest time was when she lived
  (2) how long it would take to
  (3) to show me the picture she had drawn
  (4) to where I had left

《総合》

問1 ① lay
  ② lying

問2 had never, big

問3 they let me believe they believed

問4 このスイカは孫が一晩で育てたものだ(と言った)。

Lesson 6

▶ Section 1

⑦ What if

⑩ 雪が降りそうだ

▶ Section 2

① upon[on], where

⑫ is whether, not

▶ Section 3

⑬ got, nerves

▶ Section 4

④ 危険だと知りながら

⑩ what, have done

確認問題

《語彙・表現》

1 ア、エ

2 (1) majored in
  (2) feel at home
  (3) devoted[dedicated], to
  (4) What if
  (5) work out

《文のパターン・文法》

1 (1) should have
  (2) whether, not

2 (1) must have gone
  (2) might[may] have heard
  (3) could have

3 (1) must have been a fast runner
  (2) could I have believed it

(3) was whether he was telling the truth

《総合》

問1 私は、ガウディの作品と調和する彫刻の作り方を見つけるのに必死に努力しなければならなかった。

問2 ア

問3 Gaudí's philosophy / his respect for nature / the inspiration he received from it

問4 (次から1つ選ぶ。同じ内容であれば正解) 情熱と勇気を持って挑戦する準備をしなさい。／あなたを楽観的にしてくれるよい友達を持ちなさい。／時にははめをはずしなさい。

Lesson 7

▶Section 1

③ No other animal

⑤ Without water, could

▶Section 2

⑧ Her, reminded me /
タクシーよりも(むしろ)バスを[タクシーではなくバスを]

▶Section 3

③ あなたと話しているとき

⑤ あなたと同じ大学

⑪ has been held

▶Section 4

① たばこを吸うことの危険性に気づいている

④ that, be

確認問題

《語彙・表現》

1 (1) harmful
(2) imitation
(3) rough
(4) dirt

2 ア、ウ

3 (1) far, wide
(2) In other
(3) rather than
(4) dreams about
(5) rolled off

《文のパターン・文法》

1 (1) But for
(2) To see
(3) A good doctor
(4) he take

2 (1) were to, would
(2) should be
(3) otherwise, have gone

3 (1) Were it not for this key
(2) I were to study abroad
(3) insists that the event be held

《総合》

問1 ① play ③ not

問2 私たちは環境に悪影響を及ぼし[与え]始めている

問3 survival

問4 私たちはどうすれば故郷の惑星を破壊せずにそこで生きることができるか(という問い)。

Lesson 8

▶Section 1

② 音楽に関係のある仕事に

▶Section 2

③ with tears

⑤ 失敗した(だけだった)

⑧ リーダーを選ぶ権利[発言権]がなかった

▶Section 3

① Needless, say

⑭ 弟をからかって(ばかり)いる

▶ Section 4

⑤ don't, behind

確認問題

《語彙・表現》

1 (1) awareness
(2) transformation
(3) knowledge
(4) empowerment

2 ア、エ、カ

3 (1) related to
(2) take, moment[minute]
(3) take, into account
(4) in peace
(5) Needless, say

《文のパターン・文法》

1 (1) is to
(2) to finish
(3) is to be
(4) are to be

2 (1) I woke up to find myself
(2) only to find it empty
(3) never to come back

3 (1) are to arrive in Tokyo tomorrow
(2) was never to be forgotten by them
(3) only to be late for the meeting

《総合》

問1 女性が農園の約70パーセントの仕事をして、約20パーセントの収入しか得られないこと。／女性は家事のすべてをしなければならないこと。

問2 女性には、カカオ豆を売ることについての発言権がない

問3 イ

問4 gender gap

Lesson 9

▶ Section 1

⑩ あなたがしてもらいたいことを

▶ Section 2

③ まるで私の兄弟であるかのように私と話す

⑥ come up

▶ Section 3

① 孤独だとは限らない

▶ Section 4

⑦ is being built

⑧ 私たちは、ピザの配達を注文するか外で食べる[外食する]か決める必要がある[決めなければならない]。

確認問題

《語彙・表現》

1 (1) basic
(2) reminder
(3) careless
(4) improper

2 ア、カ

3 (1) same time
(2) at least
(3) result in
(4) came up with
(5) on the basis

《文のパターン・文法》

1 (1) will be snowing heavily
(2) was being discussed (by them)
(3) Beth will have been sick in bed for a week

2 (1) will be flying
(2) will have finished

3 (1) will be attending the event
(2) will have been sent by the end
(3) is being built over there

《総合》

問1 ときどきナッジは、私たちの最善の利益にならないこと、または危険でさえあることをするように、私たちを仕向ける。

問2 her own

問3 neither

問4 もう少しで目標を達成して給料が上がるという通知。／近くに乗客がいるという通知。

Lesson 10

▶Section 1

⑪ 状況はよくなりそうもない。

▶Section 2

② すべてのメンバーがその計画を支持したというわけではない。

⑩ 全員ではないにしても、ほとんどの生徒が

▶Section 3

⑨ as tall as

⑫ two-thirds as

▶Section 4

③ 最終電車に間に合う［乗れる］ように

⑦ この本を次の日曜日までに読んでしまいたい［読み終えたい］

確認問題

《語彙・表現》

1 (1) essential
(2) scientific
(3) investigation
(4) discovery

2 ア、エ、カ

3 (1) for sure
(2) unlikely to
(3) times as, as
(4) taken the place

《文のパターン・文法》

1 (1) Lunch being
(2) Jane catching
(3) Neither[Nor] have

2 (1) It being
(2) Frankly speaking
(3) Judging from

3 (1) have I read such an interesting
(2) Little did I dream that I would
(3) had the rain stopped when we started

《総合》

問1 sum up

問2 temperature, too cold, mass, too small

問3 (宇宙には) 非常の多くの惑星があるから。

Reading 2

▶Section Ⅰ

① ほとんど乗客が乗っていなかった

④ 離陸の許可が下りていない

⑤ was identified as

▶Section Ⅱ

③ felt something moving

④ 私はそれまで一度も見たことがない昆虫を見つけた。

⑦ 豊かな想像力を持っているということがわからなかった

▶Section Ⅲ

② 2時間ずっとここで待っていた

⑤ him from going

▶Section Ⅳ

① 静かに教室を出るように頼んだ

⑧ my one and only

▶Section Ⅴ

⑤ ある女性が私に近づいてきて、(そして) かばんを運ぶのを手伝ってほしいと私に頼んだ。

⑪ including three women

確認問題

《語彙・表現》

1 イ、カ、キ、サ

2 (1) ended up
(2) touched down
(3) get in touch

(4) cut, off
(5) stick with
(6) took action

《文のパターン・文法》

1 (1) me from
(2) wasn't, as

2 (1) had talked, would have
(2) at which

3 (1) a melon no different from any other melon
(2) is Russia, followed by Canada
(3) made sure nobody was left in

《総合》

問1 was

問2 サリーはそれまでに一度もやったことも練習したことさえもないことを試そうとしていた。

問3 私が(よく)知っていること

問4 乗客に落ち着いていると思われるような声で(アナウンスをしたいと思った)。

Optional Lesson

確認問題

《語彙・表現》

1 (1) poverty
(2) importance
(3) characteristic
(4) agreement

2 オ、カ

3 (1) aware of
(2) slipped away
(3) control of
(4) my way, thinking
(5) On the contrary
(6) put, this way

《文のパターン・文法》

1 (1) nothing, much as
(2) so that
(3) in which

2 (1) the ones who have made Earth
(2) This is why we cannot stop
(3) change our way of thinking that
(4) What would happen to us if

《総合》

問1 into

問2 私たちはより多くのものを売るために寿命の短いものを作(ってい)る。

問3 経済を維持するためには過剰に消費し続けなければならず、その結果、地球を傷つけていること。

問4 It is time to start fighting for

Acknowledgments

Lesson 1 Section 3: Based on *Lost in Translation, An Illustrated Compendium of Untranslatable Words from Around the World* by Ella Frances Sanders, 2014

Reading 1 Adapted from *The Day We Planted Hope* by Conrad Kiechel, originally published in Reader's Digest. Copyright © 1994 by Trusted Media Brands, Inc. Used by permission.

Lesson 10 Reprinted with the permission of Simon & Schuster Publishing Group, a division of Simon & Schuster, Inc. from the Free Press edition of *THE MAGIC OF REALITY: How we know what's really true* (*chapter 9 Are We Alone?*) by Richard Dawkins. Copyright © 2011 by Richard Dawkins. All rights reserved.

Optional Lesson

Adapted from Discurso pronunciado por José Mujica en la cumbre Río+20
https://medios.presidencia.gub.uy/jm_portal/2012/noticias/NO_E600/mujrio.pdf